T0301877

Social Security's Investment Shortfall
$8 Trillion Plus — and The Way Forward

Plus How the US Government's Financial Deficit
Reporting = 64 Madoffs

World Scientific Series in Finance
(ISSN: 2010-1082)

Series Editor: William T. Ziemba *(University of British Columbia (Emeritus), ICMA Centre, University of Reading and Visiting Professor of University of Cyprus, Luiss Guido Carli University, Rome, Sabanci University, Istanbul and Korea Institute of Science and Technology)*

Published*

Forthcoming

World Scientific Series
in FINANCE vol. 3

Social Security's Investment Shortfall

$8 Trillion Plus — and The Way Forward

Plus How the US Government's Financial Deficit
Reporting = 64 Madoffs

Nils H Hakansson

University of California, Berkeley, USA

 **World Scientific**

NEW JERSEY · LONDON · SINGAPORE · BEIJING · SHANGHAI · HONG KONG · TAIPEI · CHENNAI

Published by

World Scientific Publishing Co. Pte. Ltd.

5 Toh Tuck Link, Singapore 596224

USA office: 27 Warren Street, Suite 401-402, Hackensack, NJ 07601

UK office: 57 Shelton Street, Covent Garden, London WC2H 9HE

British Library Cataloguing-in-Publication Data
A catalogue record for this book is available from the British Library.

World Scientific Series in Finance — Vol. 3
SOCIAL SECURITY'S INVESTMENT SHORTFALL: $8 TRILLION PLUS
— AND THE WAY FORWARD
Plus How the US Government's Financial Deficit Reporting = 64 Madoffs

Copyright © 2013 by World Scientific Publishing Co. Pte. Ltd.

ISBN 978-981-4407-96-0

In-house Editor: Sandhya Venkatesh

Typeset by Stallion Press
Email: enquiries@stallionpress.com

Printed in Singapore by B & Jo Enterprise Pte Ltd

To Joyce, Carolyn and Bill, Alex and Kirsten,
Alexandra, and Kato

CONTENTS

LIST OF TABLES AND FIGURES

Tables

Figures

PREFACE

The Social Security System of the United States is virtually unique in one especially significant respect. While other developed nations invest the excess of contributions over benefit payments and administrative expenses in both government bonds and stocks, the Social Security Trust Fund's investments have from the beginning been limited to nonmarketable US Treasury Bonds. The cost of this unnecessary and inexcusable limitation, to the Trust Fund and the nation, has been enormous.

As shown in this book, if investments had instead been made in marketable Treasury Bonds and a passive portfolio of US and international stocks, beginning when inflows first arrived in 1937, the Social Security Trust Fund, based on conservative assumptions — and on other things being equal — would have been $10.2 trillion at the end of 2010, nearly four times the actual Trust Fund's $2.61 trillion. In 2010, the actual trust fund grew by only $69 billion while the invested fund, despite negative net inflows of $36.8 billion, would have grown by $1.18 trillion, or more than 17 times as much.

But other things would of course not have been equal. The increased demand for marketable bonds and stocks would have resulted in a cumulating wealth effect — with a spillover permeating throughout the economy. The end result could only be what everyone seems to beg for — greater economic growth. In today's global markets, one nation's wealth effect spills across borders. Thus, a Social Security Trust Fund invested in marketable Treasury Bonds and a passive portfolio of global stocks would in the long term boost not only US but global economic growth — and reduce the national debt.

There is a fundamental economic reason why an intergenerational investment fund such as the one for Social Security must invest in stocks — namely, the long run risk premium. Dimson, Marsh, and Staunton have documented that the annualized risk premium for stocks over long-term government bonds for a 19-nation world index over the 111-year period 1900–2010 was 3.8%; for the United States, the risk premium was 4.4%. Compounding at an extra 4.4% per year clearly sends your ball way out of the park. Only twice in the last 200 years has the risk premium been negative for as long as 30 years.

This study ends at December 31, 2010 — for a very significant reason. Until then Social Security was not an entitlement — despite many assertions to the contrary. This is because the System's inflows (payroll taxes) and its benefit payments and administrative expenses have been kept separate and not mixed with general government inflows and outflows. In addition, only individuals who have paid into the System are entitled to benefits and no general government revenue sources had been tapped to fund the Social Security Trust Fund at that point. Furthermore, Social Security is only mildly redistributive. Warren Buffett receives about $30,000 a year in benefits, as he should. These features are consistent with the notion of a minimal safety net as expressed by Adam Smith and Friedrich Hayek.

On January 1, 2011, Social Security became in a very small sense a partial entitlement. This is because 2% of the employee portion of the payroll tax became funded by general tax revenues; the total amount for 2011 was $102.5 billion. In that year, the actual Trust Fund grew by $70 billion to $2.68 trillion while the invested Trust Fund, despite negative net inflows of $45 billion, would have grown from $10.20 trillion to $11.02 trillion, an increase of $820 billion. Of this amount, more than 90% was due to the growth in the long-term government bond portfolio.

There is also a deceptive manner in which the myth of Social Security as an entitlement has been implicitly promoted. The vehicle for this is the Unified Budget, which has been in existence since 1970. By subtracting the various trust fund surpluses from the actual federal deficits, *as if* the surpluses were available for general government expenditures and tax cuts, the US government's finances have been overstated by $4.15 trillion as of the end of 2010 and $4.25 trillion at the end of 2011. Trust funds composed of contributions dedicated to specified future benefits are then implicitly and falsely viewed as entitlements.

If the US government had reported its actual annual deficits, $605.3 billion instead of $412.7 billion in 2004 and $724.6 billion instead of $458.6 billion in 2008 to take two examples, it is unlikely that the public would have consented to a number of the government expenditures and tax cuts that were in fact implemented. This additional factor, in combination with the greater economic growth stimulated by Social Security's inclusion of stocks in its portfolio, would have significantly reduced the need for government borrowing and thus the size of the national debt.

Not surprisingly, the invested Trust Fund's powerful economies of scale, miniscule fees, low administrative costs, and other efficiencies could not be duplicated by privatized accounts, which also suffer from huge productivity losses and in many instances are subject to moral hazard. To rescue the Social Security System from being a political football, it needs to be made independent, with a status similar to that of the Federal Reserve System.

While most pension funds and other balanced funds usually rebalance between stocks and bonds within narrow bounds, a different approach suggests itself for intergenerational funds like the Social Security Trust Fund. In light of the even larger risk premium for stocks over Treasury Bills than over long-term bonds, never sell stocks or bonds, just cover occasional negative net inflows by short-term borrowing on a roll-over basis. And to hopefully benefit from mean reversion, when one category after a long run reaches a high proportion of the total portfolio, switch all new investments to the other category until the first category falls back under the boundary limit.

In the final analysis, then, the objective of this study is to detail the anatomy of how two economic policies of the United States have been enormous failures, with significant negative impacts on both world economic growth and the national debt.

Chapter 1

INTRODUCTION

This study is about one of the world's largest investment funds, the Trust Fund of the Social Security System of the United States. Hundreds of millions of people have made contributions to it over three quarters of a century. A very large number of the people who have paid into it have also received, or are receiving, retirement benefits, disability payments, or the proceeds from life insurance sent to their next of kin; all others who have made and are making contributions can expect these same types of benefits in the future.

As of December 21, 2010, the Social Security Trust Fund had assets of $2.609 trillion in the form of non-marketable Special Issue Government Bonds and no debts. Of this amount, total inflows to the Trust Fund in the form of payroll taxes exceed benefit payments and administrative expenses in the sum of $1.144 trillion. Consequently, the Trust fund's accumulation of earnings, in the form of interest income, over its first 74 years of existence, adds up to only $1.465 trillion. As of this writing, the Social Security Trust Fund has never invested a penny in stocks.

NEGATIVE EXCEPTIONALISM

This is more than remarkable because many, if not most, nations do make stock investments in their public pension funds or social security programs. A recent study by Yermo (2008) covering eight OECD countries (Canada, France, Ireland, Japan, Korea, New Zealand,

Table 1.1: Public Pension Reserve Funds in Eight OECD Countries — and the USA

Percent allocated to equities, 2006	
Canada	58.5
France	62.1
Ireland	77.1
Japan	37.3
Korea	8.9
New Zealand	60.0
Norway	40.7
Sweden	59.5
United States	0

Source: Yermo, J. (2008). Governance and Investment of Public Reserve Funds in Selected OECD Countries. OECD Working Papers on Insurance and Private Pensions, No. 15, OECD Publishing, doi: 10.1787/244270553278.

Norway, and Sweden) showed that in 2006 five of the eight kept more than half of their public pension reserve fund investments in equities, as shown in Table 1.1. In some countries, the reserve fund includes only a portion of all the public fund's assets. Canada diversified its social security investments from purely government bonds in 1998 and many countries did so much earlier. The Social Security Trust Fund, located in what is often viewed as the most capitalistic nation on earth, is clearly way behind the curve.

While many have advocated investing a portion of Social Security funds in the stock market or privatizing Social Security in part or in full, these concepts have attained no serious traction. To illustrate how important stock investments are for the future of Social Security, and in boosting future US and global economic growth, this study will examine what would have happened if stocks had been included in the Social Security Trust Fund from its beginning in 1937.

In this vein, a central purpose of this book is to show that if the Social Security Trust Fund had pursued a simple, passive strategy of investments in marketable long-term government bonds and the stocks of large companies, its earnings and assets at the end of 2010, *other things being equal*, would have been $7.595 trillion larger. In other words, the Social Security Trust Fund would have ended 2010 as by far the world's largest investment fund with assets of $10.204 trillion, dwarfing the recently expanded Federal Reserve System's balance sheet by a factor of roughly four. This translates to about $32,900 per capita for the invested fund while the corresponding number for the existing Trust Fund is only somewhat more than $8,400. In 2010, the actual Trust Fund grew by only $69 billion while the invested fund, despite negative net inflows of $36.8 billion, would have grown by $1.18 trillion, or more than 17 times as much.

But other things would clearly not be equal. The increased demand for marketable bonds and stocks would in most years have resulted in a positive wealth effect. When people and economic agents feel wealthier, they become more willing to invest in financial, physical, intangible, and intellectual assets and property — and to spend more on consumption. This in turn results in a positive influence on government revenues. The combined effect of all these ingredients can only be what everyone seems to beg for — greater economic growth. In today's global markets, one nation's wealth effect spills across borders. Thus a Social Security Trust Fund invested in marketable Treasury bonds and a passive portfolio of global stocks would in the long term boost not only US but global economic growth — and reduce the need for government borrowing.

The above cannot avoid raising the obvious question. Where has the leadership of the American business community and the US government been in the last 75 years? Does it not believe in the stock market? Does it not appreciate the purchasing power that an efficient retirement plan, life insurance plan, and disability plan combination invested in bonds *and* stocks brings to the American people? The substantial long-run outperformance of stocks over bonds has been recognized for centuries.

To save and invest for retirement and in life insurance and disability insurance plans is to provide for a personal safety net. This can be accomplished via a multitude of avenues. People can save for retirement as individuals or via corporate or group plans or a national plan or some combination. Life insurance and disability insurance can be purchased individually or as a member of a group or of a national plan.

The central objective of companies or funds receiving retirement contributions or life insurance or disability insurance premiums is to invest their inflows to make them grow — and to do so in a compounding manner. This way, when the time for benefits arrives, the payments to the beneficiary will be many times larger than his or her inputs.

And how is this compounding growth of contributions achieved? Almost universally it is executed via investments in government and corporate bonds and in common and preferred stocks, with smaller allocations to alternative assets such as real estate, infrastructure, and commodities. Historically, investments have been in domestic securities but recently a trend towards diversification into global bonds and stocks has emerged. The point to be stressed then is that whether one looks at individuals' retirement plans, the pension funds of corporations, universities, foundations, and other not-for-profit entities, or the pension funds of local and state governments and its sub-entities, or, as we saw in Table 1.1, the public pension plans of modern nations, a portfolio of stocks and bonds is the principal asset held.

Investing Social Security funds in stocks strikes many people as risky and imprudent. Over short periods stocks can indeed be quite risky. If you look at the 18-year period 1992–2009 for example the S&P 500 total return stock index did indeed lose ground when compared to long-term US Treasury Bonds. This was also the case for the 30-year period October 1, 1981 through September 30, 2011, the first such 30-year period since 1831–1861 (Eddings and Applegate, 2011). To make the case for including stocks, it is necessary to look at long periods, such as the period spanning an individual's typical working life and retirement, over which stocks outperform bonds by several multiples. That is why this study examined the full 74-year period 1937 through 2010 — over which large company US stocks outperformed long-term US Treasury Bonds by a factor of 23.8 (Table 4.1).

The economic reason why stocks outperform bonds over long periods is due to what is generally referred to as the risk premium. Since stocks are typically riskier than bonds, investors will demand higher returns, on average, when they purchase stocks than when they acquire bonds, as compensation for their higher risk, fully realizing that the realized returns for stocks over short periods may well be lower.

Dimson, Marsh, and Staunton (2002, 2011) calculated the realized risk premia of equities over long-term government bonds and over Treasury Bills for sixteen countries for the 101 years 1900–2000 and for nineteen nations for the 111 years 1900–2010. Over the 1900–2011 period, as Table 1.2 shows, the annualized realized

Table 1.2: Annualized Equity Risk Premia Relative to Long-Term Government Bonds for Nineteen Nations, 1900–2010

Country	Geometric Mean %	Arithmetic Mean %
Australia	5.9	7.8
Belgium	2.6	4.9
Canada	3.7	5.3
Denmark	2.0	3.4
Finland	5.6	9.2
France	3.2	5.6
Germany	5.4	8.8
Ireland	2.9	4.9
Italy	3.7	7.2
Japan	5.0	9.1
The Netherlands	3.5	5.8
New Zealand	3.8	5.4
Norway	2.5	5.5
South Africa	5.5	7.2
Spain	2.3	4.3
Sweden	3.8	6.1
Switzerland	2.1	3.6
United Kingdom	3.9	5.2
United States	4.4	6.4
19 Nation Index	3.8	5.0

Source: Dimson, Elroy, Paul Marsh, and Mike Staunton (2011). "Equity Premia Around the World". Available at SSRN: http://ssrn.com/abstract=1940165, October 21.

geometric equity risk premium over long-term government bonds for the 19 Nation Index was 3.8%. Australia had the highest equity premium, 5.9%, and Denmark the lowest, 2.0%. The equity risk premium for the United States was 4.4% which is the same as the equity risk premium for the 74-year Social Security period 1937–2010. Siegel (2010) has documented the risk premia all the way back to 1801.

Table 1.3 shows the realized risk premia for US equities (large company stocks) over both long-term government bonds and 30-day Treasury Bills for selected periods. As in Dimson, Marsh and Staunton (2002, 2011), an asset's risk premium is the return it earned measured as an investment in the other asset's principal and income combined. The 1982–2011 period was the first 30-year span since 1831–1861 that stocks underperformed bonds. The higher risk premia for Treasury Bills than for bonds is consistent with what is known as a generally rising term structure, the notion that longer

Table 1.3: Realized Geometric Mean Risk Premia in the United States

	Equities Over	
	Government bonds	Treasury bills
1900–2010	4.4%	5.3%
1937–2010	4.4%	6.0%
2001–2008	–11.2%	–5.5%
1831–1861	Minus	NA
1982–2011	–0.0005%	6.1%
1937–2011	4.0%	6.0%

Sources: Dimson, Elroy, Paul Marsh, and Mike Staunton (2011). Equity Premia Around the World. Available at SSRN: http://ssrn.com/abstract=1940165, October 21.

Morningstar, Inc., (2012). *Ibbotson SBBI 2011 Classic Yearbook — Market Results for Stocks, Bonds, Bills, and Inflation 1926–2011*, Chicago: Morningstar, Inc.

Eddings, Cordell and Evan Applegate (2011). Bonds Notch a Rare Win Over Stocks. *Bloomberg Businessweek*, November 7–November 13.

maturities provide higher yields, or equivalently that there is a positive risk premium for bonds over bills.

The 8-year period 2001–2008 is remarkable in that the realized risk premia for stocks were sharply negative versus both bonds *and* Treasury Bills.

THE RISK PREMIUM'S SOURCE: NEAR-UNIVERSAL AVERSION TO RISK

Among individuals, risk aversion in financial matters is virtually universal, albeit in varying degrees, an observation which has been well documented empirically. Risk aversion also holds true for most economic entities. Institutions that are seen as too big to fail are the principal exception, as the recession that began in 2008 lucidly demonstrated.

The designers of the Security System did indeed have the wisdom of creating a Trust Fund in which the excess if inflows over benefit payments and administrative expenses would earn income. This income took the form of interest since all investments were in Special Issue Government Bonds. The crucial step of separating Social Security's financing from other governmental cash flows was thus established at the System's beginning. Unfortunately, this clear-cut separation became partially obscured in 1970 with the introduction of the Unified Budget concept.

The principal finding of this study is a simple reminder of the power of compounding over long time periods, say 60 years, roughly the beginning of a person's Social Security contributions to the end of that same person's receipts of Social Security benefits. Even small differences in average compound returns generate very large differences over an active life-time. The same is true for even modest differences in annual fees.

Chapter 2 gives a very brief overview of the Social Security System. Chapter 3 then looks at how Social Security constitutes the minimal safety net portion of an individual's personal safety net and provides a short summary of how Friedrich Hayek and Adam Smith see the minimal safety net. The System's principal shortcomings are then identified in Chapter 4, including how the Unified Budget concept has severely understated the US Government's financial deficits since 1970 by reducing the reported deficits by the surpluses of its various trust funds; this in turn has permitted roughly half of the growth in the federal debt owed to the public to grow under the cover of darkness... The monthly evolution of the Social Security Trust Fund is given in Chapter 5 under the assumption of a 50–50 starting division between passive investments in marketable long-term government bonds and large company stocks, with due respect given to transaction costs, market impact, mean reversion, the opportunity to invest in international stocks beginning in 1973, and the use of (roll-over) short-term borrowing when net inflows are negative. Various countries experience with privatized social security accounts are summarized in Chapter 6 along with how such accounts contribute to economic inefficiency, moral hazard, and productivity losses. Chapter 7 then argues that the Social Security System needs to be independent and professionally managed, much like the Federal Reserve System, with some concluding observations in the Epilogue.

SOCIAL SECURITY: A VERY BRIEF OVERVIEW

The Social Security System of the United States, a child of the Great Depression, dates its birth to 1935. It was controversial then and has remained so in varying degrees ever since. The requirement since 1983 to make 75-year projections of its financial prospects, where demographic changes in the age distribution of the population play a key role, have generated sobering, and in some quarters nearly hysterical, reactions about its sustainability. It is not my intent to review these issues in any detail. Many careful studies of the problems facing Social Security have concluded that they can be solved by relatively minor adjustments. An especially cogent analysis in this vein is provided by Peter Diamond and Peter Orzag in their book *Saving Social Security — A Balanced Approach* (2004). Their adjustments to revenues and benefits are based on three components: improvements in life expectancy, changes in earnings inequality, and what they call the legacy debt that arose from the early recipients' relatively large benefits.

The theme of this inquiry is that the Social Security system currently in place, while generally comparing favorably to similar systems in other nations, has three serious flaws or shortcomings, each of which could be easily corrected. Payroll taxes are in essence mandatory contributions to, or investments in, a retirement plan and two insurance policies and should therefore be labeled as such. Second, since stocks outperform bonds over long periods and Social Security presumably has no termination date, passive equity investments belong in the Social Security Trust Fund. Finally, Social Security's financial flows need to be removed from the Unified Budget of the United States — ideally, the entire Social Security System should be granted a formally independent status similar to that of the Federal Reserve System. In addition, the Unified Budget concept itself needs to be dropped so that the public and the world can get a valid picture of the finances of the United States government.

As noted, the American Social Security System was established in 1935. Disability insurance was added to the program by the Eisenhower administration in 1957 (to the consternation of many in his party). In addition to retirement and disability benefits, Social Security provides benefits to survivors of deceased and disabled breadwinners such as spouses and in some cases children and even parents. The aggregate of these provisions constitute what is generally referred to as a social safety net. Thus, Social Security can be divided into three distinct mandatory components: a retirement plan, a life insurance policy, and a disability insurance policy, of which the latter two are often overlooked. Coverage is essentially universal, with state and local government employees the primary groups among the roughly 4 million presently outside the system. By early 2011, 54 million beneficiaries, or more than one for every six Americans, were receiving monthly checks from Social Security: 37.5 million retirees, 6.4 million survivors, and 10.2 million disabled.[1] Social Security is partially redistributive in that lower income individuals receive higher benefits relative to their contributions than higher earners but not universally so, as shown by Brown, Coronado and Fullerton (2009).

Social Security began with a payroll tax of 2% applied up to $3,000 of income. It has since risen to 6.2% (for both employee and employer) in 2010 up to a maximum of $106,800 of annual income (in 2011 the employee's contribution was temporarily lowered to 4.2% — with significant implications, as noted in Chapter 3). The surplus of inflows over benefit payments has from the beginning been placed in a Trust Fund and invested in Treasury securities (called Special Issue Government Bonds), the interest on which also is

---

[1] From Actuarial Publications, Social Security Beneficiary Statistics, available at http://ssa.gov/OACT/STATS/OASDIbenies.html.

credited to the Trust Fund. As of December 31, 2010, its balance had grown to $2.609 trillion. There were periods in the seventies and early eighties when benefit payments and administrative expenses exceeded inflows. This caused the Trust Fund to borrow $17.5 billion in fiscal year 1983, an amount that was repaid in fiscal years 1985 and 1986 (although interest payments continued until 1991). This was apparently the trigger which caused President Reagan to form the Greenspan Commission to make adjustments to some of the payroll tax and benefit parameters, adaptations which still are in effect. It is perhaps noteworthy that the three actuaries hired by President Roosevelt's Committee on Economic Security predicted in 1934 that the proportion of Americans over 65 would grow from the then 5.4 percent to 12.65 percent in 1990 — the actual figure for that year, as noted by Lowenstein, (2005, p. 45), turned out to be 12.49 percent!

While Social Security has always enjoyed strong public support, many conservatives have agitated against it, from the very beginning. A suit filed by a shareholder claiming that the payroll tax was unconstitutional went all the way to the Supreme Court, where Justice Benjamin Cardozo ruled in 1937 that "The conception of the spending power advocated by Hamilton...has prevailed over that of Madison" (Lowenstein, 2005, p.45). The list of critics and opponents is familiar: Ronald Reagan during the two decades or so before he became president, Barry Gold water, Milton Friedman (1962, Ch. XI), and various individuals and institutions leaning right. Many others, Peter Peterson among them (see e.g., Peterson, 2010), have advocated reform. Some have proposed that Social Security be made voluntary or wholly or partially privatized. These issues will be discussed in Chapter 6.

As a minimal safety net, Social Security was designed to be supplemented with additional private retirement and insurance benefits. In 2008, according to the Social Security Administration (April 2010), Social Security provided the *sole* source of income for 22.2% of beneficiaries aged 65 and older (Table 9.A1), which represents some 5.6 million Americans (Table 5.A5). And for 63.9% of the 25 million elderly beneficiary Americans in that age group, Social

Security provided the majority of their income. For the 29 million Americans 65 and older, Social Security provided more than a third, 36.5%, of their total income (Table 10.1). Even for retired upper middle-class families, the $2,000 to $4,500 monthly payment is no doubt welcome. Social Security, then, is the source of a highly significant portion of elderly Americans' purchasing power.

The above data are especially significant when viewed in light of the private resources available for retirement funding. According to the Government Accountability Office, half of American households with someone aged 55 to 64 had financial assets of $72,400 or less in 2007 — before the recession — a year in which the median family working income was $54,600 Bucks (2009) — as reported in Jeszeck (2010).

Initial retiree benefits have been indexed to wage inflation, which has tended to be higher than price inflation, to which subsequent benefit payments are indexed. Alan Greenspan, among others, has advocated that all benefits be based on price inflation alone, as a way of lowering benefits in dealing with recent pessimistic 75-year projections for the Trust Fund. An editorial in *The Financial Times* (2005) strongly disagrees, arguing that "indexing benefits to prices rather than wages produces a generation of elderly people in dire poverty. When that happens, government aid will be needed."

The administrative expenses of the Social Security System are remarkably low, especially when compared to privatized plans, as also noted by Krugman (2004). In fiscal year 1990, administrative expenses were 0.78% when measured against contributions and 0.92% if measured against benefit payments. In fiscal year 2009, the corresponding numbers were 0.86% and 0.90%.[2] Measured against historical assets, annual administrative expenses are only 0.25%.

---

[2] Author's calculations from Office of Management and Budget, 2010, Table 1.13.

Chapter 3

SAFETY NETS: INSURANCE POLICIES AND RETIREMENT PLANS

The reason for purchasing an insurance policy is to protect oneself or an economic entity from the prospect of future loss. With respect to home, auto, or other property insurance no loss may occur. But if there is damage or destruction, the insured receives a payout in some form as compensation in accordance with the terms of the policy. What the insurance policy provides is a safety net that may or may not end up being needed. The same is true for disability insurance, (discontinued) term life insurance, long-term care insurance, liability insurance, unemployment insurance, as well as event insurance written to protect against terrorist attacks, for example.

Other insurance policies do provide assured payouts. Whole life insurance is an example because it contains a savings element. Health insurance is virtually certain to provide benefits. Credit default insurance (or swap) purchased to protect against a borrower's ability to repay can be sold or held. The bottom line is that the only reason for insurance of all types to exist is to provide a safety net to the insured.

Retirement plans are also for all intents and purposes safety nets because they provide a means to cover living expenses after an individual's work-related earnings activities terminate. The two main varieties are defined benefit plans, which are group-based, and defined contribution plans in which benefits are governed by the individual's own payments into the plan. Most government retirement schemes are of the defined benefit variety while IRAs, Keoghs, and 401(k) and 403(b) plans belong in the second category. Early corporate pension plans typically began as defined benefit plans but recent years have witnessed a strong trend toward the defined contribution variety.

Safety nets can be divided into two distinct categories, voluntary and mandatory. The bulk of the insurance policies and retirement or pension plans in existence are voluntary as befits a free society. But mandatory schemes exist in virtually all countries. The US and a number of other nations mandate a minimum of automobile insurance coverage. In many nations, health insurance is mandatory. And developed nations have mandatory pension schemes financed through taxes designed to provide a minimum safety net upon retirement; some of these will be discussed in Chapter 6. Social Security, then, needs to be viewed as a mandatory retirement plan, life insurance policy, and disability insurance policy combined and designed to provide a minimal safety net, the role of which is to underlie a generally deeper, and broader, individually selected safety net.

SOCIAL SECURITY IS A SELF-FUNDED MANDATORY MINIMAL SAFETY NET, NOT AN ENTITLEMENT

Social Security is often referred to as an entitlement. But this is not technically correct, at least as of December 31, 2010, since benefits do not flow from general, unspecified tax revenues.[1] In contrast, Social Security is based on a designated tax applied to individuals and employers which enters a trust fund invested in interest-earning Treasury securities and which is the sole source of benefit payments and administrative expenses. Those who paid into the trust fund are also, along with their family members, the *sole* beneficiaries of benefits, just as in private plans. The structure of Social Security, in other words, is like that of any other triplet combination of a defined benefit retirement plan, life insurance policy, and disability insurance policy. In contrast to private plans, Social Security is partially redistributive in that lower earners receive somewhat higher benefits relative to their contributions than higher earners. But the triplet of inflation-indexed, life-time

---

[1] On January 1, 2011, when 2% of the employee portion of the payroll tax began to be funded from general tax revenues, Social Security became to a very small degree an entitlement, as also noted by for example Fleischer (2011) and Yang (2011).

annuity features of the Social Security System, combining, as it does, a retirement plan, life insurance, and disability insurance, would be difficult to duplicate in the much smaller pools of private insurers.

While one half of the contributions of the employed are by law paid by their employers, economists would argue that even the employers' portion can be viewed as contributed by the employees. This is because, if the employees paid the employers' share directly, then, in equilibrium, the employees would demand the value of those contributions in the form of higher wages. In other words, employees are giving up higher wages, roughly equal to, and in exchange for, the payroll taxes paid by employers (net of the employers' income tax deduction only if the employees were to receive a corresponding tax deduction — just as the self-employed already do).

Genuine entitlements are based on the whims of fiscal policy. Medicare is in part an entitlement because only Part A (hospitalization) is funded by a designated tax. What Congress allocates to Parts B and D also goes into a trust fund. The bottom line then is that Social Security should not be viewed as an entitlement but as a fully self-funded retirement and dual insurance plan. The notion that there are unfunded liabilities associated with Social Security assumes a highly predictable future incapable of being adapted to. The fact that Congress designates Social Security's administrative budget does not conflict with the above statement because the administrative expenses in question are *paid* by the Social Security Trust Fund.

FRIEDRICH HAYEK'S AND ADAM SMITH'S VIEWS ON MINIMAL SAFETY NETS

In Friedrich Hayek's treatise *The Constitution of Liberty* (1960), Chapter 19 is devoted to, and titled, "Social Security."[2] Two main themes emerge in his analysis. The first is that "the whole apparatus of 'social security' can probably be accepted by the most consistent defenders of liberty." "Such a program ... would involve some coercion, but only coercion intended to forestall greater coercion of the

---

[2] This chapter also deals with 'social insurance' for health, unemployment, and industrial accidents, topics which are beyond the scope of this study.

individual in the interest of others; and the argument for it rests as much on the desire of individuals to protect themselves against the consequences of the extreme misery of their fellows as on any wish to force individuals to provide more effectively for their own needs." (p. 286). He adds that "'Social insurance' thus from the beginning meant not merely compulsory insurance but compulsory membership in a unitary organization controlled by the state. The chief justification for this decision, at one time widely contested but now usually recognized as irrevocable, was the presumed greater efficiency and administrative convenience (i.e., economy) of such a unitary organization." (p. 287).

The second theme is that "A monopolistic government service... will be in a position... to redistribute income among persons or groups as seems desirable." (p. 288). "No system of monopolistic compulsory insurance", he argues, has resisted becoming "... an instrument for the compulsory redistribution of income." (p. 289). But he also recognizes that redistributions are not an inevitable result. Redistributions in a social security scheme "... can be prevented only if, from the outset, the distinction is clearly made between benefits for which the recipient has fully paid, to which he therefore has a moral as well as a legal right, and those based on need and therefore dependent on proof of need." (p. 293).

From the above it appears that Hayek, an icon among conservatives, accepts the concept of a minimal safety net based on mandatory contributions. The same appears to hold for Adam Smith as well, whose concern for the less fortunate was prominent, as reflected in both *An Inquiry Into the Nature and Causes of the Wealth of Nations* (1776) and *The Theory of Moral Sentiments* (the sixth and final edition was published in 1790).[3] But Hayek is clearly troubled by the way many countries have pursued income redistribution schemes, in the

---

[3] In *Wealth of Nations*, Smith described political economy as having "two distinct objects: first, to provide a plentiful revenue or subsistence for the people, or more properly *to enable them to provide such a revenue or subsistence for themselves*, and secondly, to supply the state or commonwealth with a revenue sufficient for the public services." (Author's italics.) (Smith, 1991, p. 320.) (Continued on next page)

name of "social security," purely as a means to politically reward the many.

The US Social Security System, as noted earlier, is partially redistributive in that high wage earners receive somewhat lower benefits relative to their contributions than low wage earners. But the middle class, then, presumably is not subject to redistribution but receiving benefits for which it has "fully paid", satisfying Hayek's criteria for a satisfactory social security system. The redistribution that occurs in the US Social Security System is that the upper middle class and high income earners partially subsidize low income earners. But Hayek also states that "It is true of course that even the provision of a uniform minimum for all those who cannot provide for themselves involves some redistribution of income" (p. 303), which suggests that he views a modest degree of redistribution as inevitable. But the penalty suffered by the higher wage earners in the Social Security System, with its low administrative expenses (about 0.25% of historical assets as noted in Chapter 2), can also be argued to be mitigated due to the national size of the pool compared to what it would be in much smaller private pools of participants — especially if the Social Security Trust Fund is properly invested...

The opening paragraph of *The Theory of Moral Sentiments* is instructive: "How selfish soever man may be supposed, there is evidently some principle in his nature, which interests him in the fortune of others and render their happiness necessary to him, though he derives nothing from it except the pleasure of seeing it. Of this kind is pity or compassion, the emotion which we feel for the misery of others, when we either see it or are made to conceive it in a very lively manner. That we often derive sorrow from the sorrow of others, is a matter of fact too obvious to require any instance to prove it; for this sentiment, like all the other original passions of human nature, is by no means confined to the virtuous and humane, though they perhaps may feel it with the most exquisite sensibility. The greatest ruffian, the most ardent violator of the laws of society, is not altogether without it." (Smith, 2009, p. 13.)

Adam Smith was remarkable in many other ways too: he was a genuine globalist, highly critical of the East India Company, believed that observed inequalities among people and nations reflected disparities that were not natural but socially generated, and defended such public services as free education.

THE MINIMAL SAFETY NET... NEEDS TAILORED PRIVATE ADD-ONS

While a surprising number of Americans rely entirely on Social Security for their retirement benefits, as noted in Chapter 2, virtually everyone aspires to have a lifestyle well above that provided by the minimal safety net. Despite the availability of a multitude of tax-deferred retirement plans at both the individual level and through corporations and other organizations, personal savings rates among Americans have been negative for some time, turning positive only recently. It is not surprising, then, as also observed in Chapter 2, that the median level of financial assets of American households with someone aged 55 to 64 was only $72,400 in 2007 (Bucks, 2009). How much of a lifetime annuity will $75,000 buy at age 65? Not much more than $400 per month...

The Employee Benefit Research Institute of Washington, D.C. (2010) reported that the proportion of workers very confident of having enough funds for a comfortable retirement was only 16%. Twenty-seven percent said they had less than $1,000 in savings and 54% had less than $25,000 excluding the value of their primary home and the value of any defined benefit plans. Clearly, the private portion of the personal safety net has a huge gap to fill for a large majority of Americans.

A thorough discussion of the interactions and relations between the various categories of safety nets in a global context may be found in Bertocchi, Schwartz, and Ziemba (2010, esp. Ch. 3).

Chapter 4

SHORTCOMINGS OF SOCIAL SECURITY

Despite being viewed as the most successful of the government's many programs, Social Security suffers from three serious shortcomings. First, contributions are labeled, and thought of, as a tax rather than as mandatory retirement and insurance contributions which is what they are. Since the contributed funds are invested in Treasury securities, they have all the properties of what we call savings or investments which, like pension funds and personal retirement accounts, are expected to grow over time. In addition, the mindset is often affected by the words used. "Taxes" tend to generate negative reactions while the word "investment" tends to elicit positive connotations.

Second, Social Security contributions have only been invested in US Treasury securities with no allocation to common stocks. Stocks of course are thought of as "risky" while Treasuries are viewed as "safe". But it is not quite as simple as that. Over a one-year period, a stock portfolio is indeed quite risky while a position in 52-week Treasury Bills is perfectly safe. But over a 50- to 60-year period, a broad-based stock portfolio is likely to be worth three or more times a portfolio invested in Treasuries. As noted in Chapter 1, there is no period of this length in US history that a broad-based portfolio of stocks has under performed a portfolio of Treasury holdings. A portfolio combining Treasuries and stocks would therefore seem worthy of consideration.

Third, the very identity of Social Security and its Trust Fund has been obscured by the adoption of the Unified Budget in 1970. In this framework, inflows to the Social Security Trust Fund, as well as to the US Government's other trust funds, are treated as income and their outflows as expenditures. Since the various trust funds' *net* inflows have been on the order of $100 billion to over $200 billion a year since 1989, the US government's operational deficits (surpluses) have been understated (overstated) by these amounts per year. In other words, the US government has presented a false picture of, and a positive spin on, its finances over the most recent four decades.

I will now address these three shortcomings in more detail.

PAYROLL TAXES VS. MANDATORY CONTRIBUTIONS

Social Security is for all intents and purposes a defined benefit plan combined with two insurance policies. It is slightly redistributive in that lower income individuals receive somewhat greater benefits relative to their contributions than higher income persons. This is in contrast to a defined contribution plan where the individual's own contributions are the sole or primary determinant of that individual's benefits. Defined benefit plans were the norm for corporate pension plans for many years but in recent years many have been converted to the defined contribution type of offering, especially the 401(k) variety. The idea is to make each individual take responsibility for his or her own retirement investments. The results have not been encouraging since participation is voluntary and about half of employees have not signed up. As noted, the 2010 Retirement Confidence Survey of the Employee Benefit Research Institute of Washington, D.C. (2010) found that 27% of workers have less than $1,000 in savings, and that, apart from the value of their primary home and any defined benefit plans, 54% had less than $25,000 in savings and investments. Even so, how one allocates one's resources between the present and the future, at least beyond a minimum of savings, is an individual matter in a free society and a deeply held belief.

Pensions have a long history. When Henry VIII broke away from the Catholic Church, he found it necessary to offer pensions to the monks and abbesses in order to prevent a revolt when the monasteries were dissolved (Cohen, 2005, p. 2). The first national pension plan was instituted by Chancellor Bismarck in 1889. By the end of roughly the first third of the twentieth century, all modern nations had followed suit. Today, many countries' pension plans are seriously underfunded and will have difficulty meeting their obligations without taking drastic steps to increase either taxes, contributions, or investment results and/or reduce benefits. The US Social Security System is in somewhat better shape than those of other nations. But many American local, state, corporate, and, as noted, individual pension plans are also in poor condition.

In the post-Reagan era in the United States, the word "taxes" has taken on an increasingly negative connotation. They have become further associated with government waste and carelessness and an unequal sharing of the tax burden via tax-avoidance by the not-so few and redistributions in reverse. It is easy to lose track of where the payroll tax actually ends up and whether anything will come of it for those paying it in light of the doomsday scenarios displayed in some of the media and in Washington concerning the future of Social Security. Since 1983 there has been a requirement to make projections 75 years into the future of Social Security's finances. Demographic projections make it possible to estimate the number of people paying in, and the number of individuals receiving benefits, within reasonable bounds. But when it comes to estimating the associated cash flows, changes in the economy are much harder to predict, and the more so the more distant the period. And possible changes in the parameters governing contributions and benefits add additional uncertainty to any projections.

Recent point projections, in other words projections which do not reflect a range of likelihoods, point to benefit payments exceeding inflows about 2017 and the trust fund being exhausted about 2033. This scenario has invigorated the system's enemies to push for cuts in benefit and alarmed much of the public, especially in the present context of current and projected huge fiscal deficits.

Since Social Security was intended to operate separately from, and not under the umbrella of, fiscal policy, what is called "payroll tax" is in fact a mandatory triplet combining a retirement contribution and two insurance premiums. It should therefore be designated as such. A simple abbreviation is preferable, such as SSC for Social Security Contribution. The old designation OASDI (Old Age, Survivors, and Disability Insurance) seems somewhat dated.

Some economists have argued that in the absence of Social Security or a mandatory savings program, people would save on their own. That appears to be true in China where individuals have been saving 28% of their income (Dickie, 2012) and there is not much of a public safety net. Recall that for some 20% of American retirees, Social Security provides their only income and that for more than half it represents the majority of their income, permitting a lifestyle which can only be described as modest at best. And that generation had a higher savings rate than the current working generation which has been more or less dissaving. A comfortable retirement lifestyle demands substantial private savings which for large numbers of pre-retirement Americans are conspicuously absent. Even conservative contemporary economists (e.g., Prescott, 2004a, 2004b) have come out in favor of mandatory savings schemes.

NOT INVESTING IN STOCKS AND MARKETABLE TREASURIES

Investing a portion of retirement contributions and insurance premiums in stocks is commonplace. Corporate, not-for-profit, state, local, and many foreign government pension plans (as illustrated in Chapter 1), along with most insurance companies, do it. So do most individuals. Social Security, in fact, is conspicuous because it is *not* investing in stocks. It is certainly not a new idea; numerous individuals have argued that Social Security should join the mainstream e.g., O'Neill (2005). The Canada Pension Plan has already done so.[1]

Some have advocated placing the whole Social Security Trust Fund in stocks since stocks do earn higher returns than bonds over long periods. But stocks represent only one piece of the securities

---

[1] Auerbach (2004) has pointed out that the government has an implicit position in the American equity market via its claim to future tax revenues.

market where bonds also constitute a very large component. Investing in the "market" therefore really requires taking positions in both stocks and bonds. Stocks and bonds also provide indirect access to holdings in commodities, real estate, and other natural resources since many corporations are engaged in, and owners of, such assets. And bonds can outperform stocks over fairly long periods. For example, over the 10-year period 2000–2009, long-term government bonds had a total compound annual return of 7.7% while the S&P 500 stock index *lost* money at a total annual compound annual rate of 0.9%. In other words, from the beginning of 2000 to the beginning of 2010, the long-term government bond portfolio was up 109.8% while the stock portfolio dropped 9.1% in value — and this over a period when inflation crept up 28.3%. Even over the 30-year period 1982–2011, the first such period since 1831–1861 (Eddings and Applegate, 2011), long-term government bonds beat the S&P 500 index by a compound total annual return of 0.0005%, as shown in Table 1.3. But over longer periods, and over most shorter spans, stocks beat bonds handsomely.

For a long-term perspective, it is instructive to review the performance of US stocks and bonds from the beginning of 1937 — when the Social Security System received its first contributions — through the end of 2010, a 74-year period, as reflected in Table 4.1. What the table reminds us is that, even though long-term government bonds outperformed large US stocks over the period 1982–2011 — and also in the first few years — large US stocks beat long-term government

Table 4.1:   Ending Value of $1 Over 74-year Period, 1937–2010

If invested in	Large US stocks	Small US stocks	Long-term gov't bonds	30-day US Treasury Bills
	$1,260	$9416	$53	$17
Annual compound return %	10.1	13.2	5.5	3.9

Source: Morningstar, Inc., 2011, *Ibbotson SBBI 2010 Classic Yearbook — Market Results for Stocks, Bonds, Bills, and Inflation 1926–2010*, Chicago: Morningstar, Inc.

bonds over the full 74-year period by a factor of 23.8 ($1,260/$53). Even fairly small differences in average annual compound returns produce huge differences in the end result. This is an example of the invisible but majestic power of compounding over long time periods...

The biggest surprise is why progressive government officials and the business community have not been more forceful in advocating equity investments by the Social Security Trust Fund in particular. Is it not obvious that the ratio of longer-run fund outputs to fund inputs is greater when stocks are part of the investment pool? If equities had been part of the mix from the beginning, or even later, current talk about unfunded liabilities (for Social Security anyway) would be replaced by discussions about whether to increase benefits or reduce contributions or both. And didn't the opponents of Social Security in the 1930's (mostly capitalists) see any value in having old people with money to spend, money that had grown with interest, dividends, and appreciation? Alan Greenspan is quoted among those opposed — and the Greenspan Commission did not propose that the Social Security Trust Fund should invest in stocks. The apparent reason for this negativity towards stock investments by Social Security is that they are viewed by many as socialism, the idea that the "government" would own stocks. But if the Social Security Trust Fund is seen as too close to the government, the simple solution is to give the whole system independent status. This is the topic of Chapter 7. With respect to the voting of the shares, the Trust Fund would presumably follow the practice of mutual funds and index funds by relying on independent advisors such as Institutional Investor Services.

In view of the out-size performance of small stocks, why not include them as well? Since their universe is quite small, there would be room for only a small portion and their inclusion in the Social Security Trust Fund portfolio will therefore be left to future studies.

TRAPPED BY THE UNIFIED BUDGET

The concept of a Unified Budget for the United States was initiated by President Lyndon Johnson who did not have the opportunity to implement it before he left office. But President Nixon did adopt it beginning with his first budget, that of 1970.

From 1789 through June 30, 1969, The United States reflected its finances through what was called the Administrative Budget. This framework recorded total government receipts and outlays by fiscal year, *excluding* all cash flows into and out of the trust funds, with the difference marked as surplus or deficit. What the Unified Budget did was to *include* the cash receipts and outlays of the trust funds in calculating the deficit or surplus. The difference is large indeed, as shown in Table 4.2. For 1970 the Unified Budget deficit was $2.8 billion while the Administrative Budget (Federal Funds) deficit was $13.2 billion. The 2008 reported deficit was $458.6 billion when the real (Federal Funds) deficit was $724.6 billion. The 2009 reported deficit was $1.41 trillion while the actual deficit was $1.54 trillion. The corresponding numbers for 2010 were $1.29 trillion and $1.42 trillion, respectively. Remember those four years of "surpluses" under President Clinton? Well, there was only one, a measly $1.6 billion in 2000; this was the first genuine surplus since 1960.

There are more than 150 trust funds with assets of more than $4 trillion at the end of fiscal year 2010, of which a little more than half belongs to the Social Security Trust Fund. Some of these trust funds go back nearly 100 years. Most of their receipts flow from dedicated taxes. The trust funds of the United States government have recorded surpluses every year since 1963 — the 2008 trust fund surplus was $266.1 billion, that of 2010 was $123.3 billion.

The problem with the Unified Budget framework, as noted by numerous individuals (see e.g., Adkins, 1996; Gokhale and Smetter, 2003; Johnston, 2004; Nataraj and Shoven, 2004; Jenkins, Jr., 2005; Rattner, 2007; Shilling, 2008), is that it implicitly views the net inflows form the trust funds as available for current government expenditures and tax cuts when they clearly are not. The government has acted as if the concept of a trust fund, dedicated to statutory benefits, was meaningless. Would the public have accepted deficits averaging $229 billion a year greater than reported over the 10-year period 1999–2008? Is this the kind of deceptive financial reporting one should expect from a modern democratic nation?

Table 4.2: US Government's Financial Surpluses or Deficits, 1970–2010 (in millions of dollars)

Fiscal year	Total	Federal funds	Trust funds	Fiscal year	Total	Federal funds	Trust funds
1970	−2,842	−13,168	10,326	1990	−221,036	−341,181	120,145
1971	−23,033	−29,896	6,863	1991	−269,238	−380,971	111,733
1972	−23,373	−29,296	5,924	1992	−290,321	−386,338	96,018
1973	−14,908	−25,683	10,774	1993	−255,051	−355,436	100,385
1974	−6,135	−20,144	14,009	1994	−203,186	−298,508	95,322
1975	−53,242	−60,664	7,422	1995	−163,952	−263,211	99,259
1976	−73,732	−76,138	2,405	1996	−107,431	−222,052	114,621
TQ	−14,744	−12,793	−1,951	1997	−21,884	−147,826	125,942
1977	−53,659	−63,155	9,495	1998	69,270	−91,927	161,197
1978	−59,185	−71,876	12,691	1999	125,610	−87,120	212,730
1979	−40,726	−59,061	18,335	2000	236,241	1,629	234,612
1980	−73,830	−82,632	8,802	2001	128,236	−100,513	228,749
1981	−78,968	−85,791	6,823	2002	−157,758	−360,156	202,398
1982	−127,977	−134,221	6,244	2003	−377,585	−555,977	178,392
1983	−207,802	−230,874	23,072	2004	−412,727	−605,365	192,638
1984	−185,367	−218,272	32,905	2005	−318,346	−555,093	236,747
1985	−212,308	−266,457	54,149	2006	−248,181	−537,271	289,090
1986	−221,227	−283,120	61,893	2007	−160,701	−409,395	248,694
1987	−149,730	−222,348	72,618	2008	−458,553	−724,621	266,068
1988	−155,178	−252,902	97,724	2009	−1,412,688	−1,539,978	127,290
1989	−152,639	−276,122	123,483	2010	−1,293,489	−1,416,821	123,332
					Total is 4,149,368		

Source: The United States Budget for Fiscal Year 2012, Historical Tables, Table 1.4.
Note: The end of the fiscal year changed from June 30 to September 30 in 1977. The period July 1 1976 — September 30 1976 became known as the transition quarter, or TQ for short.

$4,149 ÷ $65 billion = 63.8 Madoffs.

US GOVERNMENT'S FINANCIAL DEFICIT REPORTING = 64 MADOFFS

Since the trust funds of the Unified States government have run surpluses every year that the Unified Budget has been in existence, the US government, by adhering to the Unified Budget concept, has engaged in deceptive reporting with respect to its financial performance for the last 41 years. Adding up the 41 years of trust fund surpluses, or equivalently the increase in the trust fund balances over the 1970–2010 fiscal period, we obtain the sum of $4.149 trillion, as shown in Table 4.2. A recent estimate of Madoff's embezzlement comes to $65 billion which divided into $4.149 trillion equals 63.8.

THE GROWTH IN THE NATIONAL DEBT WAS PARTIALLY SHIELDED BY THE UNIFIED BUDGET

Table 4.3 contrasts the total understatements of the federal deficits from adding in the trust fund surpluses to the increases in the federal debt held by the public for each administration since president Ronald Reagan, concluding with president Barack Obama's first three budgets (ending in fiscal years 2009, 2010, and 2011), as well as for the whole 1970–2011 period. It is evident that about half of the growth in the federal debt owed to the public since president Nixon occurred under the cover of darkness — because for the voter and taxpayer, the reported (but understated) deficits was the most transparent way to estimate the federal government's need to borrow from the public trough.

Table 7.1 in the US Budget's Historical Tables also reveals that the *total* debt almost tripled under President Reagan (from $.9 trillion to $2.6 trillion) and almost doubled under President George W. Bush (from $5.6 trillion to $10 trillion).

Table 4.3: The Growth in the Federal Debt Held by the Public Shielded by the (Unified Budget's) Unreported Portion of the Deficits in Federal Funds, 1970–2011 (in millions)

Fiscal period	Understated deficits from including trust fund surpluses	Increase in federal debt held by public	
		Total	Percent shielded by understated deficits
1981–1988	355,428	1,339,693	26.5
1989–1992	451,379	948,121	47.6
1993–2000	1,144,068	410,037	279.0
2001–2008	1,842,776	2,393,246	77.0
2009–2011	347,669	4,325,156	8.0
1970–2011	4,246,415	9,416,283	45.0

Sources: The United States Budget for Fiscal Year 2013, Historical Tables, Table 1.4 and Table 7.1.

Chapter 5

IF SOCIAL SECURITY FUNDS HAD BEEN INVESTED IN MARKETABLE TREASURY BONDS AND STOCKS... WITH OTHER THINGS BEING EQUAL

Pension funds, insurance plans, and individual investors of funds for retirement share a long-term perspective in making their placement decisions. Most if not all of their allocations of capital are invested in stocks and bonds. As we observed in Chapter 1, this is true in countries outside the United States as well although in varying proportions. Historically, British funds have tended to put the highest proportion into equities, while Japan has exhibited among the highest allocations to bonds.

THE INVESTMENT STRATEGY

This chapter will address where the Social Security Trust Fund would be if the difference between inflows and outflows had been invested in stocks and bonds instead of interest-bearing US Treasury Special Purpose Bonds from the beginning in 1937 to the end of 2010, a 74-year period.

At the beginning of each month, 50% of the *previous* month's net inflows are invested in long-term US Treasury bonds and 50% in the stocks of large US companies and added to previous investments of the same type. The total monthly returns (appreciation or depreciation plus dividends or interest) for both of these categories have been tabulated by Morningstar-Ibbotson (Morningstar, 2011) since 1926 and have been widely used and accepted as a valid total return measure and as a benchmark by the investment industry.

Over time, the variable return structures of the two portfolio categories will cause the portfolio mix between bonds and stocks to vary, quite often considerably. One solution is to rebalance by selling off portions of one category and investing the proceeds in the second category; Sharpe (2010) has proposed keeping the proportions in stocks and bonds equal to their total outstanding market values which would tend to hold down needed portfolio adjustments. But rebalancing does involve a certain amount of second-guessing since a possible later reversal would give rise to unnecessary trading. Another approach is to place all new funds in the second category when the first category reaches a pre-specified maximum portfolio proportion.

Since the Social Security Trust Fund presumably is perpetual, the second approach above was adopted for the present analysis. Whenever stocks (bonds) constitute 80% or more of the total portfolio, all new funds are invested in bonds (stocks). This approach also captures the possibility of benefitting from mean reversion, the empirically observed phenomenon that prolonged periods of high, or low, returns in an investment category are typically followed by a reversal. It also saves transaction costs since there are no sales of securities.

Net inflows in any month may of course be, and have been, negative. When this is the case, a given month's deficit is assumed to be borrowed at the *beginning* of that month based on a 30-day loan at a rate 0.10 % above the 30-day Treasury Bill rate (1.2% annualized) provided by the same Morningstar-Ibbotson data base. When necessary, any debt is rolled over each month to the new 30-day borrowing rate. Both of the above timing assumptions for investments and borrowing will of course tend to understate realized Trust Fund returns.

In the second half of the previous century, investments in the stocks of other countries began to enter American equity portfolios. It therefore seems reasonable that the present model should join the main stream. Thus, beginning in 1970, when the EAFE data base became available reporting the total returns for a number of countries in Europe, Australia, and the Far East, the present model assumes that new allocations to stocks are invested in the EAFE+Canada index, for which the monthly total returns have been tabulated by MSCI/Barra. When parity between the domestic and international stock portfolios is reached, the two portfolios will receive equal allocations of new stock investments.

COMMISSIONS AND MARKET IMPACT COSTS

From 1937 through 1972, new investments are assumed to be subject to commission and market impact costs of 2% for stocks and 1% for Treasury Bonds, with these costs dropping to 1% and 0.5%, respectively, in 1973. International stock commissions are assumed to be 3% beginning in 1970, falling to 2% in 1973. Further reductions are assumed with the advent of index funds: to 0.8% for US stocks, 0.5% for Treasury Bonds, and 1.5% for international stocks in the 1980s; to 0.6%, 0.3%, and 1%, respectively, in the 1990s, and to 0.4%, 0.2%, and 0.8%, respectively, beginning in 2000. The above rates are on the high side and therefore tend to introduce a conservative bias. Index fund tracking errors are assumed to be small enough to be ignored or to be offset by securities lending fees received from short sellers.

The above strategy is clearly passive, actually doubly so since there are no sales of bonds or stocks. It is well-known that some 80% of active investors (individuals, mutual funds, pension funds, hedge funds, private equity, and others) under-perform passive index-based strategies over longer periods. This is partly because of the negative compounding effect of their fees but it also reflects the generally unmet challenges of market timing.[1] While passive investing, with its

---

[1] The 80% under-performance number is a (probably understated) guesstimate since no comprehensive study has, to my knowledge, been made. French (2008) found that investors underperformed a passive market portfolio over the period 1980–2006 by 0.67% per year via trading costs, fees, and expenses. Dichev (2007), measuring returns from investors' portfolios, which reflect their market timing ability, found annualized underperformance of 1.3% for NYSE/AMEX stocks from 1926 to 2002, 5.3% for NASDAQ stocks from 1973 to 2002, and 1.5% for 19 major international stock exchanges from 1973 to 2004. Studying 66,465 households with accounts at

essentially negligible fees, has gained a substantial following in recent years, most active investors are not aware of how their long-term net-of-fees returns compare to the returns of a net-of-fees passive strategy. (Why, you may ask, don't investors know their long-term compound returns? Because investors themselves are either unable to do the calculations or unwilling to face the facts, and investment advisors are not stepping forward... Mutual funds and others do compare their returns to chosen benchmarks but do not report individual investors' long-term returns versus a passive strategy over their holding periods which is not only relevant but would be easy to do with current technology.)

Bill Miller's Legg Mason Capital Management Value Trust provides a revealing illustration of the hazards of non-passive investing. Miller achieved legend status by handsomely beating the S&P 500 Index from 1991 through 2005, an essentially unmatched 15-year span. But five years later, as he steppped down from running the fund, virtually all of the excess return over the index was gone (see e.g., Zweig, 2011; Authers, 2011). Most investors of course piled in well after 1991, after large gains had already been achieved. If they sold as the fund under-performed, which is when the biggest exits occurred, their returns were highly likely to have lost out to the S&P 500 Index, as a study reported by Sloan (2011) indeed confirms.

---

a large discount broker, Barber and Odean (2000) found that the average household underperformed the market by 1.5% per year during 1991 to 1996 — and that those who traded most frequently lost out by 6.5% annually. In a separate study, the same authors (2001) also documented that single men, trading 67% more frequently than unmarried women, underperformed them by 1.4% per year.

At the institutional level, a study by Busse, Goyal, and Wahal (2010) of 4,617 active domestic equity institutional products managed by 1,448 investment management firms between 1991 and 2008 found little evidence of superior performance — before fees — and only modest evidence of persistence in performance. Willoughby (2010) reported that of the 248 funds with (the top) five-star rating from Morningstar on December 31, 1999, only four had retained that rating on December 31, 2009, that 87 had no stars, and that the rest had fallen below the mid-point on average.

CASH FLOWS AVAILABLE TO INVEST

Beginning in 1987, monthly data are available for the inflows to, and the outflows from, the Social Security Trust Fund; from 1937 through 1986, only annual numbers are available. Inflows consist of payroll tax receipts, taxes on benefits, and interest income from the Trust Fund securities. Since the investment strategy we are examining uses a different approach, the interest income shown for each period in the data file must be subtracted in order to obtain the actual inflows from which the outflows, benefit payments and administrative expenses, are subtracted in order to generate the net inflows available for investment.[2] Similarly, the interest expense incurred in fiscal years 1983 through 1991 must be subtracted in order to obtain the funds spent on benefit payments and administrative expenses for those years.[3]

In order to obtain monthly net inflows for 1937–1986, the annual net inflow numbers calculated above were divided by twelve. This is clearly an approximation but appears justified by the argument that it seems unreasonable to wait a whole year to invest a full year's worth of net inflows. In addition, the market impact alone of such an approach would be sufficient to motivate the employment of much smaller monthly investments.

There were periods when net inflows were negative, often for long stretches, as shown in the Appendix (Table 5.1) and summarized in Figure 5.1. Inflows did not cover outflows in fiscal years 1958 through 1966 except for 1964, nor in the 12-year period 1973–1984. From 1987 through 1998, there were occasional monthly gaps, especially in August and in the October-November time-frame. Negative inflows reappeared in August 2008 and became a regular feature in May 2009, with the exception of January and April 2010, most likely

---

[2] According to the Social Security Historian's Office, taxes began to be collected in January 1937 (DeWitt, 2007) even though the first beneficiary retirement payment did not happen until January 1940 (Diamond and Orzag, 2004, p. 14). But outlays for administrative expenses were of course present from the beginning.

[3] Beginning in 1977, the fiscal year ends at the end of September; previously the fiscal year ended in June. The July–September 1976 period is usually referred to as the transition quarter, or TQ for short.

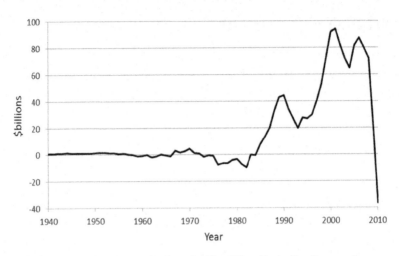

Figure 5.1:   Net Social Security Inflows by Fiscal Year Excluding Interest Income and Expense

Source for author's calculation of net inflows and outflows for 1937–1986: Office of Management and Budget, 2010, Table 1.13.

Source for 1987–2010 net inflows net outflows: Office of Chief Actuary, *Trust Fund Data*, Social Security Online, available at http://ssa.gov/cgi-bin/ops_series.cgi

as a consequence of the 2008–2009 recession. The net outflow for fiscal year 2010 was $36.8 billion. Under the investment strategy examined, negative cash flows, as noted above, give rise to short-term borrowing on a roll-over basis.

TRACKING ERRORS AND SECURITIES LENDING FEES

Index funds do not exactly duplicate the total return (appreciation or depreciation plus reinvested dividends) of the index in which it is investing but is subject to what is called a tracking error. This is due to the need to reinvest dividends and to make portfolio changes due to the occasional substitution of securities in the index itself. Tracking errors typically amount to only a few basis points[4] of return per year. But since index funds typically lend some of their securities to short

---

[4] A basis point is one hundreths of one percent.

sellers for a fee, index funds generally outperform the index slightly since the securities lending fees collected are about the size of the tracking error for bond index funds and generally exceed the tracking error for stock index funds, and often multiple times for the S&P 500 Index Fund employed in this study.

THE FIRST 19 YEARS

The monthly evolution of the Social Security Trust Fund based on the investment strategy described above, implemented with the preceding parameter assumptions, was generated via an 888 (74×12) by 35 spreadsheet, the details of which are displayed in Table 5.1 in the Appendix.

Table 5.1 shows that from 1937 through July 1955, the investment strategy gave stocks and Treasury bonds equal allocations of new investment funds. We also observe that the bond portfolio outperformed the stock portfolio through December 1942, with bonds reaching a maximum 62.79% proportion of the total portfolio at the end of March, 1938. But in the next 18 years, stocks grossly outperformed Treasury Bonds; by the end of November 1955, stocks composed 81% of the total portfolio, as also shown in Figure 5.2. The 80% boundary having been reached, new investments were shifted entirely into bonds.

Comparing the invested Trust Fund to the historical Trust Fund, we observe from Table 5.1 that the latter beat the former in the first six fiscal years (ending in June 1942), with the invested Trust Fund having reached only 90% of the historical Trust Fund's value. But by the end of the nineteenth fiscal year (ending in June 1956), as also reflected in Figure 5.3, the invested Trust Fund was worth 2.64 times as much as the historical Trust Fund.

55 YEARS OF NO NEW INVESTMENTS IN US STOCKS

The last investment in US stocks that the strategy made was in November, 1955. Thus, for the next 55 years through 2010, the stock portfolio was for practical purposes left alone, to grow by itself,

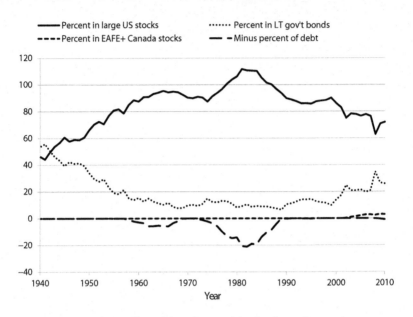

Figure 5.2: Proportions Invested in the Asset Categories

from $0.046 trillion to $7.344 trillion, multiplying its value nearly 160 times. Its maximum value, as a proportion of the total portfolio, was 116.53% as of the end July, 1982 (Figure 5.2). Not surprisingly, this high point was the beginning of stocks' 30-year under-performance. By the end of 2010, the fraction of the total portfolio composed of US stocks was down to 71.97% — recall that all new investments since that time went into Treasury Bonds and international stocks. Since the market capitalization of the S&P 500 Index on that date was $11.430 trillion, the $7.344 trillion position in US large stocks would represent 64.3% of the S&P 500 portfolio — assuming other things equal, which they could not be, as will be discussed shortly...

Note that on July 31, 1963, the first date the market value of the S&P 500 Index became available, the portfolios position in large stocks was only 29.5% ($90.522 billion/$307.089 billion) of the S&P 500 portfolio.[5] So how could the proportion grow to 64.3%

---

[5] Market capitalization values for the S&P 500 Composite Index were obtained from S&P Indices Client Services, Standard & Poors.

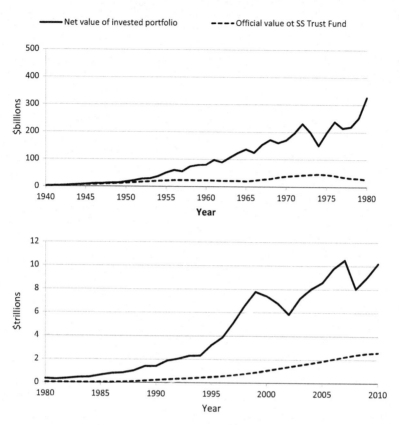

Figure 5.3:   The Values of the Invested and Historical Trust Funds Compared

by 2010 when *no* new additional investments were made by our portfolio? The index fund increased the portfolio's share of the index by the automatic reinvestment of all dividends, thereby more than doubling the Trust Fund portfolio's ownership from less than one third to almost two thirds.

NO INTERNATIONAL STOCKS UNTIL 2002

The first investment in international stocks was not made until July 2002, which was the first time since 1956 that the proportion of stocks in the portfolio fell below 80%. The maximum portfolio composition reached by international stocks was 3.15% in May 2008, falling to 3.00% at the end of 2010. The 2002–2010 period when they were purchased, the EAFE+Canada Index handily outperformed the S&P 500 Index.

THE TREASURY BOND PORTFOLIO

The Investment strategy placed funds in Treasury Bonds every year until July 1957 when net inflows turned negative, forcing the Trust Fund to borrow and roll over 30-day loans. These loans were not fully paid off until January 1970, when new bond investments resumed. Net inflows turned negative again in July 1972, resulting in new borrowing and ceased new bond investments. Not until January 1990 did the loan balance reach zero so that new Treasury Bond investments could be made. From this point on, net inflows frequently alternated between positive and negative in sign so that new bond investments were possible only a few times each year. Even though new bond investments were made only about half the time during the full 1937–2010 period, the value of the bond portfolio based on the investment strategy was $2.64 trillion at the end of 2010, which by itself is more than 101% ($2.64 trillion/$2.61 trillion) of the actual Social Security Trust Fund's value on that date! (This comparison raises the question of how well — or poorly — the historical portfolio of Treasuries (Special Issue Government Bonds) portfolio has been managed). The final Treasury Bond portfolio also represents 25.86% of the total invested portfolio at the end of 2010.

OCCASIONAL SHORT-TERM BORROWING

The investment strategy employed did not call for any sales of either stocks or bonds, only for new investments in a category to cease whenever that category reached 80% of the value of the total portfolio. Negative net inflows in a given month then required borrowing to enable the full payment of benefits and administrative expenses for that month. Since the yield curve is typically upward sloping, and one month's negative flow may be more than offset by a larger positive flow the following month, 30-day loans that could be rolled-over when necessary were employed.

After about 20 debt-free years, short-term loans became necessary in July 1957, the first month that net inflows turned negative, and continued via roll-overs until January 1970. Short-term debt reached its highest point in this interval, 7.07% of the total portfolio's net worth, in August 1966. Short-term borrowing resumed in July 1972 and continued uninterrupted through January 1990. After a very brief pause, short-term borrowing again became necessary in August 1990 and continued sporadically through September 1998. This was followed by a debt-free period until November 2007 when occasional borrowing again became necessary until May 2009, a point at which net inflows turned negative and remained so except for January and April 2010.

The debt level reached its highest point, 28.34% of the total portfolio's net worth, in July 1982. It is noteworthy that while Trust Fund's debt grew from 0 to $72.37 billion over the 10 years ending in July 1982, the trust fund's net worth still grew by more than $47 billion. And over the period from June 1972 through May 1985 when debt reached its maximum level of $92.77 billion, the Trust fund's net worth still grew from $208.27 billion to $560.30 billion, or a whopping $352 billion! After August 1990, the maximum debt level of 0.83% was reached at the end of 2010. From the above, we can see that the work of the Greenspan Commission in the early 1980s appears to have been at least partially motivated by the net cash flows out of the Social Security Trust Fund in the 1970s.

SUMMARY AND DISCUSSION

First, the investment approach has been deliberately conservative and the realized investment returns are therefore understated. This understatement is the result of several contributing factors. First, investments were delayed to the *end* of each month while all borrowing was done at the *beginning* of the month — as if the full amount needed was known in advance. Second, the commissions and market impacts employed are on the high side. Third, the excess of securities lending fees over tracking errors were ignored. And fourth, the short-term borrowing rates were overstated in view of the credit quality of the trust fund's asset base generated by the investment strategy. In addition, by never selling any assets, the strategy kept transaction costs to a minimum.

With this back-drop, the application of a simple and seemingly sensible investment strategy to the net inflows (outflows) of funds into the Social Security Trust Fund over a 74-year period has yielded some surprising results. Despite in principle equal allocations to bonds and stocks, which gave bonds a head start performance-wise, the 80% portfolio weight cap limited investments in US stocks to less than 19 years (the first 227 months). The cap also kept international stocks from entering the portfolio until July 2002. The need to cover negative net inflows with short-term loans caused new monthly bond investments to be required only about half of the time.

Even though the Treasury Bond portfolio received much larger investments than the stock portfolios, the ending stock portfolio component was more than two and three quarters as large as the final Treasury Bond portfolio. The US stock portfolio alone, coasting on old investments only for more than 55 years, outperformed the bond component by a factor of 2.78 ($7.34 trillion/$2.64 trillion as shown in Table 5.2). This despite the fact that the bond portfolio outperformed the stock portfolio over the first six years and long-term Treasury Bonds outperformed the S&P 500 Total Return Index of large company stocks over the period 1992 through 2009. The power of compounding is invisible but invincible.

The relatively high amount of short-term loans at certain times may seem troublesome. When this happens, adjustments to inflows and/or outflows would suggest themselves. This is of course exactly what was done following the Greenspan Commission's recommendations. That commission of course did not see the problem the same way that the investment strategy examined here revealed it — via sharply rising short-term debt.

The presence of short-term debt also means that the investment strategy examined here at times employed leverage. There would

Table 5.2: December 31, 2010 Balance Sheets of the Historical Social Security Trust Fund and the Invested Social Security Trust Fund

Historical Social Security Trust Fund
Balance Sheet
December 31, 2010
(in trillions of dollars)

Assets		Liabilities and Equity	
Special Issue Government		Liabilities	$0
Bonds (non-marketable)	$2.609	Equity	$2.609

Invested Social Security Trust Fund

Balance Sheet (Other things being equal)
December 31, 2010
(in trillions of dollars)

Assets			Liabilities and Equity		
US Treasury Bonds			Short-term debt	$0.085	0.83%
(marketable)	$2.639	25.86%			
Stocks (S&P 500 Index)	$7.344	71.97%			
International stocks					
(EAFE+Canada Index)	$0.306	3.00%	Equity	$10.204	100%
Total assets	$10.289		Total liabilities	$10.289	
			and equity		

seem to be no reason why this could not be done as long as it is on a limited and temporary basis. Since the yield curve is typically upward sloping, intermittent use of short-term debt would also tend to benefit the overall returns earned by the fund. But in the early 1980's, when net inflows were negative and the portfolio was borrowing heavily, 30-day borrowing rates were high, reaching a maximum of 16.9% annualized in December 1981.

More details on the effects of the short-term loans employed in the study are informative. During the first short-term borrowing period, from July 1957 through January 1970, stocks grew at a compound monthly rate of 0.70% and bonds at 0.09% while the monthly compound borrowing rate employed was 0.39%. Since stocks during the period composed more the 80% of the portfolio and short-term borrowing never exceeded 8%, it is evident that the short-term borrowing approach was a much smarter strategy than selling stocks in making up for the period's negative net inflows to the Trust Fund.

During the second continuous borrowing period, from July 1972 until January 1990, stocks grew at a compound monthly rate of return of 0.90% and bonds at a 0.68% rate while short-term borrowing occurred at a compound rate of 0.73%. Again, it is clear that asset sales, quite apart from transaction costs, would have been harmful to the Trust Fund's growth in value.

Over the 10 years and one month July 1972 through July 1982 period, short-term loans grew from 0 to 28.34% of net assets, with borrowing rates reaching as high as 16.9% annualized. During this period stocks grew at a monthly compound rate of only 0.38%, with bonds managing only 0.31% — while the monthly compound short-term borrowing rate was a steep 0.74%. Even so, the net assets of the Trust Fund, due to its much greater size than the debt, grew at a monthly compound rate of 0.17% during the period, increasing, as noted earlier, by $47 billion to $255.34 billion.

The bottom line then is that having a large asset base grow at a low rate more than compensates for paying a high rate on a relatively small loan. The overall result on the fund is still positive.

COMPARING THE INVESTED TRUST FUND WITH THE HISTORICAL TRUST FUND

As already noted, the invested Trust Fund underperformed the historical Trust Fund over the first six fiscal years, reaching only 0.90% of the latter's asset level at the end of June 1942. But from then on, the comparison heavily favors the invested Trust Fund, whose value reached 17.85 times that of the historical Trust Fund at the end of 1983, as shown in Figure 5.4. The reason for this large discrepancy is that the actual trust fund had added few new net investments and had suffered poor investment returns over a long prior period, while the invested Trust Fund had employed short-term loans to fund its shortfalls, permitting a large asset base to keep growing under the at the time very favorable return structure for equities. Beginning in 1984,

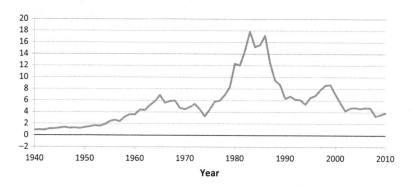

Figure 5.4: Ratio of the Value of the Invested Trust Fund to the Value of the Historical Trust Fund

two factors caused the ratio between the two funds to begin to retreat. First, the invested Trust Fund needed to repay its loans — an outlay the historical Trust Fund did not have to nearly the same extent. Second, following Paul Volcker's taming of inflation in the early 1980s, the bond market began a very long period of generating strong total returns. The result was a slow and steady decline in the ratio of value of the invested Trust Fund to that of the historical Trust Fund, ending at 3.91 at the end of 2010.

OTHER THINGS WOULD
NOT BE EQUAL...

The above scenario assumed that the Social Security Trust Fund was a small unit in a competitive market, unable to influence the prices at which it could keep on buying stocks and Treasury Bonds. What we do know, then, is where the Social Security Trust Fund would have be if it had been what economists would call a price-taker — and everything else as well would have been equal or unaffected.

It is unrealistic of course to expect the return structure in the stock market in particular but also in the bond markets, not only domestically but globally, not to be affected if the Social Security Trust Fund had implemented the above investment strategy. Each monthly impact would have been small and not particularly noticeable but the gradual buildup to a majority position in the S&P 500 portfolio would clearly have a substantial cumulative impact — and would therefore in actuality have ended as a considerably smaller proportion since more than half of the (current) investors in those stocks clearly would not have dropped out. The net new demand for stocks in particular would no doubt has added upward pressure on prices, as was the case in Chile in the early years, before additions to private accounts there began to decline. This would presumably also spill over into the psychology of other individual investors and corporations as well as consumers, all of whom would view the net result of an increase in the future purchasing power of consumers as a positive element. To quantify these changes more precisely would of course be rather difficult. The impact of Social Security investments in equities in a general equilibrium framework was analyzed by Diamond and Geanakoplos (2003) who found that heterogeneities in the population and assumptions about technology would play important roles.

Identifying contributions to the Social Security Trust Fund as mandatory investments rather than as payroll taxes would presumably also change our measurements of what we call savings — since that is what these contributions clearly are. Trashing the Unified Budget concept would add to this clarification since the current apparent "spending" of the net inflows to the various trust funds that this concept implies would no longer be feasible. This in turn would properly focus attention on the true state of the government's finances and the need for genuine fiscal discipline.

... THE WEALTH EFFECT WOULD BOOST ECONOMIC GROWTH... AND REDUCE THE NATIONAL DEBT

In view of both of the above factors — an increase in marketable bond and stock investments and a clear-cut savings element — it is difficult to conceive of a scenario in which the net result would not provide a strong positive wealth effect. When people and economic agents feel wealthier, they become more willing to invest in financial, physical, intangible, and intellectual property and assets — and to spend more on consumption. This in turn could hardly avoid spilling over into a healthier financial condition of the government via improved revenue flows. The combined effect of all these ingredients points to an upward impact on economic growth — the focal point of the contemporary economic debate. In today's global markets, one nation's wealth effect spills across borders. Thus, a Social Security Trust Fund invested in marketable Treasury Bonds and a passive portfolio of global stocks would in the long term boost not only US but global economic growth.

The boost in economic growth would also reduce the incentive for government borrowing — for two reasons. Not only would the government's revenue flows be greater but its expenses would also likely to be lower. In addition, as suggested in Chapter 4, the Unified Budget, with its side-effect of concealing approximately half of the federal government's deficits, would most likely not survive, thus hampering the government's proclivity to engage in debt financing.

Chapter 6	PRIVATIZING SOCIAL SECURITY RESULTS IN INEFFICIENCY, MORAL HAZARD, AND VERY LOW PRODUCTIVITY

The idea of privatizing Social Security or the minimum safety net in part or in full has a long history but was especially hotly debated after the second Bush administration proposed a partial privatization. To consider the merits or demerits of such a move it will be useful to first briefly review the lessons from the various countries which have implemented, and thus have experience with, privatization of public pension schemes.

PRIVATE ACCOUNTS AND CANADA — THE RECORD

Argentina and Bolivia

Argentina implemented a partial privatization in 1994. Seven percent is deducted from wages of which only 4.41% reaches private accounts; the remaining 2.59%, or 37% of the total deduction, is set aside for administrative costs and disability and survivor insurance (Mesa-Lago, 2008, p. 99). The initial popularity of the private accounts lowered the government's receipts, the common and expected result of a transition from a fully public system. But the transition soon grew out of control. In addition, tax cuts and various unexpected expenditures seriously undermined the country's finances over the following years, causing Argentina to default on its debt in December 2001. As one economist put it, the launch of "private accounts didn't create the fiscal problem, but it amplified it" (Davis and Moffett, 2005).

Bolivia implemented private accounts in 1997 and has also been plagued by unexpectedly large transition costs. There, 12.21% is deducted from wages of which 10% goes into private accounts, with the remaining 2.21% set aside for administrative costs and insurance. The situation is similar in other Latin American nations, with the administrative and insurance deductions falling between Bolivia's 18.1% and Argentina's 37% (Mesa-Lago, 2008, p. 99). These costs are in addition to the management fees charged by the investing funds. Not surprisingly, the whole region is facing strong pressure to reduce fees and administrative expenses.

Canada

The Canada Pension Plan is similar to Social Security in the US since it also provides survivor and disability benefits. As late as 1997, the plan's funds were solely invested in federal government bonds. The government then created an Investment Board to implement basic asset allocation strategies on a global scale. A recent breakdown showed the Canadian social security portfolio's holdings as follows: stocks 52%, bonds 25%, private equity 12%, and inflation sensitive assets 12%. Both passive and active strategies are employed. Canada has not succumbed to the privatization urge.

Chile

Chile launched private accounts in 1981 during the time of General Pinochet's military regime, as the brainchild of José Piñera (Moffett, 2005). Even though participation is mandatory once you opt out of the public plan, Chile's approach has been viewed as a model by advocates of privatization due to its early start and the strong performance of the Chilean stock market during the first fifteen years. But like the other Latin American systems, it is subject to high overhead. Of the 12.3% deducted from wages, only 10% enters private accounts; 2.3%, or 18.7% of the amount taken out of wages, goes to administrative fees (1.54%) and survivor and disability insurance (0.76%) (Mesa-Lago, 2008, p. 99). By September 2008, those fees had risen to 1.71% and 0.99%, respectively, for a total of 21.3% of the amount subtracted from wages (Kritzer, 2008, p. 69); the administrative fees alone added up 13.5% of the employees' contributions to future benefits. In addition, management fees can consume up to a third or more of invested funds. In 1999, the fee for annuitization could be as high as 5.4% (Kritzer, 2000); the maximum appears to have been 6% but a 2004 law limited the charges to 2.5% of the value of the annuity (Kritzer, 2008, p. 72). This seems consistent with the private plan management firms' returns on assets, which in the 1991–2004 period averaged 27% — which compares to 15.7% for Chile's financial services industry (Kritzer, 2008, p. 79). Among employees with private accounts, the proportion contributing regularly or sporadically declined from 76% in 1983 to only 54% in 2007. Among the self-employed, for whom participation has been voluntary, only 40% of the 60% with private plans have made active contributions (Kritzer, 2008, pp. 73–74). It is also noteworthy that General Pinochet excluded the military from the privatization program (Rohter, 2005).

A retiree who has contributed for at least 20 years under the private plan and whose payouts do not reach the legal minimum is entitled to any shortfall from the public plan (Piñera, 2004). Surprisingly, the Chilean *public* plan, measured by GDP, paid nearly one and a half times as much in benefits in 2003 as Social Security in the United States (Rother, 2005). Rohter gave the example of a retiree whose 24 years of contributions would only finance a 20-year pension of $315 a month while a public plan colleague having worked on the same pay scale would collect a lifetime annuity of $700 a month; large numbers of private plan retirees are finding themselves with pensions only half as large as if they had stayed in the public plan.

In 2008, Chile implemented a pension reform which is intended to strengthen benefits, broaden coverage, and gradually make participation mandatory. The added spending requirements are provided by a new pension reserve fund set up in 2006. This fund is partly financed from the budget surplus and the revenues from the sale of copper and implemented in part via employer subsidies (Kritzer, 2008, pp. 76, 81).

Poland

Individual accounts began in Poland in 1999, when nearly half a million mostly inexperienced sales agents working on commissions were authorized to funnel accounts to 21 pension funds (Davis and Moffett, 2005). This produced a somewhat chaotic beginning which has gradually been improved. The mandatory pension contribution rate is 19.52% and the account balance is annuitized at the time of retirement (Gora, 2003).

Singapore

Singapore's individual accounts began in 1955 during its colonial period. The country's 33% payroll tax is intended to fund not only old age but housing, education, hospital costs, and contingencies. The legal structure provides great flexibility in how funds are used, and so much has been tapped for housing that many retirees find themselves asset-rich and cash-poor (Davis and Moffett, 2005). A recent survey (Mercer, 2009) recommends that Singapore's system needs to increase "the percentage of contributions required to be saved for retirement".

Sweden

Beginning in 2000, Sweden allowed the top 2.5% from the 18.5% payroll tax to flow into personal investment accounts. Individuals could either put their money in up to five funds from a universe of over 600, or into a government "default fund" invested mostly in international stocks. The default fund's equity holdings are limited to between 50 and 90% (Turner, 2004). When the program started, two thirds of participants chose individualized portfolios but by 2003 92% of them had switched out of privatized fund selections (Davis and

Moffett, 2005). This change of heart is likely due to the various funds' early investment performance; over the first three years, the default fund fell 30% while the average individually chosen portfolio fell 40% (Cronqvist and Thaler, 2004). To make up for such a short-fall requires an out-performance of nearly 17%. The Swedish system is also characterized by very low fees: 0.16% for the default fund and 0.77% for the active funds (Kreuger, 2004).

United Kingdom

Personal accounts went into operation in Britain in 1988 during the Thatcher administration. Individuals were allowed to opt out the second tier of the public pension plan and even their company pension plan to fund their personal account with part of their payroll tax (Davis and Moffett, 2005). Private accounts became very popular and by 1991 4.3 million had signed up (Cohen, 2005), with 6 million eventually opening private accounts (Rice-Oxley and Ross, 2005). But much of the enthusiasm rested on over-optimistic return projections that were assumed to more than make up for the loss of employer contributions, along with commission-driven sales practices. The result came to be known as "the mis-selling scandal" and caused the insurance industry to compensate millions of people to the tune of £13billion as of 2004 (Davis and Moffett, 2005) and to also pay huge penalties and fines. It also dug a huge hole in the national pension fund of £5.9 billion. Nearly two million among those who chose private accounts had returned to the state system by 2005. In a reversal, many of the companies selling private accounts have urged their customers to return to the public plan. Even more ironically, the Confederation of British Industry has endorsed greater pension benefits via tax increases. Part of this greater need is attributable to Britain's re-indexing of initial benefits from wage inflation to price inflation (which is about 1.5% to 2% lower on an annual basis) beginning in 1979 (Cohen, 2005). In addition, fund management fees have been estimated to consume 20 to 30% of a UK private account's lifetime yield (Giles and Balls, 2005; Cohen, 2005).

Summary

To summarize, it is evident that private accounts where they have been tried suffer from excessive fees, in some cases exorbitantly so. Sweden has been the most successful by far in limiting the impact of costs and investment fees. Canada stands out by foregoing privatization and simply adding equities to its national pension fund. In our review of the above foreign countries we have also observed the presence of moral hazard, gross inefficiencies, and the consumption of enormous quantities of person-years not only in establishing private accounts but in operating them. These issues will now be addressed in more detail.

PRIVATE SOCIAL SECURITY ACCOUNTS ARE INEFFICIENT

So why leave the investing to the Social Security Trust Fund? Why not privatize all or part of the Social Security System, as many have proposed — and some countries have experimented with? There are at least five powerful reasons why privatization of the minimal safety net falls short — in sharp contrast to the personal add-on safety net where the individual's own choices clearly must reign supreme.

First, the Social Security System's national investment pool is a clear beneficiary from what is known as economies of scale, the idea that larger efficiencies are obtainable the greater the operational size. In the field of passive financial investments, economies of scale are especially significant. A handful of individuals can manage a $10 trillion portfolio of index funds when only small changes are required each month.

Second, by employing a common investment pool for retirement, life insurance, and disability insurance, the benefits from economies of scale are expanded even further. In privatized plans, these three functions are typically operated separately.

Third, the transaction costs for the periodic investments in the Trust Fund's index funds will be miniscule, the world's smallest, due to their large size. Individuals adding small amounts, some less than

$100, to their private accounts, even if they use index funds, are necessarily subject to higher transaction costs. In South America and the United Kingdom, transaction costs and fees have consumed large amounts of the funds invested in private accounts, thus sharply reducing the availability of benefits. In Chile, the companies licensed to manage privatized accounts were the main beneficiaries, not their clients. Sweden's private accounts, which are limited to only 13.5% of retirement contributions, have by far the lowest fees.

A large pool may further reduce transaction costs by more easily avoiding rebalancing between stocks and bonds by instead switching new investments at pre-set value bounds (as in Chapter 5), which may also generate benefits from mean reversion, the observed phenomenon that prolonged moves in one direction by an asset category is typically followed by prolonged moves in the opposite direction.

Fourth, the Social Security Trust Fund may (and does) at times experience negative net inflows. But the Trust Fund's very large asset base enables it to borrow at very low interest rates. By using 30-day loans on a roll-over basis, it is also most likely to benefit from the typically rising term structure of interest rates.

Fifth, the Social Security System offers inflation-adjusted lifetime annuities for retirees, survivors, and the permanently disabled based on an automated rule. It is highly unlikely that the private sector, with its much smaller pools and a profit-motive, could offer nearly comparable terms. Sloan (2009) made an analysis of his own and his wife's Social Security retirement benefits beginning in 2011. At his request, the Social Security Administration valued their benefits at $600,293. To purchase an identical life-time, inflation-protected annuity in the private sector, they were quoted a price of $774,895, nearly 13% higher, by Vanguard, a low-cost provider of investment products.

It is noteworthy that the proponents of Social Security privatization in the United States have ignored the life insurance and disability insurance components that are critical to so many millions of Americans. As noted by Kreuger (2005) for example recent years exhibit a sharp increase in Social Security disability claims. For this and other reasons, a transfer of the disability component of Social Security to the private sector poses some especially difficult challenges.

PRIVATE ACCOUNTS AND MORAL HAZARD

Moral hazard in the world of privatized Social Security accounts is a very straightforward concept. It simply means that if the benefits obtained from the private account fall below some predefined limit, the government in some way, usually from its public plan, will step in and make up the difference. The shortfall could be due to excessive risk-taking gone bad, unusually high fees, or a poorly conceived privatization plan, or some combination. Since private account holders would be able to enjoy the returns when their investments do well and be bailed out if they do poorly, they would in effect be the beneficiary of a free option offered by the government, as noted by for example Berk (2005).

If private account investors were left to subsist on the fruits of their own decisions, moral hazard due to privatization would of course disappear. But modern nations do not wish to see their citizens live in severe poverty and have therefore set minimum standards for old age income levels. Moral hazard is therefore at least potentially present in all privatization plans.

As we have seen, moral hazard has been institutionalized in the Chilean privatization system; in Britain, as we saw above, it has run amok. Sweden has circumvented the problem by limiting personal accounts to a small fraction of its public plan with no fallback; any losses below the private plan default portfolio or any other standard are not bailed out. As noted by Becker (2005) for example moral hazard can be reduced by limiting choices to index funds of stocks and bonds. Thus, it can be kept small at least in the short run. But the financial industry, in its search for profits, can always be counted on to push for weakening any portfolio constraints in the name of deregulation, thereby increasing moral hazard. It is noteworthy that the British insurance industry was the principal designer of that country's truly disastrous privatization plan (Cohen, 2005).

As a perpetual defined benefit plan, Social Security's investments, both as illustrated in Chapter 5 and as is the case in the current system, are stationary in character in that the age of any participant is not a factor. This is in contrast to personal insurance and retirement plans which tend to be life-cycle or target based. The life-cycle concept typically favors stocks over bonds in earlier years, with a gradual switch towards bonds as the individual grows older. John Bogle of Vanguard for example has proposed that the proportion of bonds should be equal to one's age. A life-cycle type of approach to private account investments, then, even if based on index funds, becomes a potential source of underperformance, and possibly moral hazard, in relation to the age-neutral approach of the extant Social Security model.

The existence of a minimal national safety net may of course cause some individuals to take on greater risks in their personal safety nets than they otherwise would. That of course is their choice to make.

PRIVATE ACCOUNTS GENERATE HUGE LOSSES IN PRODUCTIVITY

Productivity measures the number of person-hours required to make unit of product, or more generally to reach a certain economic goal. Since the beginning of the industrial revolution, manufacturing has made enormous strides in productivity and is largely responsible for the large rise in economic well-being observed in modern countries. In the service sector, on the other hand, the results are rather mixed; the internet and the ATM are probably the best examples of solid breakthroughs.

Privatizing the minimal safety net in its current form will require huge amounts of work. Some 200 million citizens will need to make personal investment and retirement plans, life insurance plans, and disability insurance plans — all of them inflation-adjusted — requiring access to hundreds of thousands of advisors and investment managers and insurance providers. In contrast, the Social Security Administration accomplishes all of these tasks, and does so much more efficiently, with administrative expenses of less than 0.25% of assets. The productivity losses from full privatization are therefore enormous. With partial privatization, along the lines proposed by the second Bush administration, the economic situation would be even worse since the existing Social Security system would continue to exist.

THE WAY FORWARD

The recent period has seen a clamor calling for reform of the Social Security System of the United States. Most proposals (see e.g., Blinder, 2010; Brandon, 2010; Farrell, 2010; Malkiel, 2010; and Peterson, 2010) have called for rather modest changes. The thrust of the present analysis, as is already evident, is that a more comprehensive, yet easily implemented, restructuring is needed.

It is evident that the Social Security Trust Fund is not in the best of hands. It clearly needs to disengage from being a political football. What is required is a change in the mindset that will view Social Security contributions as genuine (passive) investments into a minimal safety-net plan, a plan that can expect above average net-of-fees investment returns for the purpose of funding a combination of inflation-indexed, life-time annuity-based retirement, life insurance, and (when applicable) disability benefits.

MAKING THE SOCIAL SECURITY SYSTEM INDEPENDENT

The Federal Reserve Model

The Federal Reserve System appears to provide the best model. The Social Security System would then be governed by a Social Security Board (SSB) composed of seven members with 14-year staggered terms and have the same independent status as the Federal Reserve. The SSB would appoint (five?) investment trustees to run the current Trust Fund, which would gradually be converted to passive positions in US and international stock and bond markets. At some point, the SSB would also assume authority over, and responsibility for, the administration of the various Social Security offices around the country.

If we can trust the Federal Reserve to guide interest rates and inflation policy, could we not trust the same independent structure to guide passive investments generating above-average returns (net of fees) for the minimal safety net of inflation-indexed, life-time annuity-based, retirement, life insurance, and disability benefits?

In contrast to the recent history of the Fed, in which most board members leave after only a few years, it would be desirable for the SSB to have a board composed of individuals dedicated to the long-term future of the system and who expect to serve a full term.

Once the SSB is given independent status, the Unified Budget would reach the natural death it deserves, restore the other trust funds to their true status, and force the federal government to stop mimicking Madoff and engage in honest reporting of its finances.

The Transition into Stocks and (Marketable) Treasury Bonds

At a pace of say $25 billion a month, the conversion of one-half of the current Social Security Trust Fund's US government bonds (called Special Issue Government Bonds) to passive index-based holdings of stocks would take about five years and could be accomplished without noticeable market impact. Being near the end of a 30-year underperformance relative to bonds, the timing for switching into stocks could hardly be better. A similar amount of monthly conversion of the other half of the current Trust Fund's bonds into marketable long-term Treasury Bonds could also easily be accomplished. Net inflows would be invested in stocks until a 50–50 balance between stocks and bonds was reached. Negative net inflows would be financed with short-term borrowing as in Chapter 5. The market impact would then tend to be minimal since purchases would be spread, through the purchase of index funds, over thousands of securities in proportional fashion, with the new net demand tending to effect prices somewhat positively (as appeared to be the case in the early years in Chile when private accounts were still growing). In the current global environment, stock investments would sensibly be equally divided between US and international securities. The actual choices would of course be the purview of the SSB's investment team.

Annual Reports

Each year the SSB would issue a public report on its financial position, status, and cash flows. Each individual participant would have internet access to his or her contributions and receive an annual report confirming changes in his or her individual account.

Research Staff

Like the Fed, the SSB would have a staff to conduct research and to present reports to the board and the public about issues relating to the functioning of the minimal safety net. It would also at times appoint committees to address possible changes to the Social Security model currently in place. A number of such issues have of course already been noted. An obvious one to consider is possible adjustments for increasing life expectancy. Another is whether the increase in earnings inequality should generate an increase in the maximum earnings base which was initially set at 90% but which has since slipped to the 80s (Reich, 2011). A third is whether Social Security coverage should be made universal, to include the state and local government employees who are currently outside the system (and whose present safety nets are in generally sad shape). There is also the question of how to adjust for what has been called "legacy costs", the fact that those who retired in the early years of Social Security's existence received more benefits relative to their contributions than later retirees have and will. I will not belabor these issues here since they have been thoroughly addressed elsewhere. I would simply suggest that changes to the Social Security System recommended by the SSB be subject to a strict up or down vote by Congress.

Unfunded Liabilities... Goodbye?

In some future year, another significant issue will arise: whether to *lower* contributions or *raise* benefits or some combination of both. Feldstein (2007) has suggested that by investing private accounts in the stock market, contributions could be lowered by two thirds. That still falls short of what the Trust Fund could accomplish without privatization due to economies of scale alone. Since the results in Chapter 5 shows the Trust Fund invested in stocks *and* bonds beating the existing Trust Fund at the end of 2010 $10.2 trillion to $2.61 trillion, the three to one ratio suggested by Feldstein is more than in the ballpark even with bonds included, leaving room for a substantial boost in the benefit/contribution ratio for the SSB board to address sometime down the line.

With these changes, the public will begin to view its Social Security contributions very differently, as something that will grow undisturbed to provide generous benefits in the future, safe from being "apparently raided" by the federal government to pay current government expenses or to enact tax cuts as now happens under the Unified Budget.

From Payroll Taxes to Mandatory Contributions

Currently, Social Security contributions (payroll taxes) are evenly split between employee and employer, with the self-employed serving in both positions. The employer's portion is tax-deductible while the employee's is not. Since the administrative simplicity of the current contribution system is difficult to improve upon, it suggests that the employer's mandate to forward the combined contribution should be continued. But a case can be made that the *total* contribution should be clearly visible to, and *attributable* to, the employee. A simple way to do so would be for the employer to increase the employee's earnings by the amount of his or her annual Social Security tax formerly paid by the employer, as Chile did in the early years after privatization (Piñera, 2004). The employer would then gain a tax deduction for the increase in compensation that is exactly offset by the lost tax deduction for the Social Security taxes not paid, with *no* effect on the employer's before or after tax income.

Since the employee's additional income is a (50%) Social Security contribution, it should be deductible just like it is currently for self-employed individuals. Thus an employer's tax deduction would be replaced by employee tax deductions of equal value with a roughly neutral effect on federal revenues. In fact, a strong case can be made that, since Social Security benefits are taxable, 100% of an employee's Social Security contribution should be deductible just like it is for private pension plans. This would of course reduce federal tax receipts, at least in the short run, and, in view of the current fiscal environment, is best put on the back-burner — but also on the agenda of the SSB research staff.

SOME AGENDA ITEMS FOR THE SOCIAL SECURITY BOARD

As noted by Peter Diamond in his presidential address at the 2004 American Economic Association Annual Meeting, the current US Social Security System functions fairly well, especially compared to similar systems in other nations (Diamond, 2004). Paul Volcker sees it as "the bedrock of any retirement policy in this country" (Collins, 2010). But even if the three serious shortcomings addressed in Chapter 4 of this book are remedied, there are four administrative issues in particular that the new Board needs to ask its research staff to examine. The first concerns how to improve administrative efficiency, the second how to streamline the disability claim review process, the third how best to unclog the interface between private disability policies and those of the Social Security System, and finally how to deal with the Social Security contributions of illegal immigrants.

Administrative Efficiency

Service loads on Social Security Administration (SSA) personnel have grown in recent years, resulting in higher staff stress and longer waiting times for beneficiaries (Davidson, 2009). Seeking the proper balance between service levels and administrative costs appears to be a natural responsibility for the Social Security Board, along with such issues as process automation and privacy.

The Disability Insurance Backlog

A recent study found that the SSA received more than 2.8 million disability claims in 2009, a 21.3 % increase from the year before (Banham, 2010), with the number of claims doubling just between 2001 and 2007 (Basler, 2007). With Congress not having allowed the Social Security Administration to allocate sufficient funds from its own Trust Fund to administrative expenses as it relates to disability claims, some cases are taking years to resolve even though only those who have paid into the system qualify. Two-thirds of those who appeal an initial rejection eventually win, but waiting for a hearing and a judge often takes so much time — up to three years — that the individual in question may lose his home, ending up declaring bankruptcy, or die (Eckholm, 2007). The average monthly benefit check is $1,062, not nearly enough to live on for most people. Still, reducing the disability claim processing time appears to be the single most important administrative issue to be addressed. For a comprehensive analysis of the various issues facing the disability component of the Social Security System, see Autor and Duggan (2006).

The Interface with Private Disability Insurance

To add a private safety net on top of the minimal safety net, the insurance industry offers both group-based and individual disability insurance policies. These policies are generally coordinated not only with Social Security benefits but also with many other disability plans such as workers' compensation and disability pensions. The private insurers thus have an incentive to shift as much of its benefit payments as possible to these other plans.

The requirements to qualify for Social Security disability benefits are much tougher than for private plan benefits. Yet the industry apparently forces individuals who do not qualify under the rules to apply for Social Security disability benefits, and even to require them to keep on appealing upon denials (Walsh, 2008). One effect of unwarranted disability claims dumped on an already clogged Social Security System is to delay the processing of valid claims; lawsuits have been filed to end the practice. This is another area where the SSB needs to step in.

The Contributions of Illegal Immigrants

Large numbers of illegal immigrants are paying Social Security taxes based on fake Social Security cards, generating billions of inflow each year from which no benefits will be collected. The Social Security Administration even keeps a file on the earnings recorded under bad Social Security numbers (Porter, 2005). At some point the SSB will need to take a serious look at this conundrum — which also needs to be part of immigration reform.

EPILOGUE — THE LESSONS

The most surprising aspect of the Social Security System must be that after 74 years, its Trust Fund has never invested in equities — or even in marketable government bonds. It is well established that stocks outperform bonds over long periods (which in technical terms is due to their higher risk premia — recall Tables 1.2 and 1.3), which in turn implies that a passive portfolio of stocks and bonds will substantially beat a pure bond portfolio over a person's (post-child) lifetime. The key observation from this is of course that the ratio of available outputs from any given sequence of inputs, in a perpetual vehicle such as the Social Security Trust Fund, will be substantially higher based on passive stock and bond investments than from bond investments alone. This boosted ratio, in turn, translates to greater purchasing power by consumers, either via lower inputs, or higher outputs, or both in combination — and from the wealth effect, higher economic growth as well. So why then, one must ask, has this basic, and highly significant, economic observation not been acted on?

A key objection to equity investments that has been raised is that it would amount to "socialism". Socialism of course occurs when the government owns, and operates, the means of production. While the US government owns and operates the national forests, the national parks, the Department of Defense and its many assets, and many other properties as well, most people do not view this as socialism. Stock ownership by the Social Security Trust Fund could certainly be viewed as an intrusion into the private sector since share owners are asked to vote in matters of corporate governance. The simple remedy of course is to make the Social Security System independent, as discussed in Chapter 7. In recent years, index funds and mutual funds have relied on independent advisors in voting their holdings on behalf of the share owners, many of which are pension funds. Under this approach, the government would be unable to interfere in corporate governance matters via index fund ownership by the Social Security Trust Fund. Since index funds did not emerge until the 1970s, the early resistance to equity holdings by the Trust Fund is more understandable than it has been since the time of the Greenspan Commission.

As noted in Chapter 6 and elsewhere, the private sector is no match for the US Social Security System structure, as designed for a (national) minimal safety net, on the efficiency dimension, as measured by administrative expenses and manpower needs. With respect to inflation-adjusted, life-time annuity-based contracts covering retirement, life insurance, and (in part) disability insurance, a single company, or a group of companies in the private sector, is unlikely to survive long on a less than 1% margin for administrative expenses and profit. Thus, this is an area where a national pool without a profit motive becomes dominant, as even Hayek seems to recognize — if reluctantly (1960, p. 287). But for the *personal* safety net add-on to be constructed *above* the minimal safety net, an additional safety net that virtually everyone desires, and itself a huge enterprise in its scope, there is no substitute for a competitive private sector in providing the desired products in a genuine and fully informed free market environment.

There appears to be no reason for a fund as large as the one for Social Security to depart from passive investments, a deviation which would tend to increase its risk exposure. Thus, placements in private equity and in hedge funds, as employed by the Canada Pension Plan, and even fundamental indexing of the type pioneered by Robert Arnott (Tully, 2010), would therefore seem unnecessary. On the other hand, investments in corporate and international bonds and even limited positions in small company stocks should not be ruled out.

In an economy with population growth, we would expect positive net inflows as a typical pattern but not necessarily every month. When negative inflows occur, short-term loans seem preferable to asset sales, as illustrated in Chapter 5. Not only would this leave the earning power of the Fund's assets unimpaired and reduce transaction costs, but a Trust Fund with a strong asset base would have access to minimal borrowing rates.

Recall that opponents of Social Security tend to equate it with "welfare", especially those who are anxious to cut its benefit payments. Since no one is entitled to Social Security benefits without first having paid into the Social Security System, and its redistributive feature is modest, it is in fact not welfare. Applying the 'welfare" label to it would look even more out of place once Social Security has achieved independent status, as proposed in Chapter 7. Moving away from non-marketable government bonds as its only asset would further remove Social Security from the "welfare" stigma. With an independent System's Social Security Board making periodic recommendations for parameter adjustments, the notion of 75-year projections and unfunded liabilities connected with the Social Security System are likely, as Douglas MacArthur put it, to just fade away.

With mandatory contributions identified directly with individuals replacing payroll taxes, and the Social Security System assuming independent status, there appears to be no way the Unified budget concept can continue to survive, since the Social Security Trust Fund is by far the largest of the US government's trust funds. The result will be to force the government to begin reporting its finances, in particular its operating deficits or surpluses, honestly for the first time since 1969. One can only wonder what caused the Secretaries of the Treasury to misrepresent the United States government's finances to the tune of $4.246 trillion over the last four decades...

Since the public pension plans and minimal safety nets of most nations are in worse shape than Social Security is even in its current form, the approach to the minimal safety net outlined in this book may also serve as a model for other nations. A suggestion in this vein has been made by Pagrotsky and Fogde (2007).

Finally, once the Social Security Trust Fund is fully engaged in a passive investment program, with negligible, or even negative fees when the earnings from securities lending are taken into account, one cannot help but wonder to what extent the private sector will begin to clone its investment approach...

APPENDIX

Table 5.1

Monthly Evolution of the Social Security Trust Fund if It Had Been Invested in US Treasury Bonds, Large Company US Stocks, and (Since 2002) International Stocks, 1937–2010.
(other things being equal)
(Dollar amounts rounded to nearest million)

Year	Month	Soc. Sec. receipts less int. income	Soc. Sec. outlays less int. expense	Net SS cash inflow/ outflow	Amount of short term loan	Debt at end of month	30-day interest rate	Amount of debt repaid	New US stock investm.	Comm. rate for US stocks	Value of cont. stock portf.	Beg. of month US stock portfolio
1937	Jan	44	0	44	0	0						
	Feb	44	0	44	0	0			22	0.020	0	21
	Mar	44	0	44	0	0			22	0.020	22	43
	Apr	44	0	44	0	0			22	0.020	43	65
	May	44	0	44	0	0			22	0.020	59	81
	Jun	44	0	44	0	0			22	0.020	81	102
	Jul	32	0	32	0	0			22	0.020	97	119
	Aug	32	0	32	0	0			16	0.020	131	147
	Sep	32	0	32	0	0			16	0.020	139	155
	Oct	32	0	32	0	0			16	0.020	133	149
	Nov	32	0	32	0	0			16	0.020	134	150
	Dec	32	0	32	0	0			16	0.020	137	153
1938	Jan	32	0	32	0	0			16	0.020	146	161
	Feb	32	0	32	0	0			16	0.020	164	179
	Mar	32	0	32	0	0			16	0.020	191	207
	Apr	32	0	32	0	0			16	0.020	155	171
	May	32	0	32	0	0			16	0.020	196	211
	Jun	32	0	32	0	0			16	0.020	204	220
	Jul	42	1	41	0	0			16	0.020	275	291
	Aug	42	1	41	0	0			20	0.020	312	332
	Sep	42	1	41	0	0			20	0.020	325	345
	Oct	42	1	41	0	0			20	0.020	350	370
	Nov	42	1	41	0	0			20	0.020	399	419
	Dec	42	1	41	0	0			20	0.020	408	428
1939	Jan	42	1	41	0	0			20	0.020	445	465
	Feb	42	1	41	0	0			20	0.020	433	453
	Mar	42	1	41	0	0			20	0.020	471	491
	Apr	42	1	41	0	0			20	0.020	425	445
	May	42	1	41	0	0			20	0.020	444	464
	Jun	42	1	41	0	0			20	0.020	498	518
	Jul	46	2	44	0	0			20	0.020	486	506
	Aug	46	2	44	0	0			22	0.020	562	583
	Sep	46	2	44	0	0			22	0.020	546	567
	Oct	46	2	44	0	0			22	0.020	662	683
	Nov	46	2	44	0	0			22	0.020	675	696
	Dec	46	2	44	0	0			22	0.020	668	690
1940	Jan	46	2	44	0	0			22	0.020	708	730
	Feb	46	2	44	0	0			22	0.020	705	726
	Mar	46	2	44	0	0			22	0.020	736	757
	Apr	46	2	44	0	0			22	0.020	767	788
	May	46	2	44	0	0			22	0.020	786	807
	Jun	46	2	44	0	0			22	0.020	623	644
	Jul	57	8	49	0	0			22	0.020	696	717
	Aug	57	8	49	0	0			25	0.020	742	766
	Sep	57	8	49	0	0			25	0.020	793	817
	Oct	57	8	49	0	0			25	0.020	827	851
	Nov	57	8	49	0	0			25	0.020	887	912
	Dec	57	8	49	0	0			25	0.020	883	907
1941	Jan	57	8	49	0	0			25	0.020	908	932
	Feb	57	8	49	0	0			25	0.020	889	913
	Mar	57	8	49	0	0			25	0.020	908	932
	Apr	57	8	49	0	0			25	0.020	938	963
	May	57	8	49	0	0			25	0.020	904	928
	Jun	58	8	50	0	0			25	0.020	945	969
	Jul	75	11	63	0	0			25	0.020	1025	1050
	Aug	75	11	63	0	0			32	0.020	1111	1142
	Sep	75	11	63	0	0			32	0.020	1143	1174
	Oct	75	11	63	0	0			32	0.020	1166	1197
	Nov	75	11	63	0	0			32	0.020	1118	1149
	Dec	75	11	63	0	0			32	0.020	1117	1148

Table 5.1   (*Cont'd*)

Monthly Evolution of the Social Security Trust Fund if It Had Been Invested in US Treasury
Bonds, Large Company US Stocks, and (Since 2002) International Stocks, 1937–2010.
(other things being equal)
(Dollar amounts rounded to nearest million)

Year	Month	New gov't bond investm.	Market impact for bonds	Value of cont. bond portfolio	Beg. of month bond portfolio	New EAFE+ Canada investm.	Comm. for EAFE+ stocks	Value of cont. EAFE+ portfolio	Beg. of month EAFE+ portfolio	Return on large US stocks	Return on LT US gov't bonds	Return on EAFE+ stocks
1937	Jan									0.0390	-0.0013	
	Feb	22	0.010	0	22	0		0	0	0.0191	0.0086	
	Mar	22	0.010	22	44	0		0	0	-0.0077	-0.0411	
	Apr	22	0.010	42	64	0		0	0	-0.0809	0.0039	
	May	22	0.010	64	86	0		0	0	-0.0024	0.0053	
	Jun	22	0.010	86	108	0		0	0	-0.0504	-0.0018	
	Jul	22	0.010	108	129	0		0	0	0.1045	0.0138	
	Aug	16	0.010	131	147	0		0	0	-0.0483	-0.0104	
	Sep	16	0.010	145	161	0		0	0	-0.1403	0.0045	
	Oct	16	0.010	162	178	0		0	0	-0.0981	0.0042	
	Nov	16	0.010	178	194	0		0	0	-0.0866	0.0096	
	Dec	16	0.010	196	212	0		0	0	-0.0459	0.0082	
1938	Jan	16	0.010	213	229	0		0	0	0.0152	0.0057	
	Feb	16	0.010	230	246	0		0	0	0.0674	0.0052	
	Mar	16	0.010	247	263	0		0	0	-0.2487	-0.0037	
	Apr	16	0.010	262	278	0		0	0	0.1447	0.0210	
	May	16	0.010	284	300	0		0	0	-0.0330	0.0044	
	Jun	16	0.010	301	317	0		0	0	0.2503	0.0004	
	Jul	16	0.010	317	333	0		0	0	0.0744	0.0043	
	Aug	20	0.010	334	354	0		0	0	-0.0226	0.0000	
	Sep	20	0.010	354	374	0		0	0	0.0166	0.0022	
	Oct	20	0.010	375	395	0		0	0	0.0776	0.0087	
	Nov	20	0.010	399	419	0		0	0	-0.0273	-0.0022	
	Dec	20	0.010	418	438	0		0	0	0.0401	0.0080	
1939	Jan	20	0.010	442	462	0		0	0	-0.0674	0.0059	
	Feb	20	0.010	465	485	0		0	0	0.0390	0.0080	
	Mar	20	0.010	489	509	0		0	0	-0.1339	0.0125	
	Apr	20	0.010	515	535	0		0	0	-0.0027	0.0118	
	May	20	0.010	542	562	0		0	0	0.0733	0.0171	
	Jun	20	0.010	571	592	0		0	0	-0.0612	-0.0027	
	Jul	20	0.010	590	610	0		0	0	0.1105	0.0113	
	Aug	22	0.010	617	639	0		0	0	-0.0648	-0.0201	
	Sep	22	0.010	626	647	0		0	0	0.1673	-0.0545	
	Oct	22	0.010	612	634	0		0	0	-0.0123	0.0410	
	Nov	22	0.010	660	681	0		0	0	-0.0398	0.0162	
	Dec	22	0.010	692	714	0		0	0	0.0270	0.0145	
1940	Jan	22	0.010	724	746	0		0	0	-0.0336	-0.0017	
	Feb	22	0.010	744	766	0		0	0	0.0133	0.0027	
	Mar	22	0.010	768	789	0		0	0	0.0124	0.0177	
	Apr	22	0.010	803	825	0		0	0	-0.0024	-0.0035	
	May	22	0.010	822	844	0		0	0	-0.2289	-0.0299	
	Jun	22	0.010	818	840	0		0	0	0.0809	0.0258	
	Jul	22	0.010	861	883	0		0	0	0.0341	0.0052	
	Aug	25	0.010	888	912	0		0	0	0.0350	0.0028	
	Sep	25	0.010	915	939	0		0	0	0.0123	0.0110	
	Oct	25	0.010	949	974	0		0	0	0.0422	0.0031	
	Nov	25	0.010	977	1001	0		0	0	-0.0316	0.0205	
	Dec	25	0.010	1022	1046	0		0	0	0.0009	0.0067	
1941	Jan	25	0.010	1053	1078	0		0	0	-0.0463	-0.0201	
	Feb	25	0.010	1056	1081	0		0	0	-0.0060	0.0020	
	Mar	25	0.010	1083	1107	0		0	0	0.0071	0.0096	
	Apr	25	0.010	1118	1142	0		0	0	-0.0612	0.0129	
	May	25	0.010	1157	1182	0		0	0	0.0183	0.0027	
	Jun	25	0.010	1185	1209	0		0	0	0.0578	0.0066	
	Jul	25	0.010	1217	1242	0		0	0	0.0579	0.0022	
	Aug	32	0.010	1245	1276	0		0	0	0.0010	0.0018	
	Sep	32	0.010	1278	1310	0		0	0	-0.0068	-0.0012	
	Oct	32	0.010	1308	1340	0		0	0	-0.0657	0.0140	
	Nov	32	0.010	1358	1390	0		0	0	-0.0284	-0.0029	
	Dec	32	0.010	1386	1417	0		0	0	-0.0407	-0.0177	

Table 5.1   (*Cont'd*)

Monthly Evolution of the Social Security Trust Fund if It Had Been Invested in US Treasury Bonds, Large Company US Stocks, and (Since 2002) International Stocks, 1937–2010.

(other things being equal)

(Dollar amounts rounded to nearest million)

Year	Month	Ending value of US stock portfolio	Ending value of gov't bond portfolio	Ending value of EAFE+ portfolio	End Value of SS Trust Fund	Percent in large US stocks	Percent in LT gov't bonds	Percent in EAFE+ Canada stocks	Percent of debt	Official value ot SS Trust Fund	Net SS inflows by fiscal year	Ratio of invested to actual Trust Fund
1937	Jan	0	0	0	0							
	Feb	22	22	0	44	50.01	49.99	0.00	0.00			
	Mar	43	42	0	85	50.73	49.27	0.00	0.00			
	Apr	59	64	0	123	48.19	51.81	0.00	0.00			
	May	81	86	0	167	48.41	51.59	0.00	0.00			
	Jun	97	108	0	205	47.44	52.56	0.00	0.00	267	263	0.77
	Jul	131	131	0	262	49.98	50.02	0.00	0.00			
	Aug	139	145	0	285	48.98	51.02	0.00	0.00			
	Sep	133	162	0	295	45.18	54.82	0.00	0.00			
	Oct	134	178	0	313	42.97	57.03	0.00	0.00			
	Nov	137	196	0	333	41.14	58.86	0.00	0.00			
	Dec	146	213	0	359	40.55	59.45	0.00	0.00			
1938	Jan	164	230	0	394	41.51	58.49	0.00	0.00			
	Feb	191	247	0	439	43.59	56.41	0.00	0.00			
	Mar	155	262	0	418	37.21	62.79	0.00	0.00			
	Apr	196	284	0	480	40.81	59.19	0.00	0.00			
	May	204	301	0	505	40.44	59.56	0.00	0.00			
	Jun	275	317	0	592	46.47	53.53	0.00	0.00	664	382	0.89
	Jul	312	334	0	646	48.32	51.68	0.00	0.00			
	Aug	325	354	0	679	47.83	52.17	0.00	0.00			
	Sep	350	375	0	726	48.29	51.71	0.00	0.00			
	Oct	399	399	0	798	50.02	49.98	0.00	0.00			
	Nov	408	418	0	826	49.37	50.63	0.00	0.00			
	Dec	445	442	0	886	50.17	49.83	0.00	0.00			
1939	Jan	433	465	0	898	48.26	51.74	0.00	0.00			
	Feb	471	489	0	960	49.08	50.92	0.00	0.00			
	Mar	425	515	0	940	45.22	54.78	0.00	0.00			
	Apr	444	542	0	986	45.05	54.95	0.00	0.00			
	May	498	571	0	1069	46.57	53.43	0.00	0.00			
	Jun	486	590	0	1076	45.18	54.82	0.00	0.00	1180	489	0.91
	Jul	562	617	0	1179	47.67	52.33	0.00	0.00			
	Aug	546	626	0	1171	46.58	53.42	0.00	0.00			
	Sep	662	612	0	1274	51.95	48.05	0.00	0.00			
	Oct	675	660	0	1334	50.57	49.43	0.00	0.00			
	Nov	668	692	0	1360	49.13	50.87	0.00	0.00			
	Dec	708	724	0	1432	49.45	50.55	0.00	0.00			
1940	Jan	705	744	0	1449	48.65	51.35	0.00	0.00			
	Feb	736	768	0	1504	48.94	51.06	0.00	0.00			
	Mar	767	803	0	1570	48.83	51.17	0.00	0.00			
	Apr	786	822	0	1608	48.89	51.11	0.00	0.00			
	May	623	818	0	1441	43.21	56.79	0.00	0.00			
	Jun	696	861	0	1558	44.69	55.31	0.00	0.00	1745	522	0.89
	Jul	742	888	0	1630	45.53	54.47	0.00	0.00			
	Aug	793	915	0	1708	46.43	53.57	0.00	0.00			
	Sep	827	949	0	1777	46.56	53.44	0.00	0.00			
	Oct	887	977	0	1864	47.60	52.40	0.00	0.00			
	Nov	883	1022	0	1905	46.35	53.65	0.00	0.00			
	Dec	908	1053	0	1961	46.29	53.71	0.00	0.00			
1941	Jan	889	1056	0	1945	45.70	54.30	0.00	0.00			
	Feb	908	1083	0	1990	45.60	54.40	0.00	0.00			
	Mar	938	1118	0	2056	45.63	54.37	0.00	0.00			
	Apr	904	1157	0	2061	43.85	56.15	0.00	0.00			
	May	945	1185	0	2130	44.37	55.63	0.00	0.00			
	Jun	1025	1217	0	2242	45.72	54.28	0.00	0.00	2398	594	0.94
	Jul	1111	1245	0	2355	47.15	52.85	0.00	0.00			
	Aug	1143	1278	0	2421	47.20	52.80	0.00	0.00			
	Sep	1166	1308	0	2474	47.12	52.88	0.00	0.00			
	Oct	1118	1358	0	2476	45.15	54.85	0.00	0.00			
	Nov	1117	1386	0	2502	44.62	55.38	0.00	0.00			
	Dec	1101	1392	0	2493	44.16	55.84	0.00	0.00			

Table 5.1 (*Cont'd*)

Monthly Evolution of the Social Security Trust Fund if It Had Been Invested in US Treasury Bonds, Large Company US Stocks, and (Since 2002) International Stocks, 1937–2010.
(other things being equal)
(Dollar amounts rounded to nearest million)

Year	Month	Soc. Sec. receipts less int. income	Soc. Sec. outlays less int. expense	Net SS cash inflow/ outflow	Amount of short term loan	Debt at end of month	30-day interest rate	Amount of debt repaid	New US stock investm.	Comm. rate for US stocks	Value of cont. stock portf.	Beg. of month US stock portfolio
1942	Jan	75	11	63	0	0			32	0.020	1101	1132
	Feb	75	11	63	0	0			32	0.020	1150	1181
	Mar	75	11	63	0	0			32	0.020	1162	1193
	Apr	75	11	63	0	0			32	0.020	1116	1147
	May	75	11	63	0	0			32	0.020	1101	1132
	Jun	75	11	63	0	0			32	0.020	1222	1253
	Jul	94	15	79	0	0			32	0.020	1281	1312
	Aug	94	15	79	0	0			40	0.020	1356	1395
	Sep	94	15	79	0	0			40	0.020	1418	1457
	Oct	94	15	79	0	0			40	0.020	1499	1538
	Nov	94	15	79	0	0			40	0.020	1642	1681
	Dec	94	15	79	0	0			40	0.020	1677	1716
1943	Jan	94	15	79	0	0			40	0.020	1811	1849
	Feb	94	15	79	0	0			40	0.020	1986	2025
	Mar	94	15	79	0	0			40	0.020	2143	2182
	Apr	94	15	79	0	0			40	0.020	2301	2340
	May	94	15	79	0	0			40	0.020	2348	2387
	Jun	94	15	79	0	0			40	0.020	2518	2557
	Jul	108	18	90	0	0			40	0.020	2614	2653
	Aug	108	18	90	0	0			45	0.020	2514	2558
	Sep	108	18	90	0	0			45	0.020	2601	2645
	Oct	108	18	90	0	0			45	0.020	2715	2759
	Nov	108	18	90	0	0			45	0.020	2729	2773
	Dec	108	18	90	0	0			45	0.020	2591	2635
1944	Jan	108	18	90	0	0			45	0.020	2798	2842
	Feb	108	18	90	0	0			45	0.020	2890	2934
	Mar	108	18	90	0	0			45	0.020	2947	2991
	Apr	108	18	90	0	0			45	0.020	3049	3093
	May	108	18	90	0	0			45	0.020	3062	3106
	Jun	108	18	90	0	0			45	0.020	3263	3307
	Jul	109	22	87	0	0			45	0.020	3486	3530
	Aug	109	22	87	0	0			43	0.020	3462	3504
	Sep	109	22	87	0	0			43	0.020	3559	3602
	Oct	109	22	87	0	0			43	0.020	3599	3642
	Nov	109	22	87	0	0			43	0.020	3650	3693
	Dec	109	22	87	0	0			43	0.020	3742	3784
1945	Jan	109	22	87	0	0			43	0.020	3926	3969
	Feb	109	22	87	0	0			43	0.020	4031	4074
	Mar	109	22	87	0	0			43	0.020	4352	4395
	Apr	109	22	87	0	0			43	0.020	4201	4243
	May	109	22	87	0	0			43	0.020	4626	4669
	Jun	109	22	87	0	0			43	0.020	4760	4802
	Jul	103	30	73	0	0			43	0.020	4799	4842
	Aug	103	30	73	0	0			37	0.020	4755	4790
	Sep	103	30	73	0	0			37	0.020	5098	5133
	Oct	103	30	73	0	0			37	0.020	5358	5394
	Nov	103	30	73	0	0			37	0.020	5568	5604
	Dec	103	30	73	0	0			37	0.020	5826	5862
1946	Jan	103	30	73	0	0			37	0.020	5930	5966
	Feb	103	30	73	0	0			37	0.020	6392	6428
	Mar	103	30	73	0	0			37	0.020	6016	6051
	Apr	103	30	73	0	0			37	0.020	6342	6378
	May	103	30	73	0	0			37	0.020	6629	6664
	Jun	103	30	73	0	0			37	0.020	6856	6892
	Jul	122	39	83	0	0			37	0.020	6637	6673
	Aug	122	39	83	0	0			41	0.020	6514	6554
	Sep	122	39	83	0	0			41	0.020	6113	6153
	Oct	122	39	83	0	0			41	0.020	5540	5580
	Nov	122	39	83	0	0			41	0.020	5547	5587
	Dec	122	39	83	0	0			41	0.020	5572	5613

Table 5.1 (*Cont'd*)

Monthly Evolution of the Social Security Trust Fund if It Had Been Invested in US Treasury Bonds, Large Company US Stocks, and (Since 2002) International Stocks, 1937–2010.
(other things being equal)
(Dollar amounts rounded to nearest million)

Year	Month	New gov't bond investm.	Market impact for bonds	Value of cont. bond portfolio	Beg. of month bond portfolio	New EAFE+ Canada investm.	Comm. for EAFE+ stocks	Value of cont. EAFE+ portfolio	Beg. of month EAFE+ portfolio	Return on large US stocks	Return on LT US gov't bonds	Return on EAFE+ stocks
1942	Jan	32	0.010	1392	1423	0		0	0	0.0161	0.0069	
	Feb	32	0.010	1433	1464	0		0	0	-0.0159	0.0011	
	Mar	32	0.010	1466	1497	0		0	0	-0.0652	0.0092	
	Apr	32	0.010	1511	1542	0		0	0	-0.0399	-0.0029	
	May	32	0.010	1538	1569	0		0	0	0.0796	0.0075	
	Jun	32	0.010	1581	1612	0		0	0	0.0221	0.0003	
	Jul	32	0.010	1613	1644	0		0	0	0.0337	0.0018	
	Aug	40	0.010	1647	1686	0		0	0	0.0164	0.0038	
	Sep	40	0.010	1693	1732	0		0	0	0.0290	0.0003	
	Oct	40	0.010	1733	1772	0		0	0	0.0678	0.0024	
	Nov	40	0.010	1776	1816	0		0	0	-0.0021	-0.0035	
	Dec	40	0.010	1809	1849	0		0	0	0.0549	0.0049	
1943	Jan	40	0.010	1858	1897	0		0	0	0.0737	0.0033	
	Feb	40	0.010	1903	1943	0		0	0	0.0583	-0.0005	
	Mar	40	0.010	1942	1981	0		0	0	0.0545	0.0009	
	Apr	40	0.010	1983	2022	0		0	0	0.0035	0.0048	
	May	40	0.010	2032	2071	0		0	0	0.0552	0.0050	
	Jun	40	0.010	2081	2121	0		0	0	0.0223	0.0018	
	Jul	40	0.010	2125	2164	0		0	0	-0.0526	-0.0001	
	Aug	45	0.010	2164	2208	0		0	0	0.0171	0.0021	
	Sep	45	0.010	2213	2257	0		0	0	0.0263	0.0011	
	Oct	45	0.010	2260	2304	0		0	0	-0.0108	0.0005	
	Nov	45	0.010	2305	2349	0		0	0	-0.0654	0.0000	
	Dec	45	0.010	2349	2394	0		0	0	0.0617	0.0018	
1944	Jan	45	0.010	2398	2442	0		0	0	0.0171	0.0021	
	Feb	45	0.010	2448	2492	0		0	0	0.0042	0.0032	
	Mar	45	0.010	2500	2544	0		0	0	0.0195	0.0021	
	Apr	45	0.010	2550	2594	0		0	0	-0.0100	0.0013	
	May	45	0.010	2597	2642	0		0	0	0.0505	0.0028	
	Jun	45	0.010	2649	2693	0		0	0	0.0543	0.0008	
	Jul	45	0.010	2695	2740	0		0	0	-0.0193	0.0036	
	Aug	43	0.010	2750	2793	0		0	0	0.0157	0.0027	
	Sep	43	0.010	2800	2843	0		0	0	-0.0008	0.0014	
	Oct	43	0.010	2847	2890	0		0	0	0.0023	0.0012	
	Nov	43	0.010	2894	2937	0		0	0	0.0133	0.0024	
	Dec	43	0.010	2944	2987	0		0	0	0.0374	0.0042	
1945	Jan	43	0.010	2999	3042	0		0	0	0.0158	0.0127	
	Feb	43	0.010	3081	3124	0		0	0	0.0683	0.0077	
	Mar	43	0.010	3148	3191	0		0	0	-0.0441	0.0021	
	Apr	43	0.010	3198	3241	0		0	0	0.0902	0.0160	
	May	43	0.010	3293	3336	0		0	0	0.0195	0.0056	
	Jun	43	0.010	3354	3397	0		0	0	-0.0007	0.0169	
	Jul	43	0.010	3455	3498	0		0	0	-0.0180	-0.0086	
	Aug	37	0.010	3468	3504	0		0	0	0.0641	0.0026	
	Sep	37	0.010	3513	3550	0		0	0	0.0438	0.0054	
	Oct	37	0.010	3569	3605	0		0	0	0.0322	0.0104	
	Nov	37	0.010	3643	3679	0		0	0	0.0396	0.0125	
	Dec	37	0.010	3725	3761	0		0	0	0.0116	0.0194	
1946	Jan	37	0.010	3834	3870	0		0	0	0.0714	0.0025	
	Feb	37	0.010	3880	3916	0		0	0	-0.0641	0.0032	
	Mar	37	0.010	3929	3965	0		0	0	0.0480	0.0010	
	Apr	37	0.010	3969	4005	0		0	0	0.0393	-0.0135	
	May	37	0.010	3951	3988	0		0	0	0.0288	-0.0012	
	Jun	37	0.010	3983	4019	0		0	0	-0.0370	0.0070	
	Jul	37	0.010	4047	4084	0		0	0	-0.0239	-0.0040	
	Aug	41	0.010	4067	4108	0		0	0	-0.0674	-0.0111	
	Sep	41	0.010	4063	4104	0		0	0	-0.0997	-0.0009	
	Oct	41	0.010	4100	4141	0		0	0	-0.0060	0.0074	
	Nov	41	0.010	4172	4213	0		0	0	-0.0027	-0.0054	
	Dec	41	0.010	4190	4231	0		0	0	0.0457	0.0145	

Table 5.1 (*Cont'd*)

Monthly Evolution of the Social Security Trust Fund if It Had Been Invested in US Treasury
Bonds, Large Company US Stocks, and (Since 2002) International Stocks, 1937–2010.
(other things being equal)
(Dollar amounts rounded to nearest million)

Year	Month	Ending value of US stock portfolio	Ending value of gov't bond portfolio	Ending value of EAFE+ portfolio	End Value of SS Trust Fund	Percent in large US stocks	Percent in LT US gov't bonds	Percent in EAFE+ Canada stocks	Percent of debt	Official value ot SS Trust Fund	Net SS inflows by fiscal year	Ratio of invested to actual Trust Fund
1942	Jan	1150	1433	0	2583	44.52	55.48	0.00	0.00			
	Feb	1162	1466	0	2628	44.22	55.78	0.00	0.00			
	Mar	1116	1511	0	2627	42.47	57.53	0.00	0.00			
	Apr	1101	1538	0	2639	41.72	58.28	0.00	0.00			
	May	1222	1581	0	2803	43.59	56.41	0.00	0.00			
	Jun	1281	1613	0	2893	44.26	55.74	0.00	0.00	3227	760	0.90
	Jul	1356	1647	0	3003	45.15	54.85	0.00	0.00			
	Aug	1418	1693	0	3111	45.58	54.42	0.00	0.00			
	Sep	1499	1733	0	3232	46.38	53.62	0.00	0.00			
	Oct	1642	1776	0	3418	48.03	51.97	0.00	0.00			
	Nov	1677	1809	0	3487	48.11	51.89	0.00	0.00			
	Dec	1811	1858	0	3668	49.36	50.64	0.00	0.00			
1943	Jan	1986	1903	0	3889	51.06	48.94	0.00	0.00			
	Feb	2143	1942	0	4084	52.46	47.54	0.00	0.00			
	Mar	2301	1983	0	4283	53.71	46.29	0.00	0.00			
	Apr	2348	2032	0	4379	53.61	46.39	0.00	0.00			
	May	2518	2081	0	4600	54.75	45.25	0.00	0.00			
	Jun	2614	2125	0	4739	55.17	44.83	0.00	0.00	4268	953	1.11
	Jul	2514	2164	0	4677	53.74	46.26	0.00	0.00			
	Aug	2601	2213	0	4814	54.04	45.96	0.00	0.00			
	Sep	2715	2260	0	4974	54.58	45.42	0.00	0.00			
	Oct	2729	2305	0	5034	54.21	45.79	0.00	0.00			
	Nov	2591	2349	0	4941	52.45	47.55	0.00	0.00			
	Dec	2798	2398	0	5196	53.85	46.15	0.00	0.00			
1944	Jan	2890	2448	0	5338	54.15	45.85	0.00	0.00			
	Feb	2947	2500	0	5447	54.10	45.90	0.00	0.00			
	Mar	3049	2550	0	5598	54.46	45.54	0.00	0.00			
	Apr	3062	2597	0	5659	54.11	45.89	0.00	0.00			
	May	3263	2649	0	5912	55.19	44.81	0.00	0.00			
	Jun	3486	2695	0	6182	56.39	43.61	0.00	0.00	5446	1075	1.14
	Jul	3462	2750	0	6212	55.73	44.27	0.00	0.00			
	Aug	3559	2800	0	6360	55.97	44.03	0.00	0.00			
	Sep	3599	2847	0	6446	55.83	44.17	0.00	0.00			
	Oct	3650	2894	0	6544	55.78	44.22	0.00	0.00			
	Nov	3742	2944	0	6686	55.97	44.03	0.00	0.00			
	Dec	3926	2999	0	6925	56.69	43.31	0.00	0.00			
1945	Jan	4031	3081	0	7112	56.68	43.32	0.00	0.00			
	Feb	4352	3148	0	7500	58.03	41.97	0.00	0.00			
	Mar	4201	3198	0	7399	56.78	43.22	0.00	0.00			
	Apr	4626	3293	0	7919	58.42	41.58	0.00	0.00			
	May	4760	3354	0	8114	58.66	41.34	0.00	0.00			
	Jun	4799	3455	0	8254	58.14	41.86	0.00	0.00	6613	1043	1.25
	Jul	4755	3468	0	8222	57.82	42.18	0.00	0.00			
	Aug	5098	3513	0	8611	59.20	40.80	0.00	0.00			
	Sep	5358	3569	0	8927	60.02	39.98	0.00	0.00			
	Oct	5568	3643	0	9210	60.45	39.55	0.00	0.00			
	Nov	5826	3725	0	9551	61.00	39.00	0.00	0.00			
	Dec	5930	3834	0	9764	60.73	39.27	0.00	0.00			
1946	Jan	6392	3880	0	10272	62.23	37.77	0.00	0.00			
	Feb	6016	3929	0	9944	60.49	39.51	0.00	0.00			
	Mar	6342	3969	0	10311	61.51	38.49	0.00	0.00			
	Apr	6629	3951	0	10580	62.65	37.35	0.00	0.00			
	May	6856	3983	0	10839	63.25	36.75	0.00	0.00			
	Jun	6637	4047	0	10685	62.12	37.88	0.00	0.00	7641	880	1.40
	Jul	6514	4067	0	10581	61.56	38.44	0.00	0.00			
	Aug	6113	4063	0	10175	60.07	39.93	0.00	0.00			
	Sep	5540	4100	0	9640	57.47	42.53	0.00	0.00			
	Oct	5547	4172	0	9718	57.08	42.92	0.00	0.00			
	Nov	5572	4190	0	9762	57.08	42.92	0.00	0.00			
	Dec	5869	4292	0	10161	57.76	42.24	0.00	0.00			

Table 5.1 (Cont'd)

Monthly Evolution of the Social Security Trust Fund if It Had Been Invested in US Treasury
Bonds, Large Company US Stocks, and (Since 2002) International Stocks, 1937–2010.
(other things being equal)
(Dollar amounts rounded to nearest million)

Year	Month	Soc. Sec. receipts less int. income	Soc. Sec. outlays less int. expense	Net SS cash inflow/ outflow	Amount of short term loan	Debt at end of month	30-day interest rate	Amount of debt repaid	New US stock investm.	Comm. rate for US stocks	Value of cont. stock portf.	Beg. of month US stock portfolio
1947	Jan	122	39	83	0	0			41	0.020	5869	5910
	Feb	122	39	83	0	0			41	0.020	6060	6101
	Mar	122	39	83	0	0			41	0.020	6054	6095
	Apr	122	39	83	0	0			41	0.020	6004	6044
	May	122	39	83	0	0			41	0.020	5825	5865
	Jun	122	39	83	0	0			41	0.020	5874	5914
	Jul	135	47	88	0	0			41	0.020	6242	6282
	Aug	135	47	88	0	0			44	0.020	6522	6565
	Sep	135	47	88	0	0			44	0.020	6432	6475
	Oct	135	47	88	0	0			44	0.020	6403	6446
	Nov	135	47	88	0	0			44	0.020	6600	6643
	Dec	135	47	88	0	0			44	0.020	6527	6570
1948	Jan	135	47	88	0	0			44	0.020	6723	6766
	Feb	135	47	88	0	0			44	0.020	6510	6553
	Mar	135	47	88	0	0			44	0.020	6299	6342
	Apr	135	47	88	0	0			44	0.020	6845	6888
	May	135	47	88	0	0			44	0.020	7089	7132
	Jun	135	47	88	0	0			44	0.020	7759	7802
	Jul	141	55	86	0	0			44	0.020	7845	7888
	Aug	141	55	86	0	0			43	0.020	7487	7529
	Sep	141	55	86	0	0			43	0.020	7648	7690
	Oct	141	55	86	0	0			43	0.020	7478	7520
	Nov	141	55	86	0	0			43	0.020	8054	8096
	Dec	141	55	86	0	0			43	0.020	7318	7360
1949	Jan	141	55	86	0	0			43	0.020	7615	7657
	Feb	141	55	86	0	0			43	0.020	7687	7729
	Mar	141	55	86	0	0			43	0.020	7500	7542
	Apr	141	55	86	0	0			43	0.020	7790	7832
	May	141	55	86	0	0			43	0.020	7692	7734
	Jun	141	55	86	0	0			43	0.020	7534	7577
	Jul	176	65	111	0	0			43	0.020	7587	7629
	Aug	176	65	111	0	0			55	0.020	8125	8179
	Sep	176	65	111	0	0			55	0.020	8358	8413
	Oct	176	65	111	0	0			55	0.020	8634	8688
	Nov	176	65	111	0	0			55	0.020	8983	9038
	Dec	176	65	111	0	0			55	0.020	9196	9250
1950	Jan	176	65	111	0	0			55	0.020	9699	9754
	Feb	176	65	111	0	0			55	0.020	9946	10000
	Mar	176	65	111	0	0			55	0.020	10199	10253
	Apr	176	65	111	0	0			55	0.020	10325	10379
	May	176	65	111	0	0			55	0.020	10883	10937
	Jun	176	65	111	0	0			55	0.020	11494	11548
	Jul	260	131	130	0	0			55	0.020	10915	10970
	Aug	260	131	130	0	0			65	0.020	11100	11164
	Sep	260	131	130	0	0			65	0.020	11658	11722
	Oct	260	131	130	0	0			65	0.020	12416	12479
	Nov	260	131	130	0	0			65	0.020	12595	12659
	Dec	260	131	130	0	0			65	0.020	12873	12936
1951	Jan	260	131	130	0	0			65	0.020	13600	13663
	Feb	260	131	130	0	0			65	0.020	14534	14597
	Mar	260	131	130	0	0			65	0.020	14826	14890
	Apr	260	131	130	0	0			65	0.020	14657	14721
	May	260	131	130	0	0			65	0.020	15470	15534
	Jun	260	131	130	0	0			65	0.020	15069	15133
	Jul	300	172	128	0	0			65	0.020	14788	14851
	Aug	300	172	128	0	0			64	0.020	15907	15970
	Sep	300	172	128	0	0			64	0.020	16733	16796
	Oct	300	172	128	0	0			64	0.020	16817	16880
	Nov	300	172	128	0	0			64	0.020	16706	16769
	Dec	300	172	128	0	0			64	0.020	16930	16992

Table 5.1 (Cont'd)

Monthly Evolution of the Social Security Trust Fund if It Had Been Invested in US Treasury Bonds, Large Company US Stocks, and (Since 2002) International Stocks, 1937–2010.
(other things being equal)
(Dollar amounts rounded to nearest million)

Year	Month	New gov't bond investm.	Market impact for bonds	Value of cont. bond portfolio	Beg. of month bond portfolio	New EAFE+ Canada investm.	Comm. for EAFE+ stocks	Value of cont. EAFE+ portfolio	Beg. of month EAFE+ portfolio	Return on large US stocks	Return on LT US gov't bonds	Return on EAFE+ stocks
1947	Jan	41	0.010	4292	4333	0		0	0	0.0255	-0.0006	
	Feb	41	0.010	4330	4371	0		0	0	-0.0077	0.0021	
	Mar	41	0.010	4381	4422	0		0	0	-0.0149	0.0020	
	Apr	41	0.010	4430	4471	0		0	0	-0.0363	-0.0037	
	May	41	0.010	4455	4496	0		0	0	0.0014	0.0033	
	Jun	41	0.010	4511	4552	0		0	0	0.0554	0.0010	
	Jul	41	0.010	4556	4597	0		0	0	0.0381	0.0063	
	Aug	44	0.010	4626	4670	0		0	0	-0.0203	0.0081	
	Sep	44	0.010	4708	4751	0		0	0	-0.0111	-0.0044	
	Oct	44	0.010	4730	4774	0		0	0	0.0238	-0.0037	
	Nov	44	0.010	4756	4800	0		0	0	-0.0175	-0.0174	
	Dec	44	0.010	4716	4760	0		0	0	0.0233	-0.0192	
1948	Jan	44	0.010	4669	4712	0		0	0	-0.0379	0.0020	
	Feb	44	0.010	4722	4765	0		0	0	-0.0388	0.0046	
	Mar	44	0.010	4787	4831	0		0	0	0.0793	0.0034	
	Apr	44	0.010	4847	4891	0		0	0	0.0292	0.0045	
	May	44	0.010	4913	4957	0		0	0	0.0879	0.0141	
	Jun	44	0.010	5026	5070	0		0	0	0.0054	-0.0084	
	Jul	44	0.010	5028	5071	0		0	0	-0.0508	-0.0021	
	Aug	43	0.010	5061	5103	0		0	0	0.0158	0.0001	
	Sep	43	0.010	5104	5146	0		0	0	-0.0276	0.0014	
	Oct	43	0.010	5153	5196	0		0	0	0.0710	0.0007	
	Nov	43	0.010	5200	5242	0		0	0	-0.0961	0.0076	
	Dec	43	0.010	5282	5325	0		0	0	0.0346	0.0056	
1949	Jan	43	0.010	5354	5397	0		0	0	0.0039	0.0082	
	Feb	43	0.010	5441	5484	0		0	0	-0.0296	0.0049	
	Mar	43	0.010	5511	5553	0		0	0	0.0328	0.0074	
	Apr	43	0.010	5594	5637	0		0	0	-0.0179	0.0011	
	May	43	0.010	5643	5686	0		0	0	-0.0258	0.0019	
	Jun	43	0.010	5696	5739	0		0	0	0.0014	0.0167	
	Jul	43	0.010	5835	5877	0		0	0	0.0650	0.0033	
	Aug	55	0.010	5897	5952	0		0	0	0.0219	0.0111	
	Sep	55	0.010	6018	6072	0		0	0	0.0263	-0.0011	
	Oct	55	0.010	6066	6120	0		0	0	0.0340	0.0019	
	Nov	55	0.010	6132	6187	0		0	0	0.0175	0.0021	
	Dec	55	0.010	6200	6254	0		0	0	0.0486	0.0052	
1950	Jan	55	0.010	6287	6342	0		0	0	0.0197	-0.0061	
	Feb	55	0.010	6303	6358	0		0	0	0.0199	0.0021	
	Mar	55	0.010	6371	6426	0		0	0	0.0070	0.0008	
	Apr	55	0.010	6431	6485	0		0	0	0.0486	0.0030	
	May	55	0.010	6505	6560	0		0	0	0.0509	0.0033	
	Jun	55	0.010	6581	6636	0		0	0	-0.0548	-0.0025	
	Jul	55	0.010	6619	6674	0		0	0	0.0119	0.0055	
	Aug	65	0.010	6711	6775	0		0	0	0.0443	0.0014	
	Sep	65	0.010	6784	6849	0		0	0	0.0592	-0.0072	
	Oct	65	0.010	6799	6863	0		0	0	0.0093	-0.0048	
	Nov	65	0.010	6830	6895	0		0	0	0.0169	0.0035	
	Dec	65	0.010	6919	6983	0		0	0	0.0513	0.0016	
1951	Jan	65	0.010	6994	7058	0		0	0	0.0637	0.0058	
	Feb	65	0.010	7099	7163	0		0	0	0.0157	-0.0074	
	Mar	65	0.010	7110	7174	0		0	0	-0.0156	-0.0157	
	Apr	65	0.010	7062	7126	0		0	0	0.0509	-0.0063	
	May	65	0.010	7081	7145	0		0	0	-0.0299	-0.0069	
	Jun	65	0.010	7096	7160	0		0	0	-0.0228	-0.0062	
	Jul	65	0.010	7116	7180	0		0	0	0.0711	0.0138	
	Aug	64	0.010	7279	7342	0		0	0	0.0478	0.0099	
	Sep	64	0.010	7415	7478	0		0	0	0.0013	-0.0080	
	Oct	64	0.010	7418	7481	0		0	0	-0.0103	0.0010	
	Nov	64	0.010	7489	7552	0		0	0	0.0096	-0.0136	
	Dec	64	0.010	7449	7512	0		0	0	0.0424	-0.0061	

Table 5.1 (Cont'd)

Monthly Evolution of the Social Security Trust Fund if It Had Been Invested in US Treasury Bonds, Large Company US Stocks, and (Since 2002) International Stocks, 1937–2010.
(other things being equal)
(Dollar amounts rounded to nearest million)

Year	Month	Ending value of US stock portfolio	Ending value of gov't bond portfolio	Ending value of EAFE+ portfolio	End Value of SS Trust Fund	Percent in large US stocks	Percent in LT gov't bonds	Percent in EAFE+ Canada stocks	Percent of debt	Official value ot SS Trust Fund	Net SS inflows by fiscal year	Ratio of invested to actual Trust Fund
1947	Jan	6060	4330	0	10391	58.32	41.68	0.00	0.00			
	Feb	6054	4381	0	10435	58.02	41.98	0.00	0.00			
	Mar	6004	4430	0	10434	57.54	42.46	0.00	0.00			
	Apr	5825	4455	0	10280	56.66	43.34	0.00	0.00			
	May	5874	4511	0	10384	56.56	43.44	0.00	0.00			
	Jun	6242	4556	0	10798	57.81	42.19	0.00	0.00	8798	993	1.23
	Jul	6522	4626	0	11148	58.50	41.50	0.00	0.00			
	Aug	6432	4708	0	11139	57.74	42.26	0.00	0.00			
	Sep	6403	4730	0	11133	57.51	42.49	0.00	0.00			
	Oct	6600	4756	0	11356	58.12	41.88	0.00	0.00			
	Nov	6527	4716	0	11243	58.05	41.95	0.00	0.00			
	Dec	6723	4669	0	11391	59.02	40.98	0.00	0.00			
1948	Jan	6510	4722	0	11231	57.96	42.04	0.00	0.00			
	Feb	6299	4787	0	11086	56.82	43.18	0.00	0.00			
	Mar	6845	4847	0	11692	58.54	41.46	0.00	0.00			
	Apr	7089	4913	0	12002	59.07	40.93	0.00	0.00			
	May	7759	5026	0	12786	60.69	39.31	0.00	0.00			
	Jun	7845	5028	0	12872	60.94	39.06	0.00	0.00	10047	1058	1.28
	Jul	7487	5061	0	12548	59.67	40.33	0.00	0.00			
	Aug	7648	5104	0	12752	59.98	40.02	0.00	0.00			
	Sep	7478	5153	0	12631	59.20	40.80	0.00	0.00			
	Oct	8054	5200	0	13254	60.77	39.23	0.00	0.00			
	Nov	7318	5282	0	12600	58.08	41.92	0.00	0.00			
	Dec	7615	5354	0	12969	58.72	41.28	0.00	0.00			
1949	Jan	7687	5441	0	13128	58.55	41.45	0.00	0.00			
	Feb	7500	5511	0	13011	57.65	42.35	0.00	0.00			
	Mar	7790	5594	0	13384	58.20	41.80	0.00	0.00			
	Apr	7692	5643	0	13335	57.68	42.32	0.00	0.00			
	May	7534	5696	0	13231	56.95	43.05	0.00	0.00			
	Jun	7587	5835	0	13422	56.53	43.47	0.00	0.00	11310	1032	1.19
	Jul	8125	5897	0	14022	57.95	42.05	0.00	0.00			
	Aug	8358	6018	0	14376	58.14	41.86	0.00	0.00			
	Sep	8634	6066	0	14700	58.74	41.26	0.00	0.00			
	Oct	8983	6132	0	15115	59.43	40.57	0.00	0.00			
	Nov	9196	6200	0	15395	59.73	40.27	0.00	0.00			
	Dec	9699	6287	0	15986	60.67	39.33	0.00	0.00			
1950	Jan	9946	6303	0	16249	61.21	38.79	0.00	0.00			
	Feb	10199	6371	0	16570	61.55	38.45	0.00	0.00			
	Mar	10325	6431	0	16756	61.62	38.38	0.00	0.00			
	Apr	10883	6505	0	17388	62.59	37.41	0.00	0.00			
	May	11494	6581	0	18075	63.59	36.41	0.00	0.00			
	Jun	10915	6619	0	17535	62.25	37.75	0.00	0.00	12893	1326	1.36
	Jul	11100	6711	0	17811	62.32	37.68	0.00	0.00			
	Aug	11658	6784	0	18443	63.21	36.79	0.00	0.00			
	Sep	12416	6799	0	19215	64.61	35.39	0.00	0.00			
	Oct	12595	6830	0	19426	64.84	35.16	0.00	0.00			
	Nov	12873	6919	0	19791	65.04	34.96	0.00	0.00			
	Dec	13600	6994	0	20594	66.04	33.96	0.00	0.00			
1951	Jan	14534	7099	0	21633	67.18	32.82	0.00	0.00			
	Feb	14826	7110	0	21936	67.59	32.41	0.00	0.00			
	Mar	14657	7062	0	21719	67.49	32.51	0.00	0.00			
	Apr	15470	7081	0	22551	68.60	31.40	0.00	0.00			
	May	15069	7096	0	22165	67.99	32.01	0.00	0.00			
	Jun	14788	7116	0	21903	67.51	32.49	0.00	0.00	14736	1555	1.49
	Jul	15907	7279	0	23186	68.61	31.39	0.00	0.00			
	Aug	16733	7415	0	24148	69.29	30.71	0.00	0.00			
	Sep	16817	7418	0	24235	69.39	30.61	0.00	0.00			
	Oct	16706	7489	0	24195	69.05	30.95	0.00	0.00			
	Nov	16930	7449	0	24379	69.44	30.56	0.00	0.00			
	Dec	17712	7466	0	25179	70.35	29.65	0.00	0.00			

Table 5.1   (*Cont'd*)

Monthly Evolution of the Social Security Trust Fund if It Had Been Invested in US Treasury Bonds, Large Company US Stocks, and (Since 2002) International Stocks, 1937–2010.
(other things being equal)
(Dollar amounts rounded to nearest million)

Year	Month	Soc. Sec. receipts less int. income	Soc. Sec. outlays less int. expense	Net SS cash inflow/ outflow	Amount of short term loan	Debt at end of month	30-day interest rate	Amount of debt repaid	New US stock investm.	Comm. rate for US stocks	Value of cont. stock portf.	Beg. of month US stock portfolio
1952	Jan	300	172	128	0	0			64	0.020	17712	17775
	Feb	300	172	128	0	0			64	0.020	18097	18159
	Mar	300	172	128	0	0			64	0.020	17647	17710
	Apr	300	172	128	0	0			64	0.020	18600	18663
	May	300	172	128	0	0			64	0.020	17913	17975
	Jun	300	172	128	0	0			64	0.020	18592	18654
	Jul	341	226	115	0	0			64	0.020	19568	19631
	Aug	341	226	115	0	0			58	0.020	20016	20072
	Sep	341	226	115	0	0			58	0.020	19929	19986
	Oct	341	226	115	0	0			58	0.020	19634	19690
	Nov	341	226	115	0	0			58	0.020	19730	19786
	Dec	341	226	115	0	0			58	0.020	20916	20972
1953	Jan	341	226	115	0	0			58	0.020	21773	21830
	Feb	341	226	115	0	0			58	0.020	21723	21779
	Mar	341	226	115	0	0			58	0.020	21548	21605
	Apr	341	226	115	0	0			58	0.020	21147	21203
	May	341	226	115	0	0			58	0.020	20700	20757
	Jun	341	226	115	0	0			58	0.020	20917	20973
	Jul	384	280	103	0	0			58	0.020	20692	20748
	Aug	384	280	103	0	0			52	0.020	21315	21365
	Sep	384	280	103	0	0			52	0.020	20295	20345
	Oct	384	280	103	0	0			52	0.020	20415	20465
	Nov	384	280	103	0	0			52	0.020	21570	21621
	Dec	384	280	103	0	0			52	0.020	22062	22112
1954	Jan	384	280	103	0	0			52	0.020	22227	22278
	Feb	384	280	103	0	0			52	0.020	23472	23523
	Mar	384	280	103	0	0			52	0.020	23784	23834
	Apr	384	280	103	0	0			52	0.020	24609	24660
	May	384	280	103	0	0			52	0.020	25932	25982
	Jun	384	280	103	0	0			52	0.020	27069	27119
	Jul	425	370	55	0	0			52	0.020	27203	27254
	Aug	425	370	55	0	0			28	0.020	28859	28886
	Sep	425	370	55	0	0			28	0.020	28092	28119
	Oct	425	370	55	0	0			28	0.020	30511	30538
	Nov	425	370	55	0	0			28	0.020	30028	30055
	Dec	425	370	55	0	0			28	0.020	32788	32815
1955	Jan	425	370	55	0	0			28	0.020	34567	34594
	Feb	425	370	55	0	0			28	0.020	35275	35302
	Mar	425	370	55	0	0			28	0.020	35648	35675
	Apr	425	370	55	0	0			28	0.020	35568	35595
	May	425	370	55	0	0			28	0.020	37005	37032
	Jun	425	370	55	0	0			28	0.020	37235	37262
	Jul	538	457	81	0	0			28	0.020	40396	40423
	Aug	538	457	81	0	0			0	0.020	42938	42938
	Sep	538	457	81	0	0			0	0.020	42830	42830
	Oct	538	457	81	0	0			0	0.020	43387	43387
	Nov	538	457	81	0	0			40	0.020	42155	42194
	Dec	538	457	81	0	0			0	0.020	45684	45684
1956	Jan	538	457	81	0	0			0	0.020	45752	45752
	Feb	538	457	81	0	0			0	0.020	44165	44165
	Mar	538	457	81	0	0			0	0.020	45989	45989
	Apr	538	457	81	0	0			0	0.020	49254	49254
	May	538	457	81	0	0			0	0.020	49234	49234
	Jun	538	556	81	0	0			0	0.020	46314	46314
	Jul	574	556	18	0	0			0	0.020	48209	48209
	Aug	574	556	18	0	0			0	0.020	50764	50764
	Sep	574	556	18	0	0			0	0.020	49099	49099
	Oct	574	556	18	0	0			0	0.020	46938	46938
	Nov	574	556	18	0	0			0	0.020	47248	47248
	Dec	574	556	18	0	0			0	0.020	47012	47012

Table 5.1   (*Cont'd*)

Monthly Evolution of the Social Security Trust Fund if It Had Been Invested in US Treasury Bonds, Large Company US Stocks, and (Since 2002) International Stocks, 1937–2010.
(other things being equal)
(Dollar amounts rounded to nearest million)

Year	Month	New gov't bond investm.	Market impact for bonds	Value of cont. bond portfolio	Beg. of month bond portfolio	New EAFE+ Canada investm.	Comm. for EAFE+ stocks	Value of cont. EAFE+ portfolio	Beg. of month EAFE+ portfolio	Return on large US stocks	Return on LT US gov't bonds	Return on EAFE+ stocks
1952	Jan	64	0.010	7466	7530	0		0	0	0.0181	0.0028	
	Feb	64	0.010	7551	7614	0		0	0	-0.0282	0.0014	
	Mar	64	0.010	7624	7688	0		0	0	0.0503	0.0111	
	Apr	64	0.010	7773	7836	0		0	0	-0.0402	0.0171	
	May	64	0.010	7970	8033	0		0	0	0.0343	-0.0033	
	Jun	64	0.010	8007	8070	0		0	0	0.0490	0.0003	
	Jul	64	0.010	8072	8135	0		0	0	0.0196	-0.0020	
	Aug	58	0.010	8119	8176	0		0	0	-0.0071	-0.0070	
	Sep	58	0.010	8119	8176	0		0	0	-0.0176	-0.0130	
	Oct	58	0.010	8069	8126	0		0	0	0.0020	0.0148	
	Nov	58	0.010	8247	8304	0		0	0	0.0571	-0.0015	
	Dec	58	0.010	8291	8348	0		0	0	0.0382	-0.0086	
1953	Jan	58	0.010	8276	8333	0		0	0	-0.0049	0.0012	
	Feb	58	0.010	8343	8400	0		0	0	-0.0106	-0.0087	
	Mar	58	0.010	8327	8384	0		0	0	-0.0212	-0.0088	
	Apr	58	0.010	8310	8367	0		0	0	-0.0237	-0.0105	
	May	58	0.010	8279	8336	0		0	0	0.0077	-0.0148	
	Jun	58	0.010	8213	8270	0		0	0	-0.0134	0.0223	
	Jul	58	0.010	8454	8511	0		0	0	0.0273	0.0039	
	Aug	52	0.010	8544	8595	0		0	0	-0.0501	-0.0008	
	Sep	52	0.010	8588	8640	0		0	0	0.0034	0.0299	
	Oct	52	0.010	8898	8949	0		0	0	0.0540	0.0074	
	Nov	52	0.010	9015	9066	0		0	0	0.0204	-0.0049	
	Dec	52	0.010	9022	9073	0		0	0	0.0052	0.0206	
1954	Jan	52	0.010	9260	9311	0		0	0	0.0536	0.0089	
	Feb	52	0.010	9394	9445	0		0	0	0.0111	0.0240	
	Mar	52	0.010	9671	9723	0		0	0	0.0325	0.0058	
	Apr	52	0.010	9779	9830	0		0	0	0.0516	0.0104	
	May	52	0.010	9932	9983	0		0	0	0.0418	-0.0087	
	Jun	52	0.010	9896	9947	0		0	0	0.0031	0.0163	
	Jul	52	0.010	10110	10161	0		0	0	0.0589	0.0134	
	Aug	28	0.010	10297	10324	0		0	0	-0.0275	-0.0036	
	Sep	28	0.010	10287	10314	0		0	0	0.0851	-0.0010	
	Oct	28	0.010	10304	10331	0		0	0	-0.0167	0.0006	
	Nov	28	0.010	10337	10365	0		0	0	0.0909	-0.0025	
	Dec	28	0.010	10339	10366	0		0	0	0.0534	0.0064	
1955	Jan	28	0.010	10432	10460	0		0	0	0.0197	-0.0241	
	Feb	28	0.010	10208	10235	0		0	0	0.0098	-0.0078	
	Mar	28	0.010	10155	10182	0		0	0	-0.0030	0.0087	
	Apr	28	0.010	10271	10298	0		0	0	0.0396	0.0001	
	May	28	0.010	10299	10326	0		0	0	0.0055	0.0073	
	Jun	28	0.010	10402	10429	0		0	0	0.0841	-0.0076	
	Jul	28	0.010	10350	10377	0		0	0	0.0622	-0.0102	
	Aug	81	0.010	10271	10351	0		0	0	-0.0025	0.0004	
	Sep	81	0.010	10355	10435	0		0	0	0.0130	0.0073	
	Oct	81	0.010	10511	10591	0		0	0	-0.0284	0.0144	
	Nov	40	0.010	10743	10783	0		0	0	0.0827	-0.0045	
	Dec	81	0.010	10734	10814	0		0	0	0.0015	0.0037	
1956	Jan	81	0.010	10854	10934	0		0	0	-0.0347	0.0083	
	Feb	81	0.010	11025	11104	0		0	0	0.0413	-0.0002	
	Mar	81	0.010	11102	11182	0		0	0	0.0710	-0.0149	
	Apr	81	0.010	11015	11095	0		0	0	-0.0004	-0.0113	
	May	81	0.010	10969	11049	0		0	0	-0.0593	0.0225	
	Jun	81	0.010	11298	11377	0		0	0	0.0409	0.0027	
	Jul	81	0.010	11408	11488	0		0	0	0.0530	-0.0209	
	Aug	18	0.010	11248	11266	0		0	0	-0.0328	-0.0187	
	Sep	18	0.010	11056	11074	0		0	0	-0.0440	0.0050	
	Oct	18	0.010	11129	11147	0		0	0	0.0066	-0.0054	
	Nov	18	0.010	11087	11105	0		0	0	-0.0050	-0.0057	
	Dec	18	0.010	11041	11059	0		0	0	0.0370	-0.0179	

Table 5.1 (Cont'd)

Monthly Evolution of the Social Security Trust Fund if It Had Been Invested in US Treasury Bonds, Large Company US Stocks, and (Since 2002) International Stocks, 1937–2010.
(other things being equal)
(Dollar amounts rounded to nearest million)

Year	Month	Ending value of US stock portfolio	Ending value of gov't bond portfolio	Ending value of EAFE+ portfolio	End Value of SS Trust Fund	Percent in large US stocks	Percent in LT gov't bonds	Percent in EAFE+ Canada stocks	Percent of debt	Official value ot SS Trust Fund	Net SS inflows by fiscal year	Ratio of invested to actual Trust Fund
1952	Jan	18097	7551	0	25647	70.56	29.44	0.00	0.00			
	Feb	17647	7624	0	25272	69.83	30.17	0.00	0.00			
	Mar	18600	7773	0	26373	70.53	29.47	0.00	0.00			
	Apr	17913	7970	0	25883	69.21	30.79	0.00	0.00			
	May	18592	8007	0	26598	69.90	30.10	0.00	0.00			
	Jun	19568	8072	0	27641	70.80	29.20	0.00	0.00	16600	1531	1.67
	Jul	20016	8119	0	28135	71.14	28.86	0.00	0.00			
	Aug	19929	8119	0	28048	71.05	28.95	0.00	0.00			
	Sep	19634	8069	0	27704	70.87	29.13	0.00	0.00			
	Oct	19730	8247	0	27977	70.52	29.48	0.00	0.00			
	Nov	20916	8291	0	29207	71.61	28.39	0.00	0.00			
	Dec	21773	8276	0	30050	72.46	27.54	0.00	0.00			
1953	Jan	21723	8343	0	30066	72.25	27.75	0.00	0.00			
	Feb	21548	8327	0	29875	72.13	27.87	0.00	0.00			
	Mar	21147	8310	0	29457	71.79	28.21	0.00	0.00			
	Apr	20700	8279	0	28980	71.43	28.57	0.00	0.00			
	May	20917	8213	0	29129	71.81	28.19	0.00	0.00			
	Jun	20692	8454	0	29146	70.99	29.01	0.00	0.00	18366	1380	1.59
	Jul	21315	8544	0	29859	71.38	28.62	0.00	0.00			
	Aug	20295	8588	0	28883	70.27	29.73	0.00	0.00			
	Sep	20415	8898	0	29313	69.64	30.36	0.00	0.00			
	Oct	21570	9015	0	30585	70.52	29.48	0.00	0.00			
	Nov	22062	9022	0	31084	70.98	29.02	0.00	0.00			
	Dec	22227	9260	0	31487	70.59	29.41	0.00	0.00			
1954	Jan	23472	9394	0	32866	71.42	28.58	0.00	0.00			
	Feb	23784	9671	0	33455	71.09	28.91	0.00	0.00			
	Mar	24609	9779	0	34388	71.56	28.44	0.00	0.00			
	Apr	25932	9932	0	35864	72.31	27.69	0.00	0.00			
	May	27069	9896	0	36965	73.23	26.77	0.00	0.00			
	Jun	27203	10110	0	37313	72.91	27.09	0.00	0.00	20040	1238	1.86
	Jul	28859	10297	0	39156	73.70	26.30	0.00	0.00			
	Aug	28092	10287	0	38379	73.20	26.80	0.00	0.00			
	Sep	30511	10304	0	40815	74.75	25.25	0.00	0.00			
	Oct	30028	10337	0	40366	74.39	25.61	0.00	0.00			
	Nov	32788	10339	0	43126	76.03	23.97	0.00	0.00			
	Dec	34567	10432	0	44999	76.82	23.18	0.00	0.00			
1955	Jan	35275	10208	0	45483	77.56	22.44	0.00	0.00			
	Feb	35648	10155	0	45803	77.83	22.17	0.00	0.00			
	Mar	35568	10271	0	45839	77.59	22.41	0.00	0.00			
	Apr	37005	10299	0	47304	78.23	21.77	0.00	0.00			
	May	37235	10402	0	47637	78.16	21.84	0.00	0.00			
	Jun	40396	10350	0	50746	79.60	20.40	0.00	0.00	21141	661	2.40
	Jul	42938	10271	0	53209	80.70	19.30	0.00	0.00			
	Aug	42830	10355	0	53185	80.53	19.47	0.00	0.00			
	Sep	43387	10511	0	53898	80.50	19.50	0.00	0.00			
	Oct	42155	10743	0	52898	79.69	20.31	0.00	0.00			
	Nov	45684	10734	0	56418	80.97	19.03	0.00	0.00			
	Dec	45752	10854	0	56606	80.83	19.17	0.00	0.00			
1956	Jan	44165	11025	0	55189	80.02	19.98	0.00	0.00			
	Feb	45989	11102	0	57091	80.55	19.45	0.00	0.00			
	Mar	49254	11015	0	60269	81.72	18.28	0.00	0.00			
	Apr	49234	10969	0	60204	81.78	18.22	0.00	0.00			
	May	46314	11298	0	57612	80.39	19.61	0.00	0.00			
	Jun	48209	11408	0	59617	80.86	19.14	0.00	0.00	22593	967	2.64
	Jul	50764	11248	0	62012	81.86	18.14	0.00	0.00			
	Aug	49099	11056	0	60154	81.62	18.38	0.00	0.00			
	Sep	46938	11129	0	58067	80.83	19.17	0.00	0.00			
	Oct	47248	11087	0	58335	80.99	19.01	0.00	0.00			
	Nov	47012	11041	0	58053	80.98	19.02	0.00	0.00			
	Dec	48751	10861	0	59613	81.78	18.22	0.00	0.00			

Table 5.1 (Cont'd)

Monthly Evolution of the Social Security Trust Fund if It Had Been Invested in US Treasury Bonds, Large Company US Stocks, and (Since 2002) International Stocks, 1937–2010.
(other things being equal)
(Dollar amounts rounded to nearest million)

Year	Month	Soc. Sec. receipts less int. income	Soc. Sec. outlays less int. expense	Net SS cash inflow/outflow	Amount of short term loan	Debt at end of month	30-day interest rate	Amount of debt repaid	New US stock investm.	Comm. rate for US stocks	Value of cont. stock portf.	Beg. of month US stock portfolio
1957	Jan	574	556	18	0	0			0	0.020	48751	48751
	Feb	574	556	18	0	0			0	0.020	46796	46796
	Mar	574	556	18	0	0			0	0.020	45561	45561
	Apr	574	556	18	0	0			0	0.020	46541	46541
	May	574	556	18	0	0			0	0.020	48346	48346
	Jun	574	556	18	0	0			0	0.020	50459	50459
	Jul	683	685	-2	2	2	0.0040	0	0	0.020	50479	50479
	Aug	683	685	-2	2	4	0.0035	0	0	0.020	51141	51141
	Sep	683	685	-2	2	6	0.0036	0	0	0.020	48558	48558
	Oct	683	685	-2	2	8	0.0039	0	0	0.020	45635	45635
	Nov	683	685	-2	2	11	0.0038	0	0	0.020	44257	44257
	Dec	683	685	-2	2	13	0.0034	0	0	0.020	45279	45279
1958	Jan	683	685	-2	2	15	0.0038	0	0	0.020	43490	43490
	Feb	683	685	-2	2	17	0.0022	0	0	0.020	45426	45426
	Mar	683	685	-2	2	19	0.0019	0	0	0.020	44785	44785
	Apr	683	685	-2	2	21	0.0018	0	0	0.020	46254	46254
	May	683	685	-2	2	23	0.0021	0	0	0.020	47813	47813
	Jun	683	685	-2	2	25	0.0013	0	0	0.020	48827	48827
	Jul	705	812	-107	107	132	0.0017	0	0	0.020	50189	50189
	Aug	705	812	-107	107	239	0.0014	0	0	0.020	52442	52442
	Sep	705	812	-107	107	346	0.0029	0	0	0.020	53365	53365
	Oct	705	812	-107	107	454	0.0028	0	0	0.020	56039	56039
	Nov	705	812	-107	107	562	0.0021	0	0	0.020	57552	57552
	Dec	705	812	-107	107	671	0.0032	0	0	0.020	59186	59186
1959	Jan	705	812	-107	107	779	0.0031	0	0	0.020	62353	62353
	Feb	705	812	-107	107	888	0.0029	0	0	0.020	62683	62683
	Mar	705	812	-107	107	998	0.0032	0	0	0.020	62991	62991
	Apr	705	812	-107	107	1108	0.0030	0	0	0.020	63117	63117
	May	705	812	-107	107	1218	0.0032	0	0	0.020	65654	65654
	Jun	705	812	-107	107	1330	0.0035	0	0	0.020	67230	67230
	Jul	905	969	-64	64	1399	0.0035	0	0	0.020	67082	67082
	Aug	905	969	-64	64	1467	0.0029	0	0	0.020	69517	69517
	Sep	905	969	-64	64	1538	0.0041	0	0	0.020	68808	68808
	Oct	905	969	-64	64	1608	0.0040	0	0	0.020	65759	65759
	Nov	905	969	-64	64	1679	0.0036	0	0	0.020	66601	66601
	Dec	905	969	-64	64	1751	0.0044	0	0	0.020	67840	67840
1960	Jan	905	969	-64	64	1823	0.0043	0	0	0.020	69821	69821
	Feb	905	969	-64	64	1894	0.0039	0	0	0.020	64933	64933
	Mar	905	969	-64	64	1967	0.0045	0	0	0.020	65888	65888
	Apr	905	969	-64	64	2037	0.0029	0	0	0.020	65078	65078
	May	905	969	-64	64	2109	0.0037	0	0	0.020	64030	64030
	Jun	905	969	-64	64	2181	0.0034	0	0	0.020	66117	66117
	Jul	1026	1040	-13	13	2199	0.0023	0	0	0.020	67512	67512
	Aug	1026	1040	-13	13	2219	0.0027	0	0	0.020	65932	65932
	Sep	1026	1040	-13	13	2238	0.0026	0	0	0.020	68022	68022
	Oct	1026	1040	-13	13	2258	0.0032	0	0	0.020	64009	64009
	Nov	1026	1040	-13	13	2277	0.0023	0	0	0.020	63964	63964
	Dec	1026	1040	-13	13	2296	0.0026	0	0	0.020	66939	66939
1961	Jan	1026	1040	-13	13	2316	0.0029	0	0	0.020	70145	70145
	Feb	1026	1040	-13	13	2335	0.0024	0	0	0.020	74669	74669
	Mar	1026	1040	-13	13	2355	0.0030	0	0	0.020	77051	77051
	Apr	1026	1040	-13	13	2374	0.0027	0	0	0.020	79132	79132
	May	1026	1040	-13	13	2394	0.0028	0	0	0.020	79535	79535
	Jun	1026	1040	-13	13	2415	0.0030	0	0	0.020	81436	81436
	Jul	1041	1197	-156	156	2578	0.0028	0	0	0.020	79197	79197
	Aug	1041	1197	-156	156	2741	0.0024	0	0	0.020	81905	81905
	Sep	1041	1197	-156	156	2905	0.0027	0	0	0.020	83896	83896
	Oct	1041	1197	-156	156	3070	0.0029	0	0	0.020	82352	82352
	Nov	1041	1197	-156	156	3234	0.0025	0	0	0.020	84806	84806
	Dec	1041	1197	-156	156	3400	0.0029	0	0	0.020	88597	88597

Table 5.1 (*Cont'd*)

Monthly Evolution of the Social Security Trust Fund if It Had Been Invested in US Treasury Bonds, Large Company US Stocks, and (Since 2002) International Stocks, 1937–2010.
(other things being equal)
(Dollar amounts rounded to nearest million)

Year	Month	New gov't bond investm.	Market impact for bonds	Value of cont. bond portfolio	Beg. of month bond portfolio	New EAFE+ Canada investm.	Comm. for EAFE+ stocks	Value of cont. EAFE+ portfolio	Beg. of month EAFE+ portfolio	Return on large US stocks	Return on LT US gov't bonds	Return on EAFE+ stocks
1957	Jan	18	0.010	10861	10879	0		0	0	-0.0401	0.0346	
	Feb	18	0.010	11256	11274	0		0	0	-0.0264	0.0025	
	Mar	18	0.010	11302	11320	0		0	0	0.0215	-0.0024	
	Apr	18	0.010	11293	11311	0		0	0	0.0388	-0.0222	
	May	18	0.010	11060	11078	0		0	0	0.0437	-0.0023	
	Jun	18	0.010	11052	11070	0		0	0	0.0004	-0.0180	
	Jul	18	0.010	10871	10889	0		0	0	0.0131	-0.0041	
	Aug	0	0.010	10844	10844	0		0	0	-0.0505	0.0002	
	Sep	0	0.010	10846	10846	0		0	0	-0.0602	0.0076	
	Oct	0	0.010	10929	10929	0		0	0	-0.0302	-0.0050	
	Nov	0	0.010	10874	10874	0		0	0	0.0231	0.0533	
	Dec	0	0.010	11454	11454	0		0	0	-0.0395	0.0307	
1958	Jan	0	0.010	11805	11805	0		0	0	0.0445	-0.0084	
	Feb	0	0.010	11706	11706	0		0	0	-0.0141	0.0100	
	Mar	0	0.010	11823	11823	0		0	0	0.0328	0.0102	
	Apr	0	0.010	11944	11944	0		0	0	0.0337	0.0186	
	May	0	0.010	12166	12166	0		0	0	0.0212	0.0001	
	Jun	0	0.010	12167	12167	0		0	0	0.0279	-0.0160	
	Jul	0	0.010	11973	11973	0		0	0	0.0449	-0.0278	
	Aug	0	0.010	11640	11640	0		0	0	0.0176	-0.0435	
	Sep	0	0.010	11133	11133	0		0	0	0.0501	-0.0117	
	Oct	0	0.010	11003	11003	0		0	0	0.0270	0.0138	
	Nov	0	0.010	11155	11155	0		0	0	0.0284	0.0120	
	Dec	0	0.010	11289	11289	0		0	0	0.0535	-0.0181	
1959	Jan	0	0.010	11085	11085	0		0	0	0.0053	-0.0080	
	Feb	0	0.010	10996	10996	0		0	0	0.0049	0.0117	
	Mar	0	0.010	11125	11125	0		0	0	0.0020	0.0017	
	Apr	0	0.010	11143	11143	0		0	0	0.0402	-0.0117	
	May	0	0.010	11013	11013	0		0	0	0.0240	-0.0005	
	Jun	0	0.010	11008	11008	0		0	0	-0.0022	0.0010	
	Jul	0	0.010	11019	11019	0		0	0	0.0363	0.0060	
	Aug	0	0.010	11085	11085	0		0	0	-0.0102	-0.0041	
	Sep	0	0.010	11039	11039	0		0	0	-0.0443	-0.0057	
	Oct	0	0.010	10976	10976	0		0	0	0.0128	0.0150	
	Nov	0	0.010	11141	11141	0		0	0	0.0186	-0.0119	
	Dec	0	0.010	11008	11008	0		0	0	0.0292	-0.0159	
1960	Jan	0	0.010	10833	10833	0		0	0	-0.0700	0.0112	
	Feb	0	0.010	10955	10955	0		0	0	0.0147	0.0204	
	Mar	0	0.010	11178	11178	0		0	0	-0.0123	0.0282	
	Apr	0	0.010	11493	11493	0		0	0	-0.0161	-0.0170	
	May	0	0.010	11298	11298	0		0	0	0.0326	0.0152	
	Jun	0	0.010	11470	11470	0		0	0	0.0211	0.0173	
	Jul	0	0.010	11668	11668	0		0	0	-0.0234	0.0368	
	Aug	0	0.010	12098	12098	0		0	0	0.0317	-0.0067	
	Sep	0	0.010	12017	12017	0		0	0	-0.0590	0.0075	
	Oct	0	0.010	12107	12107	0		0	0	-0.0007	-0.0028	
	Nov	0	0.010	12073	12073	0		0	0	0.0465	-0.0066	
	Dec	0	0.010	11993	11993	0		0	0	0.0479	0.0279	
1961	Jan	0	0.010	12328	12328	0		0	0	0.0645	-0.0107	
	Feb	0	0.010	12196	12196	0		0	0	0.0319	0.0200	
	Mar	0	0.010	12440	12440	0		0	0	0.0270	-0.0037	
	Apr	0	0.010	12394	12394	0		0	0	0.0051	0.0115	
	May	0	0.010	12536	12536	0		0	0	0.0239	-0.0046	
	Jun	0	0.010	12479	12479	0		0	0	-0.0275	-0.0075	
	Jul	0	0.010	12385	12385	0		0	0	0.0342	0.0035	
	Aug	0	0.010	12428	12428	0		0	0	0.0243	-0.0038	
	Sep	0	0.010	12381	12381	0		0	0	-0.0184	0.0129	
	Oct	0	0.010	12541	12541	0		0	0	0.0298	0.0071	
	Nov	0	0.010	12630	12630	0		0	0	0.0447	-0.0020	
	Dec	0	0.010	12605	12605	0		0	0	0.0046	-0.0125	

Table 5.1 (*Cont'd*)

Monthly Evolution of the Social Security Trust Fund if It Had Been Invested in US Treasury Bonds, Large Company US Stocks, and (Since 2002) International Stocks, 1937–2010.
(other things being equal)
(Dollar amounts rounded to nearest million)

Year	Month	Ending value of US stock portfolio	Ending value of gov't bond portfolio	Ending value of EAFE+ portfolio	End Value of SS Trust Fund	Percent in large US stocks	Percent in LT gov't bonds	Percent in EAFE+ Canada stocks	Percent of debt	Official value ot SS Trust Fund	Net SS inflows by fiscal year	Ratio of invested to actual Trust Fund
1957	Jan	46796	11256	0	58052	80.61	19.39	0.00	0.00			
	Feb	45561	11302	0	56863	80.12	19.88	0.00	0.00			
	Mar	46541	11293	0	57833	80.47	19.53	0.00	0.00			
	Apr	48346	11060	0	59406	81.38	18.62	0.00	0.00			
	May	50459	11052	0	61511	82.03	17.97	0.00	0.00			
	Jun	50479	10871	0	61350	82.28	17.72	0.00	0.00	23066	218	2.66
	Jul	51141	10844	0	61985	82.50	17.50	0.00	0.00			
	Aug	48558	10846	0	59404	81.74	18.26	0.00	0.01			
	Sep	45635	10929	0	56564	80.68	19.32	0.00	0.01			
	Oct	44257	10874	0	55131	80.28	19.72	0.00	0.02			
	Nov	45279	11454	0	56733	79.81	20.19	0.00	0.02			
	Dec	43490	11805	0	55296	78.65	21.35	0.00	0.02	23042		2.40
1958	Jan	45426	11706	0	57132	79.51	20.49	0.00	0.03			
	Feb	44785	11823	0	56609	79.11	20.89	0.00	0.03			
	Mar	46254	11944	0	58198	79.48	20.52	0.00	0.03			
	Apr	47813	12166	0	59979	79.72	20.28	0.00	0.04			
	May	48827	12167	0	60994	80.05	19.95	0.00	0.04			
	Jun	50189	11973	0	62162	80.74	19.26	0.00	0.04		-25	
	Jul	52442	11640	0	64082	81.84	18.16	0.00	0.21			
	Aug	53365	11133	0	64499	82.74	17.26	0.00	0.37			
	Sep	56039	11003	0	67042	83.59	16.41	0.00	0.52			
	Oct	57552	11155	0	68707	83.76	16.24	0.00	0.66			
	Nov	59186	11289	0	70475	83.98	16.02	0.00	0.80			
	Dec	62353	11085	0	73438	84.91	15.09	0.00	0.91	23243		3.16
1959	Jan	62683	10996	0	72900	85.99	15.08	0.00	1.07			
	Feb	62991	11125	0	73227	86.02	15.19	0.00	1.21			
	Mar	63117	11143	0	73262	86.15	15.21	0.00	1.36			
	Apr	65654	11013	0	75559	86.89	14.58	0.00	1.47			
	May	67230	11008	0	77019	87.29	14.29	0.00	1.58			
	Jun	67082	11019	0	76771	87.38	14.35	0.00	1.73		-1278	
	Jul	69517	11085	0	79203	87.77	14.00	0.00	1.77			
	Aug	68808	11039	0	78380	87.79	14.08	0.00	1.87			
	Sep	65759	10976	0	75198	87.45	14.60	0.00	2.04			
	Oct	66601	11141	0	76134	87.48	14.63	0.00	2.11			
	Nov	67840	11008	0	77170	87.91	14.27	0.00	2.18			
	Dec	69821	10833	0	78904	88.49	13.73	0.00	2.22	21966		3.59
1960	Jan	64933	10955	0	74066	87.67	14.79	0.00	2.46			
	Feb	65888	11178	0	75172	87.65	14.87	0.00	2.52			
	Mar	65078	11493	0	74604	87.23	15.41	0.00	2.64			
	Apr	64030	11298	0	73290	87.36	15.42	0.00	2.78			
	May	66117	11470	0	75478	87.60	15.20	0.00	2.79			
	Jun	67512	11668	0	76999	87.68	15.15	0.00	2.83		-771	
	Jul	65932	12098	0	75831	86.95	15.95	0.00	2.90			
	Aug	68022	12017	0	77820	87.41	15.44	0.00	2.85			
	Sep	64009	12107	0	73878	86.64	16.39	0.00	3.03			
	Oct	63964	12073	0	73779	86.70	16.36	0.00	3.06			
	Nov	66939	11993	0	76655	87.32	15.65	0.00	2.97			
	Dec	70145	12328	0	80177	87.49	15.38	0.00	2.86	22613		3.55
1961	Jan	74669	12196	0	84549	88.31	14.42	0.00	2.74			
	Feb	77051	12440	0	87157	88.41	14.27	0.00	2.68			
	Mar	79132	12394	0	89171	88.74	13.90	0.00	2.64			
	Apr	79535	12536	0	89697	88.67	13.98	0.00	2.65			
	May	81436	12479	0	91520	88.98	13.63	0.00	2.62			
	Jun	79197	12385	0	89167	88.82	13.89	0.00	2.71		-159	
	Jul	81905	12428	0	91755	89.26	13.55	0.00	2.81			
	Aug	83896	12381	0	93536	89.69	13.24	0.00	2.93			
	Sep	82352	12541	0	91988	89.52	13.63	0.00	3.16			
	Oct	84806	12630	0	94366	89.87	13.38	0.00	3.25			
	Nov	88597	12605	0	97967	90.44	12.87	0.00	3.30			
	Dec	89004	12447	0	98051	90.77	12.69	0.00	3.47	22162		4.42

Table 5.1   (*Cont'd*)

Monthly Evolution of the Social Security Trust Fund if It Had Been Invested in US Treasury Bonds, Large Company US Stocks, and (Since 2002) International Stocks, 1937–2010.
(other things being equal)
(Dollar amounts rounded to nearest million)

Year	Month	Soc. Sec. receipts less int. income	Soc. Sec. outlays less int. expense	Net SS cash inflow/ outflow	Amount of short term loan	Debt at end of month	30-day interest rate	Amount of debt repaid	New US stock investm.	Comm. rate for US stocks	Value of cont. stock portf.	Beg. of month US stock portfolio
1962	Jan	1041	1197	-156	156	3565	0.0024	0	0	0.020	89004	89004
	Feb	1041	1197	-156	156	3728	0.0020	0	0	0.020	85747	85747
	Mar	1041	1197	-156	156	3892	0.0020	0	0	0.020	87539	87539
	Apr	1041	1197	-156	156	4062	0.0032	0	0	0.020	87136	87136
	May	1041	1197	-156	156	4232	0.0034	0	0	0.020	81847	81847
	Jun	1041	1197	-156	156	4401	0.0030	0	0	0.020	75209	75209
	Jul	1202	1316	-114	114	4532	0.0037	0	0	0.020	69170	69170
	Aug	1202	1316	-114	114	4662	0.0033	0	0	0.020	73680	73680
	Sep	1202	1316	-114	114	4791	0.0031	0	0	0.020	75212	75212
	Oct	1202	1316	-114	114	4923	0.0036	0	0	0.020	71715	71715
	Nov	1202	1316	-114	114	5052	0.0030	0	0	0.020	72174	72174
	Dec	1202	1316	-114	114	5184	0.0033	0	0	0.020	80012	80012
1963	Jan	1202	1316	-114	114	5316	0.0035	0	0	0.020	81236	81236
	Feb	1202	1316	-114	114	5448	0.0033	0	0	0.020	85347	85347
	Mar	1202	1316	-114	114	5581	0.0033	0	0	0.020	83307	83307
	Apr	1202	1316	-114	114	5715	0.0035	0	0	0.020	86389	86389
	May	1202	1316	-114	114	5849	0.0034	0	0	0.020	90709	90709
	Jun	1202	1316	-114	114	5983	0.0033	0	0	0.020	92460	92460
	Jul	1387	1385	2	0	6003	0.0037	2	0	0.020	90721	90721
	Aug	1387	1385	2	0	6022	0.0035	2	0	0.020	90522	90522
	Sep	1387	1385	2	0	6043	0.0037	2	0	0.020	95365	95365
	Oct	1387	1385	2	0	6064	0.0039	2	0	0.020	94440	94440
	Nov	1387	1385	2	0	6085	0.0037	2	0	0.020	97641	97641
	Dec	1387	1385	2	0	6106	0.0039	2	0	0.020	97192	97192
1964	Jan	1387	1385	2	0	6129	0.0040	2	0	0.020	99738	99738
	Feb	1387	1385	2	0	6149	0.0036	2	0	0.020	102561	102561
	Mar	1387	1385	2	0	6172	0.0041	2	0	0.020	104069	104069
	Apr	1387	1385	2	0	6194	0.0039	2	0	0.020	105786	105786
	May	1387	1385	2	0	6215	0.0036	2	0	0.020	106579	106579
	Jun	1387	1385	2	0	6237	0.0040	2	0	0.020	108306	108306
	Jul	1418	1455	-38	38	6300	0.0040	0	0	0.020	110234	110234
	Aug	1418	1455	-38	38	6362	0.0038	0	0	0.020	112383	112383
	Sep	1418	1455	-38	38	6424	0.0038	0	0	0.020	111057	111057
	Oct	1418	1455	-38	38	6481	0.0029	0	0	0.020	114400	114400
	Nov	1418	1455	-38	38	6537	0.0029	0	0	0.020	115498	115498
	Dec	1418	1455	-38	38	6602	0.0041	0	0	0.020	115556	115556
1965	Jan	1418	1455	-38	38	6665	0.0038	0	0	0.020	116203	116203
	Feb	1418	1455	-38	38	6730	0.0040	0	0	0.020	120212	120212
	Mar	1418	1455	-38	38	6798	0.0046	0	0	0.020	120585	120585
	Apr	1418	1455	-38	38	6864	0.0041	0	0	0.020	118981	118981
	May	1418	1455	-38	38	6930	0.0041	0	0	0.020	123216	123216
	Jun	1418	1455	-38	38	6999	0.0045	0	0	0.020	122847	122847
	Jul	1619	1725	-106	106	7135	0.0041	0	0	0.020	117036	117036
	Aug	1619	1725	-106	106	7272	0.0043	0	0	0.020	118757	118757
	Sep	1619	1725	-106	106	7408	0.0041	0	0	0.020	121987	121987
	Oct	1619	1725	-106	106	7545	0.0041	0	0	0.020	126061	126061
	Nov	1619	1725	-106	106	7685	0.0045	0	0	0.020	129704	129704
	Dec	1619	1725	-106	106	7825	0.0043	0	0	0.020	129302	129302
1966	Jan	1619	1725	-106	106	7969	0.0048	0	0	0.020	130673	130673
	Feb	1619	1725	-106	106	8111	0.0045	0	0	0.020	131483	131483
	Mar	1619	1725	-106	106	8256	0.0048	0	0	0.020	129761	129761
	Apr	1619	1725	-106	106	8399	0.0044	0	0	0.020	127100	127100
	May	1619	1725	-106	106	8548	0.0051	0	0	0.020	129897	129897
	Jun	1619	1725	-106	106	8696	0.0048	0	0	0.020	123506	123506
	Jul	2076	1811	265	0	8469	0.0045	265	0	0.020	121703	121703
	Aug	2076	1811	265	0	8247	0.0051	265	0	0.020	120242	120242
	Sep	2076	1811	265	0	8023	0.0050	265	0	0.020	111525	111525
	Oct	2076	1811	265	0	7802	0.0055	265	0	0.020	110934	110934
	Nov	2076	1811	265	0	7575	0.0050	265	0	0.020	116414	116414
	Dec	2076	1811	265	0	7348	0.0050	265	0	0.020	117520	117520

Table 5.1   (*Cont'd*)

Monthly Evolution of the Social Security Trust Fund if It Had Been Invested in US Treasury Bonds, Large Company US Stocks, and (Since 2002) International Stocks, 1937–2010.
(other things being equal)
(Dollar amounts rounded to nearest million)

Year	Month	New gov't bond investm.	Market impact for bonds	Value of cont. bond portfolio	Beg. of month bond portfolio	New EAFE+ Canada investm.	Comm. for EAFE+ stocks	Value of cont. EAFE+ portfolio	Beg. of month EAFE+ portfolio	Return on large US stocks	Return on LT US gov't bonds	Return on EAFE+ stocks
1962	Jan	0	0.010	12447	12447	0		0	0	-0.0366	-0.0014	
	Feb	0	0.010	12430	12430	0		0	0	0.0209	0.0103	
	Mar	0	0.010	12558	12558	0		0	0	-0.0046	0.0253	
	Apr	0	0.010	12875	12875	0		0	0	-0.0607	0.0082	
	May	0	0.010	12981	12981	0		0	0	-0.0811	0.0046	
	Jun	0	0.010	13041	13041	0		0	0	-0.0803	-0.0076	
	Jul	0	0.010	12941	12941	0		0	0	0.0652	-0.0109	
	Aug	0	0.010	12800	12800	0		0	0	0.0208	0.0187	
	Sep	0	0.010	13040	13040	0		0	0	-0.0465	0.0061	
	Oct	0	0.010	13119	13119	0		0	0	0.0064	0.0084	
	Nov	0	0.010	13230	13230	0		0	0	0.1086	0.0021	
	Dec	0	0.010	13257	13257	0		0	0	0.0153	0.0035	
1963	Jan	0	0.010	13304	13304	0		0	0	0.0506	-0.0001	
	Feb	0	0.010	13302	13302	0		0	0	-0.0239	0.0008	
	Mar	0	0.010	13313	13313	0		0	0	0.0370	0.0009	
	Apr	0	0.010	13325	13325	0		0	0	0.0500	-0.0012	
	May	0	0.010	13309	13309	0		0	0	0.0193	0.0023	
	Jun	0	0.010	13340	13340	0		0	0	-0.0188	0.0019	
	Jul	0	0.010	13365	13365	0		0	0	-0.0022	0.0031	
	Aug	0	0.010	13406	13406	0		0	0	0.0535	0.0021	
	Sep	0	0.010	13435	13435	0		0	0	-0.0097	0.0004	
	Oct	0	0.010	13440	13440	0		0	0	0.0339	-0.0026	
	Nov	0	0.010	13405	13405	0		0	0	-0.0046	0.0051	
	Dec	0	0.010	13473	13473	0		0	0	0.0262	-0.0006	
1964	Jan	0	0.010	13465	13465	0		0	0	0.0283	-0.0014	
	Feb	0	0.010	13446	13446	0		0	0	0.0147	-0.0011	
	Mar	0	0.010	13432	13432	0		0	0	0.0165	0.0037	
	Apr	0	0.010	13481	13481	0		0	0	0.0075	0.0047	
	May	0	0.010	13545	13545	0		0	0	0.0162	0.0050	
	Jun	0	0.010	13612	13612	0		0	0	0.0178	0.0069	
	Jul	0	0.010	13706	13706	0		0	0	0.0195	0.0008	
	Aug	0	0.010	13717	13717	0		0	0	-0.0118	0.0020	
	Sep	0	0.010	13745	13745	0		0	0	0.0301	0.0050	
	Oct	0	0.010	13813	13813	0		0	0	0.0096	0.0043	
	Nov	0	0.010	13873	13873	0		0	0	0.0005	0.0017	
	Dec	0	0.010	13896	13896	0		0	0	0.0056	0.0030	
1965	Jan	0	0.010	13938	13938	0		0	0	0.0345	0.0040	
	Feb	0	0.010	13994	13994	0		0	0	0.0031	0.0014	
	Mar	0	0.010	14013	14013	0		0	0	-0.0133	0.0054	
	Apr	0	0.010	14089	14089	0		0	0	0.0356	0.0036	
	May	0	0.010	14140	14140	0		0	0	-0.0030	0.0018	
	Jun	0	0.010	14165	14165	0		0	0	-0.0473	0.0047	
	Jul	0	0.010	14232	14232	0		0	0	0.0147	0.0022	
	Aug	0	0.010	14263	14263	0		0	0	0.0272	-0.0013	
	Sep	0	0.010	14245	14245	0		0	0	0.0334	-0.0034	
	Oct	0	0.010	14196	14196	0		0	0	0.0289	0.0027	
	Nov	0	0.010	14235	14235	0		0	0	-0.0031	-0.0062	
	Dec	0	0.010	14146	14146	0		0	0	0.0106	-0.0078	
1966	Jan	0	0.010	14036	14036	0		0	0	0.0062	-0.0104	
	Feb	0	0.010	13890	13890	0		0	0	-0.0131	-0.0250	
	Mar	0	0.010	13543	13543	0		0	0	-0.0205	0.0296	
	Apr	0	0.010	13944	13944	0		0	0	0.0220	-0.0063	
	May	0	0.010	13856	13856	0		0	0	-0.0492	-0.0059	
	Jun	0	0.010	13774	13774	0		0	0	-0.0146	-0.0016	
	Jul	0	0.010	13752	13752	0		0	0	-0.0120	-0.0037	
	Aug	0	0.010	13701	13701	0		0	0	-0.0725	-0.0206	
	Sep	0	0.010	13419	13419	0		0	0	-0.0053	0.0332	
	Oct	0	0.010	13864	13864	0		0	0	0.0494	0.0228	
	Nov	0	0.010	14180	14180	0		0	0	0.0095	-0.0148	
	Dec	0	0.010	13971	13971	0		0	0	0.0002	0.0413	

Table 5.1 (*Cont'd*)

Monthly Evolution of the Social Security Trust Fund if It Had Been Invested in US Treasury Bonds, Large Company US Stocks, and (Since 2002) International Stocks, 1937–2010.
(other things being equal)
(Dollar amounts rounded to nearest million)

Year	Month	Ending value of US stock portfolio	Ending value of gov't bond portfolio	Ending value of EAFE+ portfolio	End Value of SS Trust Fund	Percent in large US stocks	Percent in LT gov't bonds	Percent in EAFE+ Canada stocks	Percent of debt	Official value ot SS Trust Fund	Net SS inflows by fiscal year	Ratio of invested to actual Trust Fund
1962	Jan	85747	12430	0	94611	90.63	13.14	0.00	3.77			
	Feb	87539	12558	0	96368	90.84	13.03	0.00	3.87			
	Mar	87136	12875	0	96119	90.65	13.40	0.00	4.05			
	Apr	81847	12981	0	90766	90.17	14.30	0.00	4.47			
	May	75209	13041	0	84018	89.52	15.52	0.00	5.04			
	Jun	69170	12941	0	77710	89.01	16.65	0.00	5.66		-1874	
	Jul	73680	12800	0	81948	89.91	15.62	0.00	5.53			
	Aug	75212	13040	0	83590	89.98	15.60	0.00	5.58			
	Sep	71715	13119	0	80043	89.60	16.39	0.00	5.99			
	Oct	72174	13230	0	80481	89.68	16.44	0.00	6.12			
	Nov	80012	13257	0	88217	90.70	15.03	0.00	5.73			
	Dec	81236	13304	0	89356	90.91	14.89	0.00	5.80	20705		4.32
1963	Jan	85347	13302	0	93333	91.44	14.25	0.00	5.70			
	Feb	83307	13313	0	91172	91.37	14.60	0.00	5.98			
	Mar	86389	13325	0	94133	91.77	14.16	0.00	5.93			
	Apr	90709	13309	0	98303	92.28	13.54	0.00	5.81			
	May	92460	13340	0	99950	92.51	13.35	0.00	5.85			
	Jun	90721	13365	0	98103	92.48	13.62	0.00	6.10		-1371	
	Jul	90522	13406	0	97925	92.44	13.69	0.00	6.13			
	Aug	95365	13435	0	102777	92.79	13.07	0.00	5.86			
	Sep	94440	13440	0	101837	92.74	13.20	0.00	5.93			
	Oct	97641	13405	0	104982	93.01	12.77	0.00	5.78			
	Nov	97192	13473	0	104581	92.93	12.88	0.00	5.82			
	Dec	99738	13465	0	107097	93.13	12.57	0.00	5.70	20715		5.17
1964	Jan	102561	13446	0	109878	93.34	12.24	0.00	5.58			
	Feb	104069	13432	0	111351	93.46	12.06	0.00	5.52			
	Mar	105786	13481	0	113095	93.54	11.92	0.00	5.46			
	Apr	106579	13545	0	113930	93.55	11.89	0.00	5.44			
	May	108306	13612	0	115704	93.61	11.76	0.00	5.37			
	Jun	110234	13706	0	117702	93.65	11.64	0.00	5.30		24	
	Jul	112383	13717	0	119800	93.81	11.45	0.00	5.26			
	Aug	111057	13745	0	118440	93.77	11.60	0.00	5.37			
	Sep	114400	13813	0	121789	93.93	11.34	0.00	5.27			
	Oct	115498	13873	0	122890	93.98	11.29	0.00	5.27			
	Nov	115556	13896	0	122915	94.01	11.31	0.00	5.32			
	Dec	116203	13938	0	123539	94.06	11.28	0.00	5.34	21172		5.84
1965	Jan	120212	13994	0	127541	94.25	10.97	0.00	5.23			
	Feb	120585	14013	0	127868	94.30	10.96	0.00	5.26			
	Mar	118981	14089	0	126271	94.23	11.16	0.00	5.38			
	Apr	123216	14140	0	130492	94.42	10.84	0.00	5.26			
	May	122847	14165	0	130082	94.44	10.89	0.00	5.33			
	Jun	117036	14232	0	124269	94.18	11.45	0.00	5.63		-453	
	Jul	118757	14263	0	125885	94.34	11.33	0.00	5.67			
	Aug	121987	14245	0	128960	94.59	11.05	0.00	5.64			
	Sep	126061	14196	0	132849	94.89	10.69	0.00	5.58			
	Oct	129704	14235	0	136394	95.10	10.44	0.00	5.53			
	Nov	129302	14146	0	135763	95.24	10.42	0.00	5.66			
	Dec	130673	14036	0	136884	95.46	10.25	0.00	5.72	19841		6.90
1966	Jan	131483	13890	0	137404	95.69	10.11	0.00	5.80			
	Feb	129761	13543	0	135192	95.98	10.02	0.00	6.00			
	Mar	127100	13944	0	132788	95.72	10.50	0.00	6.22			
	Apr	129897	13856	0	135353	95.97	10.24	0.00	6.21			
	May	123506	13774	0	128731	95.94	10.70	0.00	6.64			
	Jun	121703	13752	0	126759	96.01	10.85	0.00	6.86		-1272	
	Jul	120242	13701	0	125474	95.83	10.92	0.00	6.75			
	Aug	111525	13419	0	116696	95.57	11.50	0.00	7.07			
	Sep	110934	13864	0	116775	95.00	11.87	0.00	6.87			
	Oct	116414	14180	0	122792	94.81	11.55	0.00	6.35			
	Nov	117520	13971	0	123915	94.84	11.27	0.00	6.11			
	Dec	117543	14548	0	124743	94.23	11.66	0.00	5.89	22308		5.59

Table 5.1 (*Cont'd*)

Monthly Evolution of the Social Security Trust Fund if It Had Been Invested in US Treasury Bonds, Large Company US Stocks, and (Since 2002) International Stocks, 1937–2010.
(other things being equal)
(Dollar amounts rounded to nearest million)

Year	Month	Soc. Sec. receipts less int. income	Soc. Sec. outlays less int. expense	Net SS cash inflow/ outflow	Amount of short term loan	Debt at end of month	30-day interest rate	Amount of debt repaid	New US stock investm.	Comm. rate for US stocks	Value of cont. stock portf.	Beg. of month US stock portfolio
1967	Jan	2076	1811	265	0	7121	0.0053	265	0	0.020	117543	117543
	Feb	2076	1811	265	0	6889	0.0046	265	0	0.020	126923	126923
	Mar	2076	1811	265	0	6657	0.0049	265	0	0.020	127837	127837
	Apr	2076	1811	265	0	6420	0.0042	265	0	0.020	133065	133065
	May	2076	1811	265	0	6182	0.0043	265	0	0.020	138880	138880
	Jun	2076	1811	265	0	5939	0.0037	265	0	0.020	132256	132256
	Jul	2122	1988	133	0	5831	0.0042	133	0	0.020	134769	134769
	Aug	2122	1988	133	0	5721	0.0041	133	0	0.020	141076	141076
	Sep	2122	1988	133	0	5612	0.0042	133	0	0.020	140088	140088
	Oct	2122	1988	133	0	5506	0.0049	133	0	0.020	144879	144879
	Nov	2122	1988	133	0	5398	0.0046	133	0	0.020	140881	140881
	Dec	2122	1988	133	0	5282	0.0033	133	0	0.020	141796	141796
1968	Jan	2122	1988	133	0	5175	0.0050	133	0	0.020	145738	145738
	Feb	2122	1988	133	0	5067	0.0049	133	0	0.020	139544	139544
	Mar	2122	1988	133	0	4958	0.0048	133	0	0.020	135902	135902
	Apr	2122	1988	133	0	4851	0.0053	133	0	0.020	137397	137397
	May	2122	1988	133	0	4744	0.0055	133	0	0.020	148856	148856
	Jun	2122	1988	133	0	4636	0.0053	133	0	0.020	151253	151253
	Jul	2492	2275	217	0	4446	0.0058	217	0	0.020	152841	152841
	Aug	2492	2275	217	0	4252	0.0052	217	0	0.020	150212	150212
	Sep	2492	2275	217	0	4053	0.0041	217	0	0.020	152675	152675
	Oct	2492	2275	217	0	3858	0.0054	217	0	0.020	158782	158782
	Nov	2492	2275	217	0	3662	0.0052	217	0	0.020	160164	160164
	Dec	2492	2275	217	0	3464	0.0053	217	0	0.020	168669	168669
1969	Jan	2492	2275	217	0	3269	0.0063	217	0	0.020	161888	161888
	Feb	2492	2275	217	0	3071	0.0056	217	0	0.020	160787	160787
	Mar	2492	2275	217	0	2871	0.0056	217	0	0.020	153938	153938
	Apr	2492	2275	217	0	2673	0.0063	217	0	0.020	159464	159464
	May	2492	2275	217	0	2471	0.0058	217	0	0.020	163116	163116
	Jun	2492	2275	217	0	2270	0.0061	217	0	0.020	163540	163540
	Jul	2880	2523	357	0	1927	0.0063	357	0	0.020	154676	154676
	Aug	2880	2523	357	0	1581	0.0060	357	0	0.020	145597	145597
	Sep	2880	2523	357	0	1236	0.0072	357	0	0.020	152207	152207
	Oct	2880	2523	357	0	887	0.0070	357	0	0.020	148615	148615
	Nov	2880	2523	357	0	536	0.0062	357	0	0.020	155436	155436
	Dec	2880	2523	357	0	183	0.0074	357	0	0.020	150820	150820
1970	Jan	2880	2523	357	0	0	0.0070	184	0	0.020	148150	148150
	Feb	2880	2523	357	0	0	0.0072	0	0	0.020	137143	137143
	Mar	2880	2523	357	0	0	0.0067	0	0	0.020	145179	145179
	Apr	2880	2523	357	0	0	0.0060	0	0	0.020	145615	145615
	May	2880	2523	357	0	0	0.0063	0	0	0.020	132669	132669
	Jun	2880	2523	357	0	0	0.0068	0	0	0.020	125412	125412
	Jul	3079	2990	90	0	0	0.0062	0	0	0.020	119368	119368
	Aug	3079	2990	90	0	0	0.0063	0	0	0.020	128344	128344
	Sep	3079	2990	90	0	0	0.0064	0	0	0.020	134877	134877
	Oct	3079	2990	90	0	0		0	0	0.020	139557	139557
	Nov	3079	2990	90	0	0		0	0	0.020	138203	138203
	Dec	3079	2990	90	0	0		0	0	0.020	145611	145611
1971	Jan	3079	2990	90	0	0		0	0	0.020	154115	154115
	Feb	3079	2990	90	0	0		0	0	0.020	160572	160572
	Mar	3079	2990	90	0	0		0	0	0.020	162836	162836
	Apr	3079	2990	90	0	0		0	0	0.020	169056	169056
	May	3079	2990	90	0	0		0	0	0.020	175430	175430
	Jun	3079	2990	90	0	0		0	0	0.020	168992	168992
	Jul	3425	3346	79	0	0		0	0	0.020	169346	169346
	Aug	3425	3346	79	0	0		0	0	0.020	162590	162590
	Sep	3425	3346	79	0	0		0	0	0.020	169288	169288
	Oct	3425	3346	79	0	0		0	0	0.020	168340	168340
	Nov	3425	3346	79	0	0		0	0	0.020	161539	161539
	Dec	3425	3346	79	0	0		0	0	0.020	161975	161975

Table 5.1 (*Cont'd*)

Monthly Evolution of the Social Security Trust Fund if It Had Been Invested in US Treasury Bonds, Large Company US Stocks, and (Since 2002) International Stocks, 1937–2010.
(other things being equal)
(Dollar amounts rounded to nearest million)

Year	Month	New gov't bond investm.	Market impact for bonds	Value of cont. bond portfolio	Beg. of month bond portfolio	New EAFE+ Canada investm.	Comm. for EAFE+ stocks	Value of cont. EAFE+ portfolio	Beg. of month EAFE+ portfolio	Return on large US stocks	Return on LT US gov't bonds	Return on EAFE+ stocks
1967	Jan	0	0.010	14548	14548	0		0	0	0.0798	0.0154	
	Feb	0	0.010	14772	14772	0		0	0	0.0072	-0.0221	
	Mar	0	0.010	14445	14445	0		0	0	0.0409	0.0198	
	Apr	0	0.010	14731	14731	0		0	0	0.0437	-0.0291	
	May	0	0.010	14302	14302	0		0	0	-0.0477	-0.0039	
	Jun	0	0.010	14247	14247	0		0	0	0.0190	-0.0312	
	Jul	0	0.010	13802	13802	0		0	0	0.0468	0.0068	
	Aug	0	0.010	13896	13896	0		0	0	-0.0070	-0.0084	
	Sep	0	0.010	13779	13779	0		0	0	0.0342	-0.0004	
	Oct	0	0.010	13774	13774	0		0	0	-0.0276	-0.0400	
	Nov	0	0.010	13223	13223	0		0	0	0.0065	-0.0196	
	Dec	0	0.010	12964	12964	0		0	0	0.0278	0.0192	
1968	Jan	0	0.010	13213	13213	0		0	0	-0.0425	0.0328	
	Feb	0	0.010	13646	13646	0		0	0	-0.0261	-0.0033	
	Mar	0	0.010	13601	13601	0		0	0	0.0110	-0.0212	
	Apr	0	0.010	13313	13313	0		0	0	0.0834	0.0227	
	May	0	0.010	13615	13615	0		0	0	0.0161	0.0043	
	Jun	0	0.010	13673	13673	0		0	0	0.0105	0.0230	
	Jul	0	0.010	13988	13988	0		0	0	-0.0172	0.0289	
	Aug	0	0.010	14392	14392	0		0	0	0.0164	-0.0003	
	Sep	0	0.010	14388	14388	0		0	0	0.0400	-0.0102	
	Oct	0	0.010	14241	14241	0		0	0	0.0087	-0.0132	
	Nov	0	0.010	14053	14053	0		0	0	0.0531	-0.0269	
	Dec	0	0.010	13675	13675	0		0	0	-0.0402	-0.0363	
1969	Jan	0	0.010	13179	13179	0		0	0	-0.0068	-0.0206	
	Feb	0	0.010	12907	12907	0		0	0	-0.0426	0.0042	
	Mar	0	0.010	12961	12961	0		0	0	0.0359	0.0010	
	Apr	0	0.010	12974	12974	0		0	0	0.0229	0.0427	
	May	0	0.010	13528	13528	0		0	0	0.0026	-0.0490	
	Jun	0	0.010	12865	12865	0		0	0	-0.0542	0.0214	
	Jul	0	0.010	13141	13141	0		0	0	-0.0587	0.0079	
	Aug	0	0.010	13245	13245	0		0	0	0.0454	-0.0069	
	Sep	0	0.010	13153	13153	0		0	0	-0.0236	-0.0531	
	Oct	0	0.010	12455	12455	0		0	0	0.0459	0.0365	
	Nov	0	0.010	12909	12909	0		0	0	-0.0297	-0.0243	
	Dec	0	0.010	12596	12596	0		0	0	-0.0177	-0.0068	
1970	Jan	0	0.010	12510	12510	0	0.030	0	0	-0.0743	-0.0021	-0.0054
	Feb	173	0.010	12484	12655	0	0.030	0	0	0.0586	0.0587	-0.0127
	Mar	357	0.010	13398	13752	0	0.030	0	0	0.0030	-0.0068	0.0152
	Apr	357	0.010	13658	14012	0	0.030	0	0	-0.0889	-0.0413	-0.0878
	May	357	0.010	13433	13786	0	0.030	0	0	-0.0547	-0.0468	-0.0566
	Jun	357	0.010	13141	13495	0	0.030	0	0	-0.0482	0.0486	0.0266
	Jul	357	0.010	14151	14504	0	0.030	0	0	0.0752	0.0319	0.0452
	Aug	90	0.010	14967	15056	0	0.030	0	0	0.0509	-0.0019	0.0108
	Sep	90	0.010	15027	15116	0	0.030	0	0	0.0347	0.0228	0.0165
	Oct	90	0.010	15461	15549	0	0.030	0	0	-0.0097	-0.0109	-0.0090
	Nov	90	0.010	15380	15469	0	0.030	0	0	0.0536	0.0791	-0.0295
	Dec	90	0.010	16692	16781	0	0.030	0	0	0.0584	-0.0084	0.0225
1971	Jan	90	0.010	16640	16729	0	0.030	0	0	0.0419	0.0506	0.0398
	Feb	90	0.010	17576	17664	0	0.030	0	0	0.0141	-0.0163	0.0077
	Mar	90	0.010	17376	17465	0	0.030	0	0	0.0382	0.0526	0.0436
	Apr	90	0.010	18384	18473	0	0.030	0	0	0.0377	-0.0283	0.0323
	May	90	0.010	17950	18039	0	0.030	0	0	-0.0367	-0.0006	0.0117
	Jun	90	0.010	18028	18117	0	0.030	0	0	0.0021	-0.0159	0.0193
	Jul	90	0.010	17829	17918	0	0.030	0	0	-0.0399	0.0030	0.0363
	Aug	79	0.010	17972	18049	0	0.030	0	0	0.0412	0.0471	-0.0069
	Sep	79	0.010	18899	18977	0	0.030	0	0	-0.0056	0.0204	-0.0140
	Oct	79	0.010	19364	19442	0	0.030	0	0	-0.0404	0.0167	-0.0335
	Nov	79	0.010	19767	19845	0	0.030	0	0	0.0027	-0.0047	0.0282
	Dec	79	0.010	19751	19829	0	0.030	0	0	0.0877	0.0044	0.0925

Table 5.1   (Cont'd)

Monthly Evolution of the Social Security Trust Fund if It Had Been Invested in US Treasury Bonds, Large Company US Stocks, and (Since 2002) International Stocks, 1937–2010.
(other things being equal)
(Dollar amounts rounded to nearest million)

Year	Month	Ending value of US stock portfolio	Ending value of gov't bond portfolio	Ending value of EAFE+ portfolio	End Value of SS Trust Fund	Percent in large US stocks	Percent in LT gov't bonds	Percent in EAFE+ Canada stocks	Percent of debt	Official value ot SS Trust Fund	Net SS inflows by fiscal year	Ratio of invested to actual Trust Fund
1967	Jan	126923	14772	0	134573	94.32	10.98	0.00	5.29			
	Feb	127837	14445	0	135393	94.42	10.67	0.00	5.09			
	Mar	133065	14731	0	141140	94.28	10.44	0.00	4.72			
	Apr	138880	14302	0	146763	94.63	9.75	0.00	4.37			
	May	132256	14247	0	140321	94.25	10.15	0.00	4.41			
	Jun	134769	13802	0	142632	94.49	9.68	0.00	4.16		3185	
	Jul	141076	13896	0	149141	94.59	9.32	0.00	3.91			
	Aug	140088	13779	0	148146	94.56	9.30	0.00	3.86			
	Sep	144879	13774	0	153041	94.67	9.00	0.00	3.67			
	Oct	140881	13223	0	148598	94.81	8.90	0.00	3.71			
	Nov	141796	12964	0	149362	94.93	8.68	0.00	3.61			
	Dec	145738	13213	0	153669	94.84	8.60	0.00	3.44	26250		5.85
1968	Jan	139544	13646	0	148015	94.28	9.22	0.00	3.50			
	Feb	135902	13601	0	144436	94.09	9.42	0.00	3.51			
	Mar	137397	13313	0	145752	94.27	9.13	0.00	3.40			
	Apr	148856	13615	0	157620	94.44	8.64	0.00	3.08			
	May	151253	13673	0	160182	94.43	8.54	0.00	2.96			
	Jun	152841	13988	0	162193	94.23	8.62	0.00	2.86		1601	
	Jul	150212	14392	0	160158	93.79	8.99	0.00	2.78			
	Aug	152675	14388	0	162811	93.77	8.84	0.00	2.61			
	Sep	158782	14241	0	168970	93.97	8.43	0.00	2.40			
	Oct	160164	14053	0	170359	94.02	8.25	0.00	2.26			
	Nov	168669	13675	0	178682	94.40	7.65	0.00	2.05			
	Dec	161888	13179	0	171602	94.34	7.68	0.00	2.02	28729		5.97
1969	Jan	160787	12907	0	170425	94.34	7.57	0.00	1.92			
	Feb	153938	12961	0	163828	93.96	7.91	0.00	1.87			
	Mar	159464	12974	0	169567	94.04	7.65	0.00	1.69			
	Apr	163116	13528	0	173971	93.76	7.78	0.00	1.54			
	May	163540	12865	0	173934	94.02	7.40	0.00	1.42			
	Jun	154676	13141	0	165547	93.43	7.94	0.00	1.37		2601	
	Jul	145597	13245	0	156914	92.79	8.44	0.00	1.23			
	Aug	152207	13153	0	163778	92.93	8.03	0.00	0.97			
	Sep	148615	12455	0	159834	92.98	7.79	0.00	0.77			
	Oct	155436	12909	0	167458	92.82	7.71	0.00	0.53			
	Nov	150820	12596	0	162879	92.60	7.73	0.00	0.33			
	Dec	148150	12510	0	160477	92.32	7.80	0.00	0.11	34182		4.69
1970	Jan	137143	12484	0	149626	91.66	8.34	0.00	0.00			
	Feb	145179	13398	0	158577	91.55	8.45	0.00	0.00			
	Mar	145615	13658	0	159273	91.42	8.58	0.00	0.00			
	Apr	132669	13433	0	146102	90.81	9.19	0.00	0.00			
	May	125412	13141	0	138554	90.52	9.48	0.00	0.00			
	Jun	119368	14151	0	133518	89.40	10.60	0.00	0.00		4285	
	Jul	128344	14967	0	143311	89.56	10.44	0.00	0.00			
	Aug	134877	15027	0	149904	89.98	10.02	0.00	0.00			
	Sep	139557	15461	0	155017	90.03	9.97	0.00	0.00			
	Oct	138203	15380	0	153583	89.99	10.01	0.00	0.00			
	Nov	145611	16692	0	162303	89.72	10.28	0.00	0.00			
	Dec	154115	16640	0	170755	90.25	9.75	0.00	0.00	38068		4.49
1971	Jan	160572	17576	0	178148	90.13	9.87	0.00	0.00			
	Feb	162836	17376	0	180213	90.36	9.64	0.00	0.00			
	Mar	169056	18384	0	187440	90.19	9.81	0.00	0.00			
	Apr	175430	17950	0	193380	90.72	9.28	0.00	0.00			
	May	168992	18028	0	187020	90.36	9.64	0.00	0.00			
	Jun	169346	17829	0	187175	90.47	9.53	0.00	0.00		1077	
	Jul	162590	17972	0	180561	90.05	9.95	0.00	0.00			
	Aug	169288	18899	0	188188	89.96	10.04	0.00	0.00			
	Sep	168340	19364	0	187705	89.68	10.32	0.00	0.00			
	Oct	161539	19767	0	181306	89.10	10.90	0.00	0.00			
	Nov	161975	19751	0	181727	89.13	10.87	0.00	0.00			
	Dec	176181	19916	0	196097	89.84	10.16	0.00	0.00	40434		4.85

Table 5.1   (*Cont'd*)

Monthly Evolution of the Social Security Trust Fund if It Had Been Invested in US Treasury Bonds, Large Company US Stocks, and (Since 2002) International Stocks, 1937–2010.
(other things being equal)
(Dollar amounts rounded to nearest million)

Year	Month	Soc. Sec. receipts less int. income	Soc. Sec. outlays less int. expense	Net SS cash inflow/ outflow	Amount of short term loan	Debt at end of month	30-day interest rate	Amount of debt repaid	New US stock investm.	Comm. rate for US stocks	Value of cont. stock portf.	Beg. of month US stock portfolio
1972	Jan	3425	3346	79	0	0		0	0	0.020	176181	176181
	Feb	3425	3346	79	0	0		0	0	0.020	179599	179599
	Mar	3425	3346	79	0	0		0	0	0.020	184969	184969
	Apr	3425	3346	79	0	0		0	0	0.020	186300	186300
	May	3425	3346	79	0	0		0	0	0.020	187362	187362
	Jun	3425	3346	79	0	0		0	0	0.020	191465	191465
	Jul	3942	4091	-149	149	149	0.0041	0	0	0.020	187540	187540
	Aug	3942	4091	-149	149	299	0.0039	0	0	0.020	188216	188216
	Sep	3942	4091	-149	149	450	0.0044	0	0	0.020	195575	195575
	Oct	3942	4091	-149	149	602	0.0050	0	0	0.020	194871	194871
	Nov	3942	4091	-149	149	754	0.0047	0	0	0.020	196956	196956
	Dec	3942	4091	-149	149	907	0.0047	0	0	0.020	206902	206902
1973	Jan	3942	4091	-149	149	1061	0.0054	0	0	0.010	209613	209613
	Feb	3942	4091	-149	149	1216	0.0051	0	0	0.010	206280	206280
	Mar	3942	4091	-149	149	1373	0.0056	0	0	0.010	199411	199411
	Apr	3942	4091	-149	149	1529	0.0052	0	0	0.010	199371	199371
	May	3942	4091	-149	149	1688	0.0061	0	0	0.010	191496	191496
	Jun	3942	4091	-149	149	1848	0.0061	0	0	0.010	188834	188834
	Jul	4599	4656	-57	57	1920	0.0074	0	0	0.010	187871	187871
	Aug	4599	4656	-57	57	1992	0.0080	0	0	0.010	195273	195273
	Sep	4599	4656	-57	57	2066	0.0078	0	0	0.010	189063	189063
	Oct	4599	4656	-57	57	2139	0.0075	0	0	0.010	196909	196909
	Nov	4599	4656	-57	57	2210	0.0066	0	0	0.010	196968	196968
	Dec	4599	4656	-57	57	2284	0.0074	0	0	0.010	175656	175656
1974	Jan	4599	4656	-57	57	2358	0.0073	0	0	0.010	178871	178871
	Feb	4599	4656	-57	57	2432	0.0068	0	0	0.010	177350	177350
	Mar	4599	4656	-57	57	2505	0.0066	0	0	0.010	177687	177687
	Apr	4599	4656	-57	57	2584	0.0085	0	0	0.010	173832	173832
	May	4599	4656	-57	57	2664	0.0085	0	0	0.010	167348	167348
	Jun	4599	4656	-57	57	2740	0.0070	0	0	0.010	162796	162796
	Jul	5323	5388	-66	66	2828	0.0080	0	0	0.010	160712	160712
	Aug	5323	5388	-66	66	2913	0.0070	0	0	0.010	148514	148514
	Sep	5323	5388	-66	66	3006	0.0091	0	0	0.010	136217	136217
	Oct	5323	5388	-66	66	3090	0.0061	0	0	0.010	120280	120280
	Nov	5323	5388	-66	66	3176	0.0064	0	0	0.010	140210	140210
	Dec	5323	5388	-66	66	3267	0.0080	0	0	0.010	133929	133929
1975	Jan	5323	5388	-66	66	3355	0.0068	0	0	0.010	131558	131558
	Feb	5323	5388	-66	66	3439	0.0053	0	0	0.010	148016	148016
	Mar	5323	5388	-66	66	3522	0.0051	0	0	0.010	157992	157992
	Apr	5323	5388	-66	66	3607	0.0054	0	0	0.010	161737	161737
	May	5323	5388	-66	66	3693	0.0054	0	0	0.010	169710	169710
	Jun	5323	5388	-66	66	3777	0.0051	0	0	0.010	178349	178349
	Jul	5656	6159	-503	503	4305	0.0058	0	0	0.010	186588	186588
	Aug	5656	6159	-503	503	4835	0.0058	0	0	0.010	174292	174292
	Sep	5656	6159	-503	503	5372	0.0063	0	0	0.010	171782	171782
	Oct	5656	6159	-503	503	5913	0.0066	0	0	0.010	166148	166148
	Nov	5656	6159	-503	503	6449	0.0051	0	0	0.010	176731	176731
	Dec	5656	6159	-503	503	6992	0.0058	0	0	0.010	182263	182263
1976	Jan	5656	6159	-503	503	7537	0.0057	0	0	0.010	180513	180513
	Feb	5656	6159	-503	503	8075	0.0044	0	0	0.010	202157	202157
	Mar	5656	6159	-503	503	8620	0.0050	0	0	0.010	200984	200984
	Apr	5656	6159	-503	503	9171	0.0052	0	0	0.010	207537	207537
	May	5656	6159	-503	503	9719	0.0047	0	0	0.010	205482	205482
	Jun	5656	6159	-503	503	10276	0.0053	0	0	0.010	203982	203982
	Jul	6088	6588	-499	499	10836	0.0057	0	0	0.010	212692	212692
	Aug	6088	6588	-499	499	11395	0.0052	0	0	0.010	211246	211246
	Sep	6088	6588	-499	499	11958	0.0054	0	0	0.010	211541	211541
	Oct	6543	7089	-546	546	12568	0.0051	0	0	0.010	216766	216766
	Nov	6543	7089	-546	546	13179	0.0050	0	0	0.010	212301	212301
	Dec	6543	7089	-546	546	13794	0.0050	0	0	0.010	212110	212110

Table 5.1 (*Cont'd*)

Monthly Evolution of the Social Security Trust Fund if It Had Been Invested in US Treasury
Bonds, Large Company US Stocks, and (Since 2002) International Stocks, 1937–2010.
(other things being equal)
(Dollar amounts rounded to nearest million)

Year	Month	New gov't bond investm.	Market impact for bonds	Value of cont. bond portfolio	Beg. of month bond portfolio	New EAFE+ Canada investm.	Comm. for EAFE+ stocks	Value of cont. EAFE+ portfolio	Beg. of month EAFE+ portfolio	Return on large US stocks	Return on LT US gov't bonds	Return on EAFE+ stocks
1972	Jan	79	0.010	19916	19994	0	0.030	0	0	0.0194	-0.0063	0.0567
	Feb	79	0.010	19868	19946	0	0.030	0	0	0.0299	0.0088	0.0613
	Mar	79	0.010	20122	20199	0	0.030	0	0	0.0072	-0.0082	0.0288
	Apr	79	0.010	20034	20112	0	0.030	0	0	0.0057	0.0027	0.0215
	May	79	0.010	20166	20244	0	0.030	0	0	0.0219	0.0270	0.0355
	Jun	79	0.010	20790	20868	0	0.030	0	0	-0.0205	-0.0065	-0.0204
	Jul	79	0.010	20733	20810	0	0.030	0	0	0.0036	0.0216	0.0461
	Aug	0	0.010	21260	21260	0	0.030	0	0	0.0391	0.0029	0.0186
	Sep	0	0.010	21322	21322	0	0.030	0	0	-0.0036	-0.0083	-0.0290
	Oct	0	0.010	21145	21145	0	0.030	0	0	0.0107	0.0234	0.0064
	Nov	0	0.010	21639	21639	0	0.030	0	0	0.0505	0.0226	0.0634
	Dec	0	0.010	22128	22128	0	0.030	0	0	0.0131	-0.0229	0.0343
1973	Jan	0	0.005	21622	21622	0	0.020	0	0	-0.0159	-0.0321	0.0153
	Feb	0	0.005	20928	20928	0	0.020	0	0	-0.0333	0.0014	0.0711
	Mar	0	0.005	20957	20957	0	0.020	0	0	-0.0002	0.0082	0.0060
	Apr	0	0.005	21129	21129	0	0.020	0	0	-0.0395	0.0046	-0.0546
	May	0	0.005	21226	21226	0	0.020	0	0	-0.0139	-0.0105	0.0175
	Jun	0	0.005	21003	21003	0	0.020	0	0	-0.0051	-0.0021	0.0244
	Jul	0	0.005	20959	20959	0	0.020	0	0	0.0394	-0.0433	-0.0057
	Aug	0	0.005	20051	20051	0	0.020	0	0	-0.0318	0.0391	-0.0459
	Sep	0	0.005	20835	20835	0	0.020	0	0	0.0415	0.0318	-0.0026
	Oct	0	0.005	21498	21498	0	0.020	0	0	0.0003	0.0215	0.0268
	Nov	0	0.005	21960	21960	0	0.020	0	0	-0.1082	-0.0183	-0.1391
	Dec	0	0.005	21558	21558	0	0.020	0	0	0.0183	-0.0082	-0.0375
1974	Jan	0	0.005	21382	21382	0	0.020	0	0	-0.0085	-0.0083	0.0099
	Feb	0	0.005	21204	21204	0	0.020	0	0	0.0019	-0.0024	0.0341
	Mar	0	0.005	21153	21153	0	0.020	0	0	-0.0217	-0.0292	-0.0254
	Apr	0	0.005	20536	20536	0	0.020	0	0	-0.0373	-0.0253	0.0137
	May	0	0.005	20016	20016	0	0.020	0	0	-0.0272	0.0123	-0.0438
	Jun	0	0.005	20262	20262	0	0.020	0	0	-0.0128	0.0045	-0.0437
	Jul	0	0.005	20353	20353	0	0.020	0	0	-0.0759	-0.0029	-0.0425
	Aug	0	0.005	20294	20294	0	0.020	0	0	-0.0828	-0.0232	-0.1022
	Sep	0	0.005	19823	19823	0	0.020	0	0	-0.1170	0.0247	-0.0760
	Oct	0	0.005	20313	20313	0	0.020	0	0	0.1657	0.0489	0.0208
	Nov	0	0.005	21306	21306	0	0.020	0	0	-0.0448	0.0295	0.0158
	Dec	0	0.005	21935	21935	0	0.020	0	0	-0.0177	0.0171	-0.0079
1975	Jan	0	0.005	22310	22310	0	0.020	0	0	0.1251	0.0225	0.1761
	Feb	0	0.005	22812	22812	0	0.020	0	0	0.0674	0.0131	0.1199
	Mar	0	0.005	23111	23111	0	0.020	0	0	0.0237	-0.0267	-0.0124
	Apr	0	0.005	22494	22494	0	0.020	0	0	0.0493	-0.0182	0.0441
	May	0	0.005	22084	22084	0	0.020	0	0	0.0509	0.0212	-0.0044
	Jun	0	0.005	22553	22553	0	0.020	0	0	0.0462	0.0292	-0.0321
	Jul	0	0.005	23211	23211	0	0.020	0	0	-0.0659	-0.0087	-0.0374
	Aug	0	0.005	23009	23009	0	0.020	0	0	-0.0144	-0.0068	-0.0021
	Sep	0	0.005	22853	22853	0	0.020	0	0	-0.0328	-0.0098	-0.0456
	Oct	0	0.005	22629	22629	0	0.020	0	0	0.0637	0.0475	0.0721
	Nov	0	0.005	23704	23704	0	0.020	0	0	0.0313	-0.0109	0.0295
	Dec	0	0.005	23445	23445	0	0.020	0	0	-0.0096	0.0390	0.0159
1976	Jan	0	0.005	24360	24360	0	0.020	0	0	0.1199	0.0090	0.0585
	Feb	0	0.005	24579	24579	0	0.020	0	0	-0.0058	0.0062	-0.0012
	Mar	0	0.005	24731	24731	0	0.020	0	0	0.0326	0.0166	-0.0163
	Apr	0	0.005	25142	25142	0	0.020	0	0	-0.0099	0.0018	-0.0020
	May	0	0.005	25187	25187	0	0.020	0	0	-0.0073	-0.0158	-0.0232
	Jun	0	0.005	24789	24789	0	0.020	0	0	0.0427	0.0208	0.0143
	Jul	0	0.005	25305	25305	0	0.020	0	0	-0.0068	0.0078	-0.0118
	Aug	0	0.005	25502	25502	0	0.020	0	0	0.0014	0.0211	-0.0003
	Sep	0	0.005	26040	26040	0	0.020	0	0	0.0247	0.0145	-0.0165
	Oct	0	0.005	26418	26418	0	0.020	0	0	-0.0206	0.0084	-0.0606
	Nov	0	0.005	26640	26640	0	0.020	0	0	-0.0009	0.0339	-0.0030
	Dec	0	0.005	27543	27543	0	0.020	0	0	0.0540	0.0327	0.1153

Table 5.1 (Cont'd)

Monthly Evolution of the Social Security Trust Fund if It Had Been Invested in US Treasury Bonds, Large Company US Stocks, and (Since 2002) International Stocks, 1937–2010.
(other things being equal)
(Dollar amounts rounded to nearest million)

Year	Month	Ending value of US stock portfolio	Ending value of gov't bond portfolio	Ending value of EAFE+ portfolio	End Value of SS Trust Fund	Percent in large US stocks	Percent in LT gov't bonds	Percent in EAFE+ Canada stocks	Percent of debt	Official value ot SS Trust Fund	Net SS inflows by fiscal year	Ratio of invested to actual Trust Fund
1972	Jan	179599	19868	0	199467	90.04	9.96	0.00	0.00			
	Feb	184969	20122	0	205090	90.19	9.81	0.00	0.00			
	Mar	186300	20034	0	206334	90.29	9.71	0.00	0.00			
	Apr	187362	20166	0	207528	90.28	9.72	0.00	0.00			
	May	191465	20790	0	212256	90.21	9.79	0.00	0.00			
	Jun	187540	20733	0	208273	90.05	9.95	0.00	0.00		943	
	Jul	188216	21260	0	209326	89.92	10.16	0.00	0.07			
	Aug	195575	21322	0	216597	90.29	9.84	0.00	0.14			
	Sep	194871	21145	0	215565	90.40	9.81	0.00	0.21			
	Oct	196956	21639	0	217993	90.35	9.93	0.00	0.28			
	Nov	206902	22128	0	228276	90.64	9.69	0.00	0.33			
	Dec	209613	21622	0	230327	91.01	9.39	0.00	0.39	42775		5.38
1973	Jan	206280	20928	0	226146	91.22	9.25	0.00	0.47			
	Feb	199411	20957	0	219151	90.99	9.56	0.00	0.56			
	Mar	199371	21129	0	219127	90.98	9.64	0.00	0.63			
	Apr	191496	21226	0	211192	90.67	10.05	0.00	0.72			
	May	188834	21003	0	208148	90.72	10.09	0.00	0.81			
	Jun	187871	20959	0	206981	90.77	10.13	0.00	0.89		-1785	
	Jul	195273	20051	0	213405	91.50	9.40	0.00	0.90			
	Aug	189063	20835	0	207906	90.94	10.02	0.00	0.96			
	Sep	196909	21498	0	216342	91.02	9.94	0.00	0.95			
	Oct	196968	21960	0	216790	90.86	10.13	0.00	0.99			
	Nov	175656	21558	0	195005	90.08	11.06	0.00	1.13			
	Dec	178871	21382	0	197968	90.35	10.80	0.00	1.15	44414		4.46
1974	Jan	177350	21204	0	196196	90.39	10.81	0.00	1.20			
	Feb	177687	21153	0	196409	90.47	10.77	0.00	1.24			
	Mar	173832	20536	0	191862	90.60	10.70	0.00	1.31			
	Apr	167348	20016	0	184780	90.57	10.83	0.00	1.40			
	May	162796	20262	0	180394	90.24	11.23	0.00	1.48			
	Jun	160712	20353	0	178326	90.12	11.41	0.00	1.54		-685	
	Jul	148514	20294	0	165981	89.48	12.23	0.00	1.70			
	Aug	136217	19823	0	153127	88.96	12.95	0.00	1.90			
	Sep	120280	20313	0	137587	87.42	14.76	0.00	2.18			
	Oct	140210	21306	0	158426	88.50	13.45	0.00	1.95			
	Nov	133929	21935	0	152688	87.71	14.37	0.00	2.08			
	Dec	131558	22310	0	150601	87.36	14.81	0.00	2.17	45866		3.28
1975	Jan	148016	22812	0	167473	88.38	13.62	0.00	2.00			
	Feb	157992	23111	0	177664	88.93	13.01	0.00	1.94			
	Mar	161737	22494	0	180708	89.50	12.45	0.00	1.95			
	Apr	169710	22084	0	188187	90.18	11.74	0.00	1.92			
	May	178349	22553	0	197208	90.44	11.44	0.00	1.87			
	Jun	186588	23211	0	206022	90.57	11.27	0.00	1.83		-786	
	Jul	174292	23009	0	192996	90.31	11.92	0.00	2.23			
	Aug	171782	22853	0	189800	90.51	12.04	0.00	2.55			
	Sep	166148	22629	0	183405	90.59	12.34	0.00	2.93			
	Oct	176731	23704	0	194522	90.85	12.19	0.00	3.04			
	Nov	182263	23445	0	199260	91.47	11.77	0.00	3.24			
	Dec	180513	24360	0	197882	91.22	12.31	0.00	3.53	44342		4.46
1976	Jan	202157	24579	0	219199	92.23	11.21	0.00	3.44			
	Feb	200984	24731	0	217641	92.35	11.36	0.00	3.71			
	Mar	207537	25142	0	224058	92.63	11.22	0.00	3.85			
	Apr	205482	25187	0	221498	92.77	11.37	0.00	4.14			
	May	203982	24789	0	219052	93.12	11.32	0.00	4.44			
	Jun	212692	25305	0	227721	93.40	11.11	0.00	4.51			
	Jul	211246	25502	0	225911	93.51	11.29	0.00	4.80			
	Aug	211541	26040	0	226187	93.53	11.51	0.00	5.04			
	Sep	216766	26418	0	231226	93.75	11.43	0.00	5.17		-7530	
	Oct	212301	26640	0	226473	93.78	11.77	0.00	5.55			
	Nov	212110	27543	0	226473	93.66	12.16	0.00	5.82			
	Dec	223564	28443	0	238213	93.85	11.94	0.00	5.79	41133		5.79

Table 5.1   (Cont'd)

Monthly Evolution of the Social Security Trust Fund if It Had Been Invested in US Treasury Bonds, Large Company US Stocks, and (Since 2002) International Stocks, 1937–2010.
(other things being equal)
(Dollar amounts rounded to nearest million)

Year	Month	Soc. Sec. receipts less int. income	Soc. Sec. outlays less int. expense	Net SS cash inflow/ outflow	Amount of short term loan	Debt at end of month	30-day interest rate	Amount of debt repaid	New US stock investm.	Comm. rate for US stocks	Value of cont. stock portf.	Beg. of month US stock portfolio
1977	Jan	6543	7089	-546	546	14406	0.0046	0	0	0.010	223564	223564
	Feb	6543	7089	-546	546	15019	0.0045	0	0	0.010	212632	212632
	Mar	6543	7089	-546	546	15640	0.0048	0	0	0.010	209421	209421
	Apr	6543	7089	-546	546	16263	0.0048	0	0	0.010	206929	206929
	May	6543	7089	-546	546	16888	0.0047	0	0	0.010	207218	207218
	Jun	6543	7089	-546	546	17521	0.0050	0	0	0.010	204110	204110
	Jul	6543	7089	-546	546	18161	0.0052	0	0	0.010	213805	213805
	Aug	6543	7089	-546	546	18808	0.0054	0	0	0.010	210577	210577
	Sep	6543	7089	-546	546	19456	0.0053	0	0	0.010	207776	207776
	Oct	7266	7822	-556	556	20130	0.0059	0	0	0.010	207776	207776
	Nov	7266	7822	-556	556	20810	0.0060	0	0	0.010	199154	199154
	Dec	7266	7822	-556	556	21491	0.0059	0	0	0.010	206522	206522
1978	Jan	7266	7822	-556	556	22177	0.0059	0	0	0.010	207514	207514
	Feb	7266	7822	-556	556	22860	0.0056	0	0	0.010	195146	195146
	Mar	7266	7822	-556	556	23563	0.0063	0	0	0.010	192004	192004
	Apr	7266	7822	-556	556	24273	0.0064	0	0	0.010	197303	197303
	May	7266	7822	-556	556	24980	0.0061	0	0	0.010	214469	214469
	Jun	7266	7822	-556	556	25699	0.0064	0	0	0.010	217385	217385
	Jul	7266	7822	-556	556	26428	0.0066	0	0	0.010	214081	214081
	Aug	7266	7822	-556	556	27159	0.0065	0	0	0.010	226070	226070
	Sep	7266	7822	-556	556	27914	0.0072	0	0	0.010	233756	233756
	Oct	8322	8673	-351	351	28485	0.0078	0	0	0.010	232634	232634
	Nov	8322	8673	-351	351	29067	0.0080	0	0	0.010	211906	211906
	Dec	8322	8673	-351	351	29676	0.0088	0	0	0.010	217416	217416
1979	Jan	8322	8673	-351	351	30288	0.0087	0	0	0.010	221155	221155
	Feb	8322	8673	-351	351	30893	0.0083	0	0	0.010	230466	230466
	Mar	8322	8673	-351	351	31529	0.0091	0	0	0.010	223921	223921
	Apr	8322	8673	-351	351	32166	0.0090	0	0	0.010	236796	236796
	May	8322	8673	-351	351	32816	0.0092	0	0	0.010	237649	237649
	Jun	8322	8673	-351	351	33469	0.0091	0	0	0.010	233656	233656
	Jul	8322	8673	-351	351	34114	0.0087	0	0	0.010	243236	243236
	Aug	8322	8673	-351	351	34764	0.0087	0	0	0.010	245912	245912
	Sep	8322	8673	-351	351	35442	0.0093	0	0	0.010	260937	260937
	Oct	9592	9880	-288	288	36076	0.0097	0	0	0.010	261589	261589
	Nov	9592	9880	-288	288	36761	0.0109	0	0	0.010	244429	244429
	Dec	9592	9880	-288	288	37439	0.0105	0	0	0.010	256993	256993
1980	Jan	9592	9880	-288	288	38066	0.0090	0	0	0.008	261927	261927
	Feb	9592	9880	-288	288	38734	0.0099	0	0	0.008	277905	277905
	Mar	9592	9880	-288	288	39534	0.0131	0	0	0.008	278766	278766
	Apr	9592	9880	-288	288	40364	0.0136	0	0	0.008	251252	251252
	May	9592	9880	-288	288	41022	0.0091	0	0	0.008	262031	262031
	Jun	9592	9880	-288	288	41604	0.0071	0	0	0.008	276757	276757
	Jul	9592	9880	-288	288	42156	0.0063	0	0	0.008	284949	284949
	Aug	9592	9880	-288	288	42759	0.0074	0	0	0.008	304211	304211
	Sep	9592	9880	-288	288	43413	0.0085	0	0	0.008	308196	308196
	Oct	11023	11632	-609	609	44484	0.0105	0	0	0.008	316857	316857
	Nov	11023	11632	-609	609	45571	0.0106	0	0	0.008	322782	322782
	Dec	11023	11632	-609	609	46831	0.0141	0	0	0.008	358126	358126
1981	Jan	11023	11632	-609	609	47981	0.0114	0	0	0.008	346845	346845
	Feb	11023	11632	-609	609	49158	0.0117	0	0	0.008	331654	331654
	Mar	11023	11632	-609	609	50419	0.0131	0	0	0.008	338552	338552
	Apr	11023	11632	-609	609	51722	0.0136	0	0	0.008	351417	351417
	May	11023	11632	-609	609	52808	0.0091	0	0	0.008	343932	343932
	Jun	11023	11632	-609	609	53796	0.0071	0	0	0.008	346064	346064
	Jul	11023	11632	-609	609	54748	0.0063	0	0	0.008	343296	343296
	Aug	11023	11632	-609	609	55766	0.0074	0	0	0.008	343536	343536
	Sep	11023	11632	-609	609	56854	0.0085	0	0	0.008	324504	324504
	Oct	12163	12997	-834	834	58294	0.0105	0	0	0.008	308214	308214
	Nov	12163	12997	-834	834	59755	0.0106	0	0	0.008	324488	324488
	Dec	12163	12997	-834	834	61443	0.0141	0	0	0.008	338798	338798

Table 5.1   (*Cont'd*)

Monthly Evolution of the Social Security Trust Fund if It Had Been Invested in US Treasury Bonds, Large Company US Stocks, and (Since 2002) International Stocks, 1937–2010.
(other things being equal)
(Dollar amounts rounded to nearest million)

Year	Month	New gov't bond investm.	Market impact for bonds	Value of cont. bond portfolio	Beg. of month bond portfolio	New EAFE+ Canada investm.	Comm. for EAFE+ stocks	Value of cont. EAFE+ portfolio	Beg. of month EAFE+ portfolio	Return on large US stocks	Return on LT US gov't bonds	Return on EAFE+ stocks
1977	Jan	0	0.005	28443	28443	0	0.020	0	0	-0.0489	-0.0388	-0.0081
	Feb	0	0.005	27340	27340	0	0.020	0	0	-0.0151	-0.0049	0.0193
	Mar	0	0.005	27206	27206	0	0.020	0	0	-0.0119	0.0091	0.0038
	Apr	0	0.005	27453	27453	0	0.020	0	0	0.0014	0.0071	0.0244
	May	0	0.005	27648	27648	0	0.020	0	0	-0.0150	0.0125	-0.0052
	Jun	0	0.005	27994	27994	0	0.020	0	0	0.0475	0.0164	0.0243
	Jul	0	0.005	28453	28453	0	0.020	0	0	-0.0151	-0.0070	-0.0138
	Aug	0	0.005	28254	28254	0	0.020	0	0	-0.0133	0.0198	0.0364
	Sep	0	0.005	28813	28813	0	0.020	0	0	0.0000	-0.0029	0.0278
	Oct	0	0.005	28730	28730	0	0.020	0	0	-0.0415	-0.0093	0.0173
	Nov	0	0.005	28463	28463	0	0.020	0	0	0.0370	0.0093	-0.0031
	Dec	0	0.005	28727	28727	0	0.020	0	0	0.0048	-0.0168	0.0392
1978	Jan	0	0.005	28245	28245	0	0.020	0	0	-0.0596	-0.0080	0.0060
	Feb	0	0.005	28019	28019	0	0.020	0	0	-0.0161	0.0004	0.0107
	Mar	0	0.005	28030	28030	0	0.020	0	0	0.0276	-0.0021	0.0710
	Apr	0	0.005	27971	27971	0	0.020	0	0	0.0870	-0.0005	-0.0050
	May	0	0.005	27957	27957	0	0.020	0	0	0.0136	-0.0058	0.0235
	Jun	0	0.005	27795	27795	0	0.020	0	0	-0.0152	-0.0062	0.0414
	Jul	0	0.005	27623	27623	0	0.020	0	0	0.0560	0.0143	0.0851
	Aug	0	0.005	28018	28018	0	0.020	0	0	0.0340	0.0218	0.0206
	Sep	0	0.005	28628	28628	0	0.020	0	0	-0.0048	-0.0106	0.0306
	Oct	0	0.005	28325	28325	0	0.020	0	0	-0.0891	-0.0200	0.0504
	Nov	0	0.005	27758	27758	0	0.020	0	0	0.0260	0.0189	-0.0826
	Dec	0	0.005	28283	28283	0	0.020	0	0	0.0172	-0.0130	0.0483
1979	Jan	0	0.005	27915	27915	0	0.020	0	0	0.0421	0.0191	0.0077
	Feb	0	0.005	28449	28449	0	0.020	0	0	-0.0284	-0.0135	-0.0020
	Mar	0	0.005	28065	28065	0	0.020	0	0	0.0575	0.0129	0.0287
	Apr	0	0.005	28427	28427	0	0.020	0	0	0.0036	-0.0112	-0.0011
	May	0	0.005	28108	28108	0	0.020	0	0	-0.0168	0.0261	-0.0166
	Jun	0	0.005	28842	28842	0	0.020	0	0	0.0410	0.0311	0.0226
	Jul	0	0.005	29739	29739	0	0.020	0	0	0.0110	-0.0085	0.0066
	Aug	0	0.005	29486	29486	0	0.020	0	0	0.0611	-0.0035	0.0312
	Sep	0	0.005	29383	29383	0	0.020	0	0	0.0025	-0.0122	0.0461
	Oct	0	0.005	29024	29024	0	0.020	0	0	-0.0656	-0.0841	-0.0818
	Nov	0	0.005	26583	26583	0	0.020	0	0	0.0514	0.0311	0.0198
	Dec	0	0.005	27410	27410	0	0.020	0	0	0.0192	0.0057	0.0370
1980	Jan	0	0.005	27566	27566	0	0.015	0	0	0.0610	-0.0741	0.0578
	Feb	0	0.005	25524	25524	0	0.015	0	0	0.0031	-0.0467	0.0102
	Mar	0	0.005	24332	24332	0	0.015	0	0	-0.0987	-0.0315	-0.1194
	Apr	0	0.005	23565	23565	0	0.015	0	0	0.0429	0.1523	0.0884
	May	0	0.005	27154	27154	0	0.015	0	0	0.0562	0.0419	0.0507
	Jun	0	0.005	28292	28292	0	0.015	0	0	0.0296	0.0359	0.0648
	Jul	0	0.005	29308	29308	0	0.015	0	0	0.0676	-0.0476	-0.0001
	Aug	0	0.005	27913	27913	0	0.015	0	0	0.0131	-0.0432	0.0328
	Sep	0	0.005	26707	26707	0	0.015	0	0	0.0281	-0.0262	0.0307
	Oct	0	0.005	26007	26007	0	0.015	0	0	0.0187	-0.0263	0.0348
	Nov	0	0.005	25323	25323	0	0.015	0	0	0.1095	0.0100	-0.0143
	Dec	0	0.005	25576	25576	0	0.015	0	0	-0.0315	0.0352	-0.0013
1981	Jan	0	0.005	26477	26477	0	0.015	0	0	-0.0438	-0.0115	-0.0132
	Feb	0	0.005	26172	26172	0	0.015	0	0	0.0208	-0.0435	-0.0141
	Mar	0	0.005	25034	25034	0	0.015	0	0	0.0380	0.0384	0.0400
	Apr	0	0.005	25995	25995	0	0.015	0	0	-0.0213	-0.0518	0.0225
	May	0	0.005	24648	24648	0	0.015	0	0	0.0062	0.0622	-0.0347
	Jun	0	0.005	26182	26182	0	0.015	0	0	-0.0080	-0.0179	0.0065
	Jul	0	0.005	25713	25713	0	0.015	0	0	0.0007	-0.0353	-0.0431
	Aug	0	0.005	24805	24805	0	0.015	0	0	-0.0554	-0.0386	0.0216
	Sep	0	0.005	23848	23848	0	0.015	0	0	-0.0502	-0.0145	-0.1037
	Oct	0	0.005	23502	23502	0	0.015	0	0	0.0528	0.0829	0.0129
	Nov	0	0.005	25450	25450	0	0.015	0	0	0.0441	0.1410	0.1132
	Dec	0	0.005	29039	29039	0	0.015	0	0	-0.0265	-0.0713	-0.0127

Table 5.1 (*Cont'd*)

Monthly Evolution of the Social Security Trust Fund if It Had Been Invested in US Treasury Bonds, Large Company US Stocks, and (Since 2002) International Stocks, 1937–2010.
(other things being equal)
(Dollar amounts rounded to nearest million)

Year	Month	Ending value of US stock portfolio	Ending value of gov't bond portfolio	Ending value of EAFE+ portfolio	End Value of SS Trust Fund	Percent in large US stocks	Percent in LT gov't bonds	Percent in EAFE+ Canada stocks	Percent of debt	Official value ot SS Trust Fund	Net SS inflows by fiscal year	Ratio of invested to actual Trust Fund
1977	Jan	212632	27340	0	225566	94.27	12.12	0.00	6.39			
	Feb	209421	27206	0	221608	94.50	12.28	0.00	6.78			
	Mar	206929	27453	0	218743	94.60	12.55	0.00	7.15			
	Apr	207218	27648	0	218604	94.79	12.65	0.00	7.44			
	May	204110	27994	0	215216	94.84	13.01	0.00	7.85			
	Jun	213805	28453	0	224737	95.14	12.66	0.00	7.80			
	Jul	210577	28254	0	220670	95.43	12.80	0.00	8.23			
	Aug	207776	28813	0	217782	95.41	13.23	0.00	8.64			
	Sep	207776	28730	0	217050	95.73	13.24	0.00	8.96		-6551	
	Oct	199154	28463	0	207486	95.98	13.72	0.00	9.70			
	Nov	206522	28727	0	214440	96.31	13.40	0.00	9.70			
	Dec	207514	28245	0	214267	96.85	13.18	0.00	10.03	35861		5.97
1978	Jan	195146	28019	0	200987	97.09	13.94	0.00	11.03			
	Feb	192004	28030	0	197174	97.38	14.22	0.00	11.59			
	Mar	197303	27971	0	201711	97.81	13.87	0.00	11.68			
	Apr	214469	27957	0	218153	98.31	12.82	0.00	11.13			
	May	217385	27795	0	220200	98.72	12.62	0.00	11.34			
	Jun	214081	27623	0	216005	99.11	12.79	0.00	11.90			
	Jul	226070	28018	0	227659	99.30	12.31	0.00	11.61			
	Aug	233756	28628	0	235225	99.38	12.17	0.00	11.55			
	Sep	232634	28325	0	233045	99.82	12.15	0.00	11.98		-6667	
	Oct	211906	27758	0	211179	100.34	13.14	0.00	13.49			
	Nov	217416	28283	0	216632	100.36	13.06	0.00	13.42			
	Dec	221155	27915	0	219394	100.80	12.72	0.00	13.53	31746		6.91
1979	Jan	230466	28449	0	228626	100.80	12.44	0.00	13.25			
	Feb	223921	28065	0	221092	101.28	12.69	0.00	13.97			
	Mar	236796	28427	0	233694	101.33	12.16	0.00	13.49			
	Apr	237649	28108	0	233591	101.74	12.03	0.00	13.77			
	May	233656	28842	0	229682	101.73	12.56	0.00	14.29			
	Jun	243236	29739	0	239506	101.56	12.42	0.00	13.97			
	Jul	245912	29486	0	241284	101.92	12.22	0.00	14.14			
	Aug	260937	29383	0	255556	102.11	11.50	0.00	13.60			
	Sep	261589	29024	0	255172	102.51	11.37	0.00	13.89		-4209	
	Oct	244429	26583	0	234936	104.04	11.32	0.00	15.36			
	Nov	256993	27410	0	247642	103.78	11.07	0.00	14.84			
	Dec	261927	27566	0	252055	103.92	10.94	0.00	14.85	30291		8.32
1980	Jan	277905	25524	0	265362	104.73	9.62	0.00	14.35			
	Feb	278766	24332	0	264363	105.45	9.20	0.00	14.65			
	Mar	251252	23565	0	235283	106.79	10.02	0.00	16.80			
	Apr	262031	27154	0	248821	105.31	10.91	0.00	16.22			
	May	276757	28292	0	264026	104.82	10.72	0.00	15.54			
	Jun	284949	29308	0	272652	104.51	10.75	0.00	15.26			
	Jul	304211	27913	0	289968	104.91	9.63	0.00	14.54			
	Aug	308196	26707	0	292145	105.49	9.14	0.00	14.64			
	Sep	316852	26007	0	299451	105.81	8.68	0.00	14.50		-3460	
	Oct	322782	25323	0	303621	106.31	8.34	0.00	14.65			
	Nov	358126	25576	0	338132	105.91	7.56	0.00	13.48			
	Dec	346845	26477	0	326491	106.23	8.11	0.00	14.34	26453		12.34
1981	Jan	331654	26172	0	309845	107.04	8.45	0.00	15.49			
	Feb	338552	25034	0	314427	107.67	7.96	0.00	15.63			
	Mar	351417	25995	0	326993	107.47	7.95	0.00	15.42			
	Apr	343932	24648	0	316858	108.54	7.78	0.00	16.32			
	May	346064	26182	0	319438	108.34	8.20	0.00	16.53			
	Jun	343296	25713	0	315213	108.91	8.16	0.00	17.07			
	Jul	343536	24805	0	313594	109.55	7.91	0.00	17.46			
	Aug	324504	23848	0	292586	110.91	8.15	0.00	19.06			
	Sep	308214	23502	0	274862	112.13	8.55	0.00	20.68		-7308	
	Oct	324488	25450	0	291644	111.26	8.73	0.00	19.99			
	Nov	338798	29039	0	308082	110.97	9.43	0.00	19.40			
	Dec	329819	26968	0	295345	111.67	9.13	0.00	20.80	24539		12.04

Table 5.1   (*Cont'd*)

Monthly Evolution of the Social Security Trust Fund if It Had Been Invested in US Treasury Bonds, Large Company US Stocks, and (Since 2002) International Stocks, 1937–2010.
(other things being equal)
(Dollar amounts rounded to nearest million)

Year	Month	Soc. Sec. receipts less int. income	Soc. Sec. outlays less int. expense	Net SS cash inflow/ outflow	Amount of short term loan	Debt at end of month	30-day interest rate	Amount of debt repaid	New US stock investm.	Comm. rate for US stocks	Value of cont. stock portf.	Beg. of month US stock portfolio
1982	Jan	12163	12997	-834	834	62837	0.0090	0	0	0.008	329819	329819
	Feb	12163	12997	-834	834	64321	0.0102	0	0	0.008	324443	324443
	Mar	12163	12997	-834	834	65858	0.0108	0	0	0.008	307832	307832
	Apr	12163	12997	-834	834	67513	0.0123	0	0	0.008	305985	305985
	May	12163	12997	-834	834	69139	0.0116	0	0	0.008	318653	318653
	Jun	12163	12997	-834	834	70715	0.0106	0	0	0.008	309476	309476
	Jul	12163	12997	-834	834	72372	0.0115	0	0	0.008	304091	304091
	Aug	12163	12997	-834	834	73835	0.0086	0	0	0.008	297553	297553
	Sep	12163	12997	-834	834	75125	0.0061	0	0	0.008	335253	335253
	Oct	14221	14227	-6	6	75649	0.0069	0	0	0.008	338940	338940
	Nov	14221	14227	-6	6	76208	0.0073	0	0	0.008	377105	377105
	Dec	14221	14227	-6	6	76801	0.0077	0	0	0.008	393622	393622
1983	Jan	14221	14227	-6	6	77414	0.0079	0	0	0.008	400432	400432
	Feb	14221	14227	-6	6	77978	0.0072	0	0	0.008	414367	414367
	Mar	14221	14227	-6	6	78553	0.0073	0	0	0.008	425141	425141
	Apr	14221	14227	-6	6	79196	0.0081	0	0	0.008	440658	440658
	May	14221	14227	-6	6	79828	0.0079	0	0	0.008	474060	474060
	Jun	14221	14227	-6	6	80449	0.0077	0	0	0.008	471595	471595
	Jul	14221	14227	-6	6	81131	0.0084	0	0	0.008	489610	489610
	Aug	14221	14227	-6	6	81835	0.0086	0	0	0.008	474285	474285
	Sep	14221	14227	-6	6	82545	0.0086	0	0	0.008	482348	482348
	Oct	14289	14852	-34	34	83289	0.0086	0	0	0.008	488908	488908
	Nov	14818	14852	-34	34	83989	0.0080	0	0	0.008	482356	482356
	Dec	14818	14852	-34	34	84720	0.0083	0	0	0.008	493595	493595
1984	Jan	14818	14852	-34	34	85483	0.0086	0	0	0.008	490584	490584
	Feb	14818	14852	-34	34	86210	0.0081	0	0	0.008	487396	487396
	Mar	14818	14852	-34	34	86959	0.0083	0	0	0.008	471409	471409
	Apr	14818	14852	-34	34	87785	0.0091	0	0	0.008	479470	479470
	May	14818	14852	-34	34	88592	0.0088	0	0	0.008	482778	482778
	Jun	14818	14852	-34	34	89379	0.0085	0	0	0.008	456998	456998
	Jul	14818	14852	-34	34	90235	0.0092	0	0	0.008	467098	467098
	Aug	14818	14852	-34	34	91108	0.0093	0	0	0.008	460418	460418
	Sep	14818	14852	-34	34	92017	0.0096	0	0	0.008	512215	512215
	Oct	16353	15719	634	0	92303	0.0100	634	0	0.008	512318	512318
	Nov	16353	15719	634	0	92436	0.0083	634	0	0.008	513650	513650
	Dec	16353	15719	634	0	92486	0.0074	634	0	0.008	508462	508462
1985	Jan	16353	15719	634	0	92545	0.0075	634	0	0.008	521326	521326
	Feb	16353	15719	634	0	92541	0.0068	634	0	0.008	561364	561364
	Mar	16353	15719	634	0	92573	0.0072	634	0	0.008	569055	569055
	Apr	16353	15719	634	0	92698	0.0082	634	0	0.008	570079	570079
	May	16353	15719	634	0	92768	0.0076	634	0	0.008	568255	568255
	Jun	16353	15719	634	0	92737	0.0065	634	0	0.008	603202	603202
	Jul	16353	15719	634	0	92771	0.0072	634	0	0.008	612793	612793
	Aug	16353	15719	634	0	92740	0.0065	634	0	0.008	611200	611200
	Sep	16353	15719	634	0	92755	0.0070	634	0	0.008	607472	607472
	Oct	17685	16563	1122	0	92329	0.0075	1122	0	0.008	587972	587972
	Nov	17685	16563	1122	0	91863	0.0071	1122	0	0.008	614254	614254
	Dec	17685	16563	1122	0	91431	0.0075	1122	0	0.008	658235	658235
1986	Jan	17685	16563	1122	0	90913	0.0066	1122	0	0.008	688974	688974
	Feb	17685	16563	1122	0	90364	0.0063	1122	0	0.008	692006	692006
	Mar	17685	16563	1122	0	89875	0.0070	1122	0	0.008	744667	744667
	Apr	17685	16563	1122	0	89310	0.0062	1122	0	0.008	785922	785922
	May	17685	16563	1122	0	88716	0.0059	1122	0	0.008	776177	776177
	Jun	17685	16563	1122	0	88144	0.0062	1122	0	0.008	818789	818789
	Jul	17685	16563	1122	0	87569	0.0062	1122	0	0.008	832381	832381
	Aug	17685	16563	1122	0	86938	0.0056	1122	0	0.008	785018	785018
	Sep	17685	16563	1122	0	86294	0.0055	1122	0	0.008	843737	843737
	Oct	18529	17282	1247	0	85530	0.0056	1247	0	0.008	774382	774382
	Nov	18529	17282	1247	0	84702	0.0049	1247	0	0.008	817438	817438
	Dec	18529	17282	1247	0	83955	0.0059	1247	0	0.008	838364	838364

Table 5.1   (*Cont'd*)

Monthly Evolution of the Social Security Trust Fund if It Had Been Invested in US Treasury Bonds, Large Company US Stocks, and (Since 2002) International Stocks, 1937–2010.
(other things being equal)
(Dollar amounts rounded to nearest million)

Year	Month	New gov't bond investm.	Market impact for bonds	Value of cont. bond portfolio	Beg. of month bond portfolio	New EAFE+ Canada investm.	Comm. for EAFE+ stocks	Value of cont. EAFE+ portfolio	Beg. of month EAFE+ portfolio	Return on large US stocks	Return on LT US gov't bonds	Return on EAFE+ stocks
1982	Jan	0	0.005	26968	26968	0	0.015	0	0	-0.0163	0.0046	-0.0136
	Feb	0	0.005	27092	27092	0	0.015	0	0	-0.0512	0.0182	-0.0646
	Mar	0	0.005	27585	27585	0	0.015	0	0	-0.0060	0.0231	-0.0493
	Apr	0	0.005	28223	28223	0	0.015	0	0	0.0414	0.0373	0.0596
	May	0	0.005	29275	29275	0	0.015	0	0	-0.0288	0.0034	-0.0134
	Jun	0	0.005	29375	29375	0	0.015	0	0	-0.0174	-0.0223	-0.0790
	Jul	0	0.005	28720	28720	0	0.015	0	0	-0.0215	0.0501	-0.0062
	Aug	0	0.005	30159	30159	0	0.015	0	0	0.1267	0.0781	0.0139
	Sep	0	0.005	32514	32514	0	0.015	0	0	0.0110	0.0618	-0.0068
	Oct	0	0.005	34524	34524	0	0.015	0	0	0.1126	0.0634	0.0136
	Nov	0	0.005	36712	36712	0	0.015	0	0	0.0438	-0.0002	0.0737
	Dec	0	0.005	36705	36705	0	0.015	0	0	0.0173	0.0312	0.0814
1983	Jan	0	0.005	37850	37850	0	0.015	0	0	0.0348	-0.0309	-0.0048
	Feb	0	0.005	36681	36681	0	0.015	0	0	0.0260	0.0492	0.0288
	Mar	0	0.005	38485	38485	0	0.015	0	0	0.0365	-0.0094	0.0377
	Apr	0	0.005	38124	38124	0	0.015	0	0	0.0758	0.0350	0.0619
	May	0	0.005	39458	39458	0	0.015	0	0	-0.0052	-0.0386	-0.0017
	Jun	0	0.005	37935	37935	0	0.015	0	0	0.0382	0.0039	0.0229
	Jul	0	0.005	38083	38083	0	0.015	0	0	-0.0313	-0.0486	0.0029
	Aug	0	0.005	36232	36232	0	0.015	0	0	0.0170	0.0020	-0.0135
	Sep	0	0.005	36304	36304	0	0.015	0	0	0.0136	0.0505	0.0363
	Oct	0	0.005	38138	38138	0	0.015	0	0	-0.0134	-0.0132	-0.0068
	Nov	0	0.005	37634	37634	0	0.015	0	0	0.0233	0.0183	0.0304
	Dec	0	0.005	38323	38323	0	0.015	0	0	-0.0061	-0.0059	0.0375
1984	Jan	0	0.005	38097	38097	0	0.015	0	0	-0.0065	0.0244	0.0356
	Feb	0	0.005	39026	39026	0	0.015	0	0	-0.0328	-0.0178	0.0075
	Mar	0	0.005	38332	38332	0	0.015	0	0	0.0171	-0.0156	0.0829
	Apr	0	0.005	37734	37734	0	0.015	0	0	0.0069	-0.0105	-0.0171
	May	0	0.005	37338	37338	0	0.015	0	0	-0.0534	-0.0516	-0.0964
	Jun	0	0.005	35411	35411	0	0.015	0	0	0.0221	0.0150	-0.0024
	Jul	0	0.005	35942	35942	0	0.015	0	0	-0.0143	0.0693	-0.0608
	Aug	0	0.005	38433	38433	0	0.015	0	0	0.1125	0.0266	0.0905
	Sep	0	0.005	39455	39455	0	0.015	0	0	0.0002	0.0342	-0.0085
	Oct	0	0.005	40805	40805	0	0.015	0	0	0.0026	0.0561	0.0213
	Nov	0	0.005	43094	43094	0	0.015	0	0	-0.0101	0.0118	0.0038
	Dec	0	0.005	43602	43602	0	0.015	0	0	0.0253	0.0091	0.0201
1985	Jan	0	0.005	43999	43999	0	0.015	0	0	0.0768	0.0364	0.0279
	Feb	0	0.005	45601	45601	0	0.015	0	0	0.0137	-0.0493	-0.0090
	Mar	0	0.005	43353	43353	0	0.015	0	0	0.0018	0.0307	0.0731
	Apr	0	0.005	44683	44683	0	0.015	0	0	-0.0032	0.0242	-0.0023
	May	0	0.005	45765	45765	0	0.015	0	0	0.0615	0.0896	0.0418
	Jun	0	0.005	49865	49865	0	0.015	0	0	0.0159	0.0142	0.0233
	Jul	0	0.005	50573	50573	0	0.015	0	0	-0.0026	-0.0180	0.0516
	Aug	0	0.005	49663	49663	0	0.015	0	0	-0.0061	0.0259	0.0288
	Sep	0	0.005	50949	50949	0	0.015	0	0	-0.0321	-0.0021	0.0490
	Oct	0	0.005	50842	50842	0	0.015	0	0	0.0447	0.0338	0.0647
	Nov	0	0.005	52561	52561	0	0.015	0	0	0.0716	0.0401	0.0430
	Dec	0	0.005	54669	54669	0	0.015	0	0	0.0467	0.0541	0.0447
1986	Jan	0	0.005	57626	57626	0	0.015	0	0	0.0044	-0.0025	0.0208
	Feb	0	0.005	57482	57482	0	0.015	0	0	0.0761	0.1145	0.1050
	Mar	0	0.005	64064	64064	0	0.015	0	0	0.0554	0.0770	0.1380
	Apr	0	0.005	68997	68997	0	0.015	0	0	-0.0124	-0.0080	0.0632
	May	0	0.005	68445	68445	0	0.015	0	0	0.0549	-0.0505	-0.0413
	Jun	0	0.005	64988	64988	0	0.015	0	0	0.0166	0.0613	0.0639
	Jul	0	0.005	68972	68972	0	0.015	0	0	-0.0569	-0.0108	0.0567
	Aug	0	0.005	68227	68227	0	0.015	0	0	0.0748	0.0499	0.0963
	Sep	0	0.005	71632	71632	0	0.015	0	0	-0.0822	-0.0500	-0.0099
	Oct	0	0.005	68050	68050	0	0.015	0	0	0.0556	0.0289	-0.0628
	Nov	0	0.005	70017	70017	0	0.015	0	0	0.0256	0.0267	0.0557
	Dec	0	0.005	71886	71886	0	0.015	0	0	-0.0264	-0.0018	0.0516

Table 5.1 (*Cont'd*)

Monthly Evolution of the Social Security Trust Fund if It Had Been Invested in US Treasury Bonds, Large Company US Stocks, and (Since 2002) International Stocks, 1937–2010.
(other things being equal)
(Dollar amounts rounded to nearest million)

Year	Month	Ending value of US stock portfolio	Ending value of gov't bond portfolio	Ending value of EAFE+ portfolio	End Value of SS Trust Fund	Percent in large US stocks	Percent in LT gov't bonds	Percent in EAFE+ Canada stocks	Percent of debt	Official value ot SS Trust Fund	Net SS inflows by fiscal year	Ratio of invested to actual Trust Fund
1982	Jan	324443	27092	0	288698	112.38	9.38	0.00	21.77			
	Feb	307832	27585	0	271097	113.55	10.18	0.00	23.73			
	Mar	305985	28223	0	268349	114.02	10.52	0.00	24.54			
	Apr	318653	29275	0	280415	113.64	10.44	0.00	24.08			
	May	309476	29375	0	269711	114.74	10.89	0.00	25.63			
	Jun	304091	28720	0	262096	116.02	10.96	0.00	26.98			
	Jul	297553	30159	0	255340	116.53	11.81	0.00	28.34			
	Aug	335253	32514	0	293932	114.06	11.06	0.00	25.12			
	Sep	338940	34524	0	298339	113.61	11.57	0.00	25.18		-10007	
	Oct	377105	36712	0	338168	111.51	10.86	0.00	22.37			
	Nov	393622	36705	0	354119	111.16	10.37	0.00	21.52			
	Dec	400432	37850	0	361481	110.78	10.47	0.00	21.25	24778		14.59
1983	Jan	414367	36681	0	373634	110.90	9.82	0.00	20.72			
	Feb	425141	38485	0	385648	110.24	9.98	0.00	20.22			
	Mar	440658	38124	0	400229	110.10	9.53	0.00	19.63			
	Apr	474060	39458	0	434322	109.15	9.08	0.00	18.23			
	May	471595	37935	0	429702	109.75	8.83	0.00	18.58			
	Jun	489610	38083	0	447244	109.47	8.51	0.00	17.99			
	Jul	474285	36232	0	429386	110.46	8.44	0.00	18.89			
	Aug	482348	36304	0	436818	110.42	8.31	0.00	18.73			
	Sep	488908	38138	0	444501	109.99	8.58	0.00	18.57		-75	
	Oct	482356	37634	0	436702	110.45	8.62	0.00	19.07			
	Nov	493595	38323	0	447929	110.19	8.56	0.00	18.75			
	Dec	490584	38097	0	443961	110.50	8.58	0.00	19.08	24867		17.85
1984	Jan	487396	39026	0	440939	110.54	8.85	0.00	19.39			
	Feb	471409	38332	0	423531	111.30	9.05	0.00	20.35			
	Mar	479470	37734	0	430245	111.44	8.77	0.00	20.21			
	Apr	482778	37338	0	432331	111.67	8.64	0.00	20.31			
	May	456998	35411	0	403818	113.17	8.77	0.00	21.94			
	Jun	467098	35942	0	413661	112.92	8.69	0.00	21.61			
	Jul	460418	38433	0	408616	112.68	9.41	0.00	22.08			
	Aug	512215	39455	0	460562	111.22	8.57	0.00	19.78			
	Sep	512318	40805	0	461105	111.11	8.85	0.00	19.96		-406	
	Oct	513650	43094	0	464440	110.60	9.28	0.00	19.87			
	Nov	508462	43602	0	459629	110.62	9.49	0.00	20.11			
	Dec	521326	43999	0	472840	110.25	9.31	0.00	19.56	31075		15.22
1985	Jan	561364	45601	0	514419	109.13	8.86	0.00	17.99			
	Feb	569055	43353	0	519867	109.46	8.34	0.00	17.80			
	Mar	570079	44683	0	522189	109.17	8.56	0.00	17.73			
	Apr	568255	45765	0	521321	109.00	8.78	0.00	17.78			
	May	603202	49865	0	560299	107.66	8.90	0.00	16.56			
	Jun	612793	50573	0	570629	107.39	8.86	0.00	16.25			
	Jul	611200	49663	0	568092	107.59	8.74	0.00	16.33			
	Aug	607472	50949	0	565681	107.39	9.01	0.00	16.39			
	Sep	587972	50842	0	546059	107.68	9.31	0.00	16.99		7608	
	Oct	614254	52561	0	574486	106.92	9.15	0.00	16.07			
	Nov	658235	54669	0	621040	105.99	8.80	0.00	14.79			
	Dec	688974	57626	0	655170	105.16	8.80	0.00	13.96	42163		15.54
1986	Jan	692006	57482	0	658575	105.08	8.73	0.00	13.80			
	Feb	744667	64064	0	718367	103.66	8.92	0.00	12.58			
	Mar	785922	68997	0	765044	102.73	9.02	0.00	11.75			
	Apr	776177	68445	0	755311	102.76	9.06	0.00	11.82			
	May	818789	64988	0	795061	102.98	8.17	0.00	11.16			
	Jun	832381	68972	0	813208	102.36	8.48	0.00	10.84			
	Jul	785018	68227	0	765676	102.53	8.91	0.00	11.44			
	Aug	843737	71632	0	828431	101.85	8.65	0.00	10.49			
	Sep	774382	68050	0	756138	102.41	9.00	0.00	11.41		13459	
	Oct	817438	70017	0	801924	101.93	8.73	0.00	10.67			
	Nov	838364	71886	0	825548	101.55	8.71	0.00	10.26			
	Dec	816231	71757	0	804033	101.52	8.92	0.00	10.44	46861		17.16

Table 5.1 (Cont'd)

Monthly Evolution of the Social Security Trust Fund if It Had Been Invested in US Treasury Bonds, Large Company US Stocks, and (Since 2002) International Stocks, 1937–2010.
(other things being equal)
(Dollar amounts rounded to nearest million)

Year	Month	Soc. Sec. receipts less int. income	Soc. Sec. outlays less int. expense	Net SS cash inflow/ outflow	Amount of short term loan	Debt at end of month	30-day interest rate	Amount of debt repaid	New US stock investm.	Comm. rate for US stocks	Value of cont. stock portf.	Beg. of month US stock portfolio
1987	Jan	20002	16947	3055	0	81336	0.0052	3055	0	0.008	816231	816231
	Feb	17931	17054	877	0	80890	0.0053	877	0	0.008	925851	925851
	Mar	18415	16998	1417	0	79934	0.0057	1417	0	0.008	964089	964089
	Apr	25744	17045	8699	0	71667	0.0054	8699	0	0.008	990312	990312
	May	17864	17487	377	0	71634	0.0048	377	0	0.008	981597	981597
	Jun	19213	19704	-491	491	72543	0.0058	0	0	0.008	991708	991708
	Jul	17864	17254	610	0	72339	0.0056	610	0	0.008	1041194	1041194
	Aug	17009	17089	-80	80	72832	0.0057	0	0	0.008	1093046	1093046
	Sep	19175	17152	2023	0	71210	0.0055	2023	0	0.008	1135128	1135128
	Oct	17515	17339	176	0	71532	0.0070	176	0	0.008	1110155	1110155
	Nov	16723	17114	-391	391	72246	0.0045	0	0	0.008	871250	871250
	Dec	18277	17227	1050	0	71550	0.0049	1050	0	0.008	799894	799894
1988	Jan	22556	18187	4369	0	67460	0.0039	4369	0	0.008	858927	858927
	Feb	20072	18035	2037	0	65801	0.0056	2037	0	0.008	895603	895603
	Mar	21245	18439	2806	0	63350	0.0054	2806	0	0.008	937696	937696
	Apr	29693	18266	11427	0	52277	0.0056	11427	0	0.008	909378	909378
	May	20433	18191	2242	0	50354	0.0061	2242	0	0.008	919199	919199
	Jun	22162	21014	1148	0	49502	0.0059	1148	0	0.008	926369	926369
	Jul	21165	18210	2955	0	46849	0.0061	2955	0	0.008	969352	969352
	Aug	18880	18223	657	0	46515	0.0069	657	0	0.008	965475	965475
	Sep	22868	18190	4678	0	42171	0.0072	4678	0	0.008	933517	933517
	Oct	18987	18206	781	0	41690	0.0071	781	0	0.008	973099	973099
	Nov	17758	18403	-645	645	42618	0.0067	0	0	0.008	999664	999664
	Dec	19483	18237	1246	0	41683	0.0073	1246	0	0.008	985469	985469
1989	Jan	25666	19051	6615	0	35338	0.0065	6615	0	0.008	1003306	1003306
	Feb	24097	19065	5032	0	30557	0.0071	5032	0	0.008	1075845	1075845
	Mar	24152	19579	4573	0	26219	0.0077	4573	0	0.008	1049056	1049056
	Apr	31763	19326	12437	0	13983	0.0077	12437	0	0.008	1073814	1073814
	May	22175	19221	2954	0	11153	0.0089	2954	0	0.008	1129223	1129223
	Jun	24895	22252	2643	0	8600	0.0081	2643	0	0.008	1174618	1174618
	Jul	22103	19327	2776	0	5893	0.0080	2776	0	0.008	1168275	1168275
	Aug	19305	19343	-38	38	5980	0.0084	0	0	0.008	1273186	1273186
	Sep	24243	19443	4800	0	1225	0.0075	4800	0	0.008	1297758	1297758
	Oct	18289	19399	-1110	1110	2353	0.0078	0	0	0.008	1292697	1292697
	Nov	19600	19686	-86	86	2458	0.0079	0	0	0.008	1262577	1262577
	Dec	20470	19472	998	0	1474	0.0061	998	0	0.008	1288839	1288839
1990	Jan	27027	20208	6819	0	0	0.0067	1484	0	0.006	1319256	1319256
	Feb	21684	20545	1139	0	0	0.0067	0	0	0.006	1230733	1230733
	Mar	26439	20401	6038	0	0	0.0074	0	0	0.006	1246610	1246610
	Apr	35378	20865	14513	0	0	0.0079	0	0	0.006	1279396	1279396
	May	24311	20656	3655	0	0	0.0078	0	0	0.006	1247795	1247795
	Jun	27341	23891	3450	0	0	0.0073	0	0	0.006	1369455	1369455
	Jul	23979	20693	3286	0	0	0.0078	0	0	0.006	1359869	1359869
	Aug	22656	41094	-18438	18438	18578	0.0076	0	0	0.006	1355517	1355517
	Sep	24741	614	24127	0	0	0.0070	18708	0	0.006	1233114	1233114
	Oct	21894	20953	941	0	0	0.0078	0	0	0.006	1172445	1172445
	Nov	25375	21020	4355	0	0	0.0067	0	0	0.006	1168107	1168107
	Dec	17375	21267	-3892	3892	3920	0.0070	0	0	0.006	1243333	1243333
1991	Jan	32517	22165	10352	0	0	0.0062	3944	0	0.006	1277400	1277400
	Feb	22551	22199	352	0	0	0.0058	0	0	0.006	1333861	1333861
	Mar	26282	22365	3917	0	0	0.0054	0	0	0.006	1429365	1429365
	Apr	33425	22447	10978	0	0	0.0063	0	0	0.006	1463384	1463384
	May	22091	22525	-434	434	437	0.0057	0	0	0.006	1467482	1467482
	Jun	27537	25880	1657	0	0	0.0052	439	0	0.006	1530290	1530290
	Jul	24845	22582	2263	0	0	0.0059	0	0	0.006	1460356	1460356
	Aug	22272	22617	-345	345	347	0.0056	0	0	0.006	1528700	1528700
	Sep	26688	22606	4082	0	0	0.0056	349	0	0.006	1564625	1564625
	Oct	22936	22651	285	0	0	0.0052	0	0	0.006	1538965	1538965
	Nov	22713	22942	-229	229	230	0.0049	0	0	0.006	1559587	1559587
	Dec	23926	22874	1052	0	0	0.0048	231	0	0.006	1496580	1496580

Table 5.1 (*Cont'd*)

Monthly Evolution of the Social Security Trust Fund if It Had Been Invested in US Treasury Bonds, Large Company US Stocks, and (Since 2002) International Stocks, 1937–2010.
(other things being equal)
(Dollar amounts rounded to nearest million)

Year	Month	New gov't bond investm.	Market impact for bonds	Value of cont. bond portfolio	Beg. of month bond portfolio	New EAFE+ Canada investm.	Comm. for EAFE+ stocks	Value of cont. EAFE+ portfolio	Beg. of month EAFE+ portfolio	Return on large US stocks	Return on LT US gov't bonds	Return on EAFE+ stocks
1987	Jan	0	0.005	71757	71757	0	0.015	0	0	0.1343	0.0161	0.1079
	Feb	0	0.005	72912	72912	0	0.015	0	0	0.0413	0.0202	0.0310
	Mar	0	0.005	74385	74385	0	0.015	0	0	0.0272	-0.0223	0.0827
	Apr	0	0.005	72726	72726	0	0.015	0	0	-0.0088	-0.0473	0.1000
	May	0	0.005	69286	69286	0	0.015	0	0	0.0103	-0.0105	0.0000
	Jun	0	0.005	68559	68559	0	0.015	0	0	0.0499	0.0098	-0.0292
	Jul	0	0.005	69230	69230	0	0.015	0	0	0.0498	-0.0178	0.0020
	Aug	0	0.005	67998	67998	0	0.015	0	0	0.0385	-0.0165	0.0718
	Sep	0	0.005	66876	66876	0	0.015	0	0	-0.0220	-0.0369	-0.0155
	Oct	0	0.005	64408	64408	0	0.015	0	0	-0.2152	0.0623	-0.1433
	Nov	0	0.005	68421	68421	0	0.015	0	0	-0.0819	0.0037	0.0088
	Dec	0	0.005	68674	68674	0	0.015	0	0	0.0738	0.0165	0.0316
1988	Jan	0	0.005	69807	69807	0	0.015	0	0	0.0427	0.0666	0.0169
	Feb	0	0.005	74457	74457	0	0.015	0	0	0.0470	0.0052	0.0669
	Mar	0	0.005	74844	74844	0	0.015	0	0	-0.0302	-0.0307	0.0611
	Apr	0	0.005	72546	72546	0	0.015	0	0	0.0108	-0.0160	0.0148
	May	0	0.005	71385	71385	0	0.015	0	0	0.0078	-0.0102	-0.0320
	Jun	0	0.005	70657	70657	0	0.015	0	0	0.0464	0.0368	-0.0220
	Jul	0	0.005	73257	73257	0	0.015	0	0	-0.0040	-0.0170	0.0295
	Aug	0	0.005	72012	72012	0	0.015	0	0	-0.0331	0.0058	-0.0643
	Sep	0	0.005	72430	72430	0	0.015	0	0	0.0424	0.0345	0.0430
	Oct	0	0.005	74928	74928	0	0.015	0	0	0.0273	0.0308	0.0838
	Nov	0	0.005	77236	77236	0	0.015	0	0	-0.0142	-0.0196	0.0574
	Dec	0	0.005	75722	75722	0	0.015	0	0	0.0181	0.0110	0.0066
1989	Jan	0	0.005	76555	76555	0	0.015	0	0	0.0723	0.0203	0.0201
	Feb	0	0.005	78109	78109	0	0.015	0	0	-0.0249	-0.0179	0.0040
	Mar	0	0.005	76711	76711	0	0.015	0	0	0.0236	0.0122	-0.0183
	Apr	0	0.005	77647	77647	0	0.015	0	0	0.0516	0.0159	0.0101
	May	0	0.005	78882	78882	0	0.015	0	0	0.0402	0.0401	-0.0520
	Jun	0	0.005	82045	82045	0	0.015	0	0	-0.0054	0.0550	-0.0150
	Jul	0	0.005	86557	86557	0	0.015	0	0	0.0898	0.0238	0.1238
	Aug	0	0.005	88617	88617	0	0.015	0	0	0.0193	-0.0259	-0.0423
	Sep	0	0.005	86322	86322	0	0.015	0	0	-0.0039	0.0019	0.0431
	Oct	0	0.005	86486	86486	0	0.015	0	0	-0.0233	0.0379	-0.0383
	Nov	0	0.005	89764	89764	0	0.015	0	0	0.0208	0.0078	0.0488
	Dec	0	0.005	90464	90464	0	0.015	0	0	0.0236	-0.0006	0.0365
1990	Jan	0	0.003	90410	90410	0	0.010	0	0	-0.0671	-0.0343	-0.0392
	Feb	5335	0.003	87309	92628	0	0.010	0	0	0.0129	-0.0025	-0.0669
	Mar	1139	0.003	92396	93532	0	0.010	0	0	0.0263	-0.0044	-0.0995
	Apr	6038	0.003	93120	99140	0	0.010	0	0	-0.0247	-0.0202	-0.0106
	May	14513	0.003	97138	111607	0	0.010	0	0	0.0975	0.0415	0.1128
	Jun	3655	0.003	116239	119883	0	0.010	0	0	-0.0070	0.0230	-0.0084
	Jul	3450	0.003	122641	126080	0	0.010	0	0	-0.0032	0.0107	0.0146
	Aug	3286	0.003	127430	130706	0	0.010	0	0	-0.0903	-0.0419	-0.0950
	Sep	0	0.003	125229	125229	0	0.010	0	0	-0.0492	0.0117	-0.1351
	Oct	5419	0.003	126694	132097	0	0.010	0	0	-0.0037	0.0215	0.1476
	Nov	941	0.003	134937	135875	0	0.010	0	0	0.0644	0.0402	-0.0554
	Dec	4355	0.003	141337	145679	0	0.010	0	0	0.0274	0.0187	0.0177
1991	Jan	0	0.003	148403	148403	0	0.010	0	0	0.0442	0.0130	0.0312
	Feb	6408	0.003	150332	156721	0	0.010	0	0	0.0716	0.0030	0.1058
	Mar	352	0.003	157191	157541	0	0.010	0	0	0.0238	0.0038	-0.0574
	Apr	3917	0.003	158140	162045	0	0.010	0	0	0.0028	0.0140	0.0102
	May	10978	0.003	164313	175258	0	0.010	0	0	0.0428	0.0000	0.0118
	Jun	0	0.003	175258	175258	0	0.010	0	0	-0.0457	-0.0063	-0.0711
	Jul	1217	0.003	174154	175368	0	0.010	0	0	0.0468	0.0157	0.0479
	Aug	2263	0.003	178121	180377	0	0.010	0	0	0.0235	0.0340	-0.0186
	Sep	0	0.003	186510	186510	0	0.010	0	0	-0.0164	0.0303	0.0529
	Oct	3732	0.003	192161	195882	0	0.010	0	0	0.0134	0.0054	0.0157
	Nov	285	0.003	196940	197224	0	0.010	0	0	-0.0404	0.0082	-0.0455
	Dec	0	0.003	198841	198841	0	0.010	0	0	0.1143	0.0581	0.0498

Table 5.1 (*Cont'd*)

Monthly Evolution of the Social Security Trust Fund if It Had Been Invested in US Treasury Bonds, Large Company US Stocks, and (Since 2002) International Stocks, 1937–2010.
(other things being equal)
(Dollar amounts rounded to nearest million)

Year	Month	Ending value of US stock portfolio	Ending value of gov't bond portfolio	Ending value of EAFE+ portfolio	End Value of SS Trust Fund	Percent in large US stocks	Percent in LT gov't bonds	Percent in EAFE+ Canada stocks	Percent of debt	Official value ot SS Trust Fund	Net SS inflows by fiscal year	Ratio of invested to actual Trust Fund
1987	Jan	925851	72912	0	917427	100.92	7.95	0.00	8.87			
	Feb	964089	74385	0	957583	100.68	7.77	0.00	8.45			
	Mar	990312	72726	0	983104	100.73	7.40	0.00	8.13			
	Apr	981597	69286	0	979217	100.24	7.08	0.00	7.32			
	May	991708	68559	0	988633	100.31	6.93	0.00	7.25			
	Jun	1041194	69230	0	1037881	100.32	6.67	0.00	6.99			
	Jul	1093046	67998	0	1088704	100.40	6.25	0.00	6.64			
	Aug	1135128	66876	0	1129172	100.53	5.92	0.00	6.45			
	Sep	1110155	64408	0	1103354	100.62	5.84	0.00	6.45		20229	
	Oct	871250	68421	0	868139	100.36	7.88	0.00	8.24			
	Nov	799894	68674	0	796322	100.45	8.62	0.00	9.07			
	Dec	858927	69807	0	857183	100.20	8.14	0.00	8.35	68807		12.46
1988	Jan	895603	74457	0	902599	99.22	8.25	0.00	7.47			
	Feb	937696	74844	0	946739	99.04	7.91	0.00	6.95			
	Mar	909378	72546	0	918574	99.00	7.90	0.00	6.90			
	Apr	919199	71385	0	938307	97.96	7.61	0.00	5.57			
	May	926369	70657	0	946672	97.86	7.46	0.00	5.32			
	Jun	969352	73257	0	993107	97.61	7.38	0.00	4.98			
	Jul	965475	72012	0	990638	97.46	7.27	0.00	4.73			
	Aug	933517	72430	0	959432	97.30	7.55	0.00	4.85			
	Sep	973099	74928	0	1005856	96.74	7.45	0.00	4.19		33157	
	Oct	999664	77236	0	1035211	96.57	7.46	0.00	4.03			
	Nov	985469	75722	0	1018574	96.75	7.43	0.00	4.18			
	Dec	1003306	76555	0	1038179	96.64	7.37	0.00	4.01	109762		9.46
1989	Jan	1075845	78109	0	1118616	96.18	6.98	0.00	3.16			
	Feb	1049056	76711	0	1095211	95.79	7.00	0.00	2.79			
	Mar	1073814	77647	0	1125243	95.43	6.90	0.00	2.33			
	Apr	1129223	78882	0	1194121	94.57	6.61	0.00	1.17			
	May	1174618	82045	0	1245509	94.31	6.59	0.00	0.90			
	Jun	1168275	86557	0	1246232	93.74	6.95	0.00	0.69			
	Jul	1273186	88617	0	1355910	93.90	6.54	0.00	0.43			
	Aug	1297758	86322	0	1378100	94.17	6.26	0.00	0.43			
	Sep	1292697	86486	0	1377958	93.81	6.28	0.00	0.09		43178	
	Oct	1262577	89764	0	1349989	93.53	6.65	0.00	0.17			
	Nov	1288839	90464	0	1376845	93.61	6.57	0.00	0.18			
	Dec	1319256	90410	0	1408191	93.68	6.42	0.00	0.10	162968		8.64
1990	Jan	1230733	87309	0	1318042	93.38	6.62	0.00	0.00			
	Feb	1246610	92396	0	1339006	93.10	6.90	0.00	0.00			
	Mar	1279396	93120	0	1372516	93.22	6.78	0.00	0.00			
	Apr	1247795	97138	0	1344933	92.78	7.22	0.00	0.00			
	May	1369455	116239	0	1485694	92.18	7.82	0.00	0.00			
	Jun	1359869	122641	0	1482509	91.73	8.27	0.00	0.00			
	Jul	1355517	127430	0	1482946	91.41	8.59	0.00	0.00			
	Aug	1233114	125229	0	1339765	92.04	9.35	0.00	1.39			
	Sep	1172445	126694	0	1299139	90.25	9.75	0.00	0.00		44393	
	Oct	1168107	134937	0	1303044	89.64	10.36	0.00	0.00			
	Nov	1243333	141237	0	1384670	89.79	10.21	0.00	0.00			
	Dec	1277400	148403	0	1421883	89.84	10.44	0.00	0.28	225277		6.31
1991	Jan	1333861	150332	0	1484193	89.87	10.13	0.00	0.00			
	Feb	1429365	157191	0	1586556	90.09	9.91	0.00	0.00			
	Mar	1463384	158140	0	1621524	90.25	9.75	0.00	0.00			
	Apr	1467482	164313	0	1631795	89.93	10.07	0.00	0.00			
	May	1530290	175258	0	1705111	89.75	10.28	0.00	0.03			
	Jun	1460356	174154	0	1634510	89.35	10.65	0.00	0.00			
	Jul	1528700	178121	0	1706821	89.56	10.44	0.00	0.00			
	Aug	1564625	186510	0	1750787	89.37	10.65	0.00	0.02			
	Sep	1538965	192161	0	1731126	88.90	11.10	0.00	0.00		34221	
	Oct	1559587	196940	0	1756527	88.79	11.21	0.00	0.00			
	Nov	1496580	198841	0	1695191	88.28	11.73	0.00	0.01			
	Dec	1667639	210394	0	1878033	88.80	11.20	0.00	0.00	280747		6.69

Table 5.1 (Cont'd)

Monthly Evolution of the Social Security Trust Fund if It Had Been Invested in US Treasury Bonds, Large Company US Stocks, and (Since 2002) International Stocks, 1937–2010.
(other things being equal)
(Dollar amounts rounded to nearest million)

Year	Month	Soc. Sec. receipts less int. income	Soc. Sec. outlays less int. expense	Net SS cash inflow/ outflow	Amount of short term loan	Debt at end of month	30-day interest rate	Amount of debt repaid	New US stock investm.	Comm. rate for US stocks	Value of cont. stock portf.	Beg. of month US stock portfolio
1992	Jan	25797	23739	2058	0	0	0.0044	0	0	0.006	1667639	1667639
	Feb	24285	23731	554	0	0	0.0038	0	0	0.006	1636621	1636621
	Mar	27147	23862	3285	0	0	0.0044	0	0	0.006	1657570	1657570
	Apr	37004	23972	13032	0	0	0.0042	0	0	0.006	1625081	1625081
	May	25867	24076	1791	0	0	0.0038	0	0	0.006	1672371	1672371
	Jun	30125	27230	2895	0	0	0.0042	0	0	0.006	1681402	1681402
	Jul	25488	24202	1286	0	0	0.0041	0	0	0.006	1657022	1657022
	Aug	23298	24098	-800	800	803	0.0036	0	0	0.006	1723799	1723799
	Sep	26047	24148	1899	0	0	0.0036	806	0	0.006	1688979	1688979
	Oct	23744	24301	-557	557	559	0.0033	0	0	0.006	1708402	1708402
	Nov	23863	24146	-283	283	845	0.0033	0	0	0.006	1714552	1714552
	Dec	24562	24361	201	0	647	0.0038	201	0	0.006	1772333	1772333
1993	Jan	24645	25353	-708	708	1359	0.0033	0	0	0.006	1795550	1795550
	Feb	25650	25068	582	0	782	0.0032	582	0	0.006	1808658	1808658
	Mar	26690	25277	1413	0	0	0.0035	784	0	0.006	1833075	1833075
	Apr	37746	25417	12329	0	0	0.0034	0	0	0.006	1872486	1872486
	May	26639	25288	1351	0	0	0.0032	0	0	0.006	1826610	1826610
	Jun	30422	28724	1698	0	0	0.0035	0	0	0.006	1875928	1875928
	Jul	25901	25567	334	0	0	0.0034	0	0	0.006	1882119	1882119
	Aug	25237	25451	-214	214	215	0.0035	0	0	0.006	1873273	1873273
	Sep	29467	25614	3853	0	0	0.0036	216	0	0.006	1944645	1944645
	Oct	24252	25538	-1286	1286	1290	0.0032	0	0	0.006	1930254	1930254
	Nov	24885	25552	-667	667	1964	0.0035	0	0	0.006	1969438	1969438
	Dec	26183	25917	266	0	1704	0.0033	266	0	0.006	1950926	1950926
1994	Jan	30703	26149	4554	0	0	0.0035	1710	0	0.006	1974922	1974922
	Feb	26483	26324	159	0	0	0.0031	0	0	0.006	2041082	2041082
	Mar	28985	26503	2482	0	0	0.0037	0	0	0.006	1985973	1985973
	Apr	39084	26627	12457	0	0	0.0037	0	0	0.006	1899583	1899583
	May	28700	26525	2175	0	0	0.0042	0	0	0.006	1924277	1924277
	Jun	32631	30088	2543	0	0	0.0041	0	0	0.006	1955643	1955643
	Jul	27059	26698	361	0	0	0.0038	0	0	0.006	1907339	1907339
	Aug	26924	26718	206	0	0	0.0047	0	0	0.006	1970472	1970472
	Sep	31217	26912	4305	0	0	0.0047	0	0	0.006	2050670	2050670
	Oct	24733	26702	-1969	1969	1978	0.0048	0	0	0.006	2001249	2001249
	Nov	26061	26612	-551	551	2541	0.0047	0	0	0.006	2047077	2047077
	Dec	27429	27155	274	0	2281	0.0054	274	0	0.006	1971950	1971950
1995	Jan	32865	27809	5056	0	0	0.0052	2293	0	0.006	2000740	2000740
	Feb	28670	27634	1036	0	0	0.0050	0	0	0.006	2052759	2052759
	Mar	31093	27800	3293	0	0	0.0056	0	0	0.006	2132406	2132406
	Apr	41341	27953	13388	0	0	0.0054	0	0	0.006	2195526	2195526
	May	29927	27999	1928	0	0	0.0064	0	0	0.006	2259415	2259415
	Jun	32420	32048	372	0	0	0.0057	0	0	0.006	2348662	2348662
	Jul	29355	27999	1356	0	0	0.0055	0	0	0.006	2403856	2403856
	Aug	27833	27949	-116	116	117	0.0057	0	0	0.006	2483904	2483904
	Sep	31247	28171	3076	0	0	0.0053	117	0	0.006	2490611	2490611
	Oct	24824	28060	-3236	3236	3254	0.0057	0	0	0.006	2594967	2594967
	Nov	26844	27888	-1044	1044	4321	0.0052	0	0	0.006	2585885	2585885
	Dec	28103	28504	-401	401	4750	0.0059	0	0	0.006	2699664	2699664
1996	Jan	34520	28704	5816	0	0	0.0053	4775	0	0.006	2749608	2749608
	Feb	28987	28831	156	0	0	0.0049	0	0	0.006	2844194	2844194
	Mar	32740	29112	3628	0	0	0.0049	0	0	0.006	2871499	2871499
	Apr	44802	29090	15712	0	0	0.0056	0	0	0.006	2899065	2899065
	May	30468	29155	1313	0	0	0.0052	0	0	0.006	2941681	2941681
	Jun	35732	32680	3052	0	0	0.0050	0	0	0.006	3017577	3017577
	Jul	31121	29263	1858	0	0	0.0055	0	0	0.006	3029949	3029949
	Aug	29022	29221	-199	199	200	0.0051	0	0	0.006	2895116	2895116
	Sep	32393	29145	3248	0	0	0.0054	201	0	0.006	2956492	2956492
	Oct	28165	29353	-1188	1188	1194	0.0052	0	0	0.006	3122647	3122647
	Nov	28325	29459	-1134	1134	2340	0.0051	0	0	0.006	3208208	3208208
	Dec	29458	29556	-98	98	2452	0.0056	0	0	0.006	3451711	3451711

Table 5.1   (*Cont'd*)

Monthly Evolution of the Social Security Trust Fund if It Had Been Invested in US Treasury Bonds, Large Company US Stocks, and (Since 2002) International Stocks, 1937–2010.
(other things being equal)
(Dollar amounts rounded to nearest million)

Year	Month	New gov't bond investm.	Market impact for bonds	Value of cont. bond portfolio	Beg. of month bond portfolio	New EAFE+ Canada investm.	Comm. for EAFE+ stocks	Value of cont. EAFE+ portfolio	Beg. of month EAFE+ portfolio	Return on large US stocks	Return on LT US gov't bonds	Return on EAFE+ stocks
1992	Jan	821	0.003	210394	211212	0	0.010	0	0	-0.0186	-0.0324	-0.0196
	Feb	2058	0.003	204369	206421	0	0.010	0	0	0.0128	0.0051	-0.0343
	Mar	554	0.003	207473	208026	0	0.010	0	0	-0.0196	-0.0094	-0.0652
	Apr	3285	0.003	206070	209345	0	0.010	0	0	0.0291	0.0016	0.0042
	May	13032	0.003	209680	222673	0	0.010	0	0	0.0054	0.0243	0.0645
	Jun	1791	0.003	228084	229870	0	0.010	0	0	-0.0145	0.0200	-0.0449
	Jul	2895	0.003	234467	237354	0	0.010	0	0	0.0403	0.0398	-0.0231
	Aug	1286	0.003	246800	248082	0	0.010	0	0	-0.0202	0.0067	0.0591
	Sep	0	0.003	249745	249745	0	0.010	0	0	0.0115	0.0185	-0.0217
	Oct	1093	0.003	254365	255455	0	0.010	0	0	0.0036	-0.0198	-0.0490
	Nov	0	0.003	250397	250397	0	0.010	0	0	0.0337	0.0010	0.0074
	Dec	0	0.003	250647	250647	0	0.010	0	0	0.0131	0.0246	0.0064
1993	Jan	0	0.003	256813	256813	0	0.010	0	0	0.0073	0.0280	-0.0006
	Feb	0	0.003	264004	264004	0	0.010	0	0	0.0135	0.0354	0.0316
	Mar	0	0.003	273350	273350	0	0.010	0	0	0.0215	0.0021	0.0849
	Apr	629	0.003	273924	274550	0	0.010	0	0	-0.0245	0.0072	0.0928
	May	12329	0.003	276527	288819	0	0.010	0	0	0.0270	0.0047	0.0211
	Jun	1351	0.003	290177	291524	0	0.010	0	0	0.0033	0.0449	-0.0151
	Jul	1698	0.003	304613	306306	0	0.010	0	0	-0.0047	0.0191	0.0337
	Aug	334	0.003	312156	312489	0	0.010	0	0	0.0381	0.0434	0.0525
	Sep	0	0.003	326051	326051	0	0.010	0	0	-0.0074	0.0005	-0.0232
	Oct	3637	0.003	326214	329841	0	0.010	0	0	0.0203	0.0096	0.0331
	Nov	0	0.003	333007	333007	0	0.010	0	0	-0.0094	-0.0259	-0.0849
	Dec	0	0.003	324382	324382	0	0.010	0	0	0.0123	0.0020	0.0714
1994	Jan	0	0.003	325031	325031	0	0.010	0	0	0.0335	0.0257	0.0839
	Feb	2844	0.003	333385	336220	0	0.010	0	0	-0.0270	-0.0450	-0.0043
	Mar	159	0.003	321090	321248	0	0.010	0	0	-0.0435	-0.0395	-0.0429
	Apr	2482	0.003	308559	311034	0	0.010	0	0	0.0130	-0.0150	0.0407
	May	12457	0.003	306368	318788	0	0.010	0	0	0.0163	-0.0082	-0.0049
	Jun	2175	0.003	316174	318342	0	0.010	0	0	-0.0247	-0.0100	0.0116
	Jul	2543	0.003	315159	317694	0	0.010	0	0	0.0331	0.0363	0.0110
	Aug	361	0.003	329226	329586	0	0.010	0	0	0.0407	-0.0086	0.0250
	Sep	206	0.003	326752	326957	0	0.010	0	0	-0.0241	-0.0331	-0.0294
	Oct	4305	0.003	316135	320427	0	0.010	0	0	0.0229	-0.0025	0.0319
	Nov	0	0.003	319626	319626	0	0.010	0	0	-0.0367	0.0066	-0.0481
	Dec	0	0.003	321735	321735	0	0.010	0	0	0.0146	0.0161	0.0069
1995	Jan	0	0.003	326915	326915	0	0.010	0	0	0.0260	0.0273	-0.0386
	Feb	2763	0.003	335840	338595	0	0.010	0	0	0.0388	0.0287	-0.0006
	Mar	1036	0.003	348313	349346	0	0.010	0	0	0.0296	0.0091	0.0619
	Apr	3293	0.003	352525	355808	0	0.010	0	0	0.0291	0.0169	0.0372
	May	13388	0.003	361821	375169	0	0.010	0	0	0.0395	0.0790	-0.0098
	Jun	1928	0.003	404807	406729	0	0.010	0	0	0.0235	0.0139	-0.0160
	Jul	372	0.003	412383	412754	0	0.010	0	0	0.0333	-0.0168	0.0608
	Aug	1356	0.003	405819	407171	0	0.010	0	0	0.0027	0.0236	-0.0365
	Sep	0	0.003	416781	416781	0	0.010	0	0	0.0419	0.0175	0.0189
	Oct	2959	0.003	424074	427024	0	0.010	0	0	-0.0035	0.0294	-0.0259
	Nov	0	0.003	439579	439579	0	0.010	0	0	0.0440	0.0249	0.0284
	Dec	0	0.003	450524	450524	0	0.010	0	0	0.0185	0.0272	0.0394
1996	Jan	0	0.003	462778	462778	0	0.010	0	0	0.0344	-0.0011	0.0061
	Feb	1041	0.003	462269	463307	0	0.010	0	0	0.0096	-0.0483	0.0032
	Mar	156	0.003	440930	441085	0	0.010	0	0	0.0096	-0.0210	0.0214
	Apr	3628	0.003	431822	435439	0	0.010	0	0	0.0147	-0.0165	0.0298
	May	15712	0.003	428255	443920	0	0.010	0	0	0.0258	-0.0054	-0.0168
	Jun	1313	0.003	441522	442831	0	0.010	0	0	0.0041	0.0203	0.0046
	Jul	3052	0.003	451821	454864	0	0.010	0	0	-0.0445	0.0018	-0.0290
	Aug	1858	0.003	455682	457535	0	0.010	0	0	0.0212	-0.0139	0.0041
	Sep	0	0.003	451175	451175	0	0.010	0	0	0.0562	0.0290	0.0273
	Oct	3047	0.003	464259	467297	0	0.010	0	0	0.0274	0.0404	-0.0064
	Nov	0	0.003	486176	486176	0	0.010	0	0	0.0759	0.0351	0.0415
	Dec	0	0.003	503241	503241	0	0.010	0	0	-0.0196	-0.0256	-0.0136

Table 5.1 (*Cont'd*)

Monthly Evolution of the Social Security Trust Fund if It Had Been Invested in US Treasury Bonds, Large Company US Stocks, and (Since 2002) International Stocks, 1937–2010.
(other things being equal)
(Dollar amounts rounded to nearest million)

Year	Month	Ending value of US stock portfolio	Ending value of gov't bond portfolio	Ending value of EAFE+ portfolio	End Value of SS Trust Fund	Percent in large US stocks	Percent in LT gov't bonds	Percent in EAFE+ Canada stocks	Percent of debt	Official value ot SS Trust Fund	Net SS inflows by fiscal year	Ratio of invested to actual Trust Fund
1992	Jan	1636621	204369	0	1840990	88.90	11.10	0.00	0.00			
	Feb	1657570	207473	0	1865043	88.88	11.12	0.00	0.00			
	Mar	1625081	206070	0	1831151	88.75	11.25	0.00	0.00			
	Apr	1672371	209680	0	1882051	88.86	11.14	0.00	0.00			
	May	1681402	228084	0	1909486	88.06	11.94	0.00	0.00			
	Jun	1657022	234467	0	1891489	87.60	12.40	0.00	0.00			
	Jul	1723799	246800	0	1970600	87.48	12.52	0.00	0.00			
	Aug	1688979	249745	0	1937920	87.15	12.89	0.00	0.04			
	Sep	1708402	254365	0	1962767	87.04	12.96	0.00	0.00		27108	
	Oct	1714552	250397	0	1964390	87.28	12.75	0.00	0.03			
	Nov	1772333	250647	0	2022135	87.65	12.40	0.00	0.04			
	Dec	1795550	256813	0	2051716	87.51	12.52	0.00	0.03	331743		6.18
1993	Jan	1808658	264004	0	2071302	87.32	12.75	0.00	0.07			
	Feb	1833075	273350	0	2105643	87.06	12.98	0.00	0.04			
	Mar	1872486	273924	0	2146409	87.24	12.76	0.00	0.00			
	Apr	1826610	276527	0	2103137	86.85	13.15	0.00	0.00			
	May	1875928	290177	0	2166105	86.60	13.40	0.00	0.00			
	Jun	1882119	304613	0	2186732	86.07	13.93	0.00	0.00			
	Jul	1873273	312156	0	2185429	85.72	14.28	0.00	0.00			
	Aug	1944645	326051	0	2270481	85.65	14.36	0.00	0.01			
	Sep	1930254	326214	0	2256469	85.54	14.46	0.00	0.00		19999	
	Oct	1969438	333007	0	2301156	85.58	14.47	0.00	0.06			
	Nov	1950926	324382	0	2273344	85.82	14.27	0.00	0.09			
	Dec	1974922	325031	0	2298249	85.93	14.14	0.00	0.07	378285		6.08
1994	Jan	2041082	333385	0	2374466	85.96	14.04	0.00	0.00			
	Feb	1985973	321090	0	2307062	86.08	13.92	0.00	0.00			
	Mar	1899583	308559	0	2208142	86.03	13.97	0.00	0.00			
	Apr	1924277	306368	0	2230645	86.27	13.73	0.00	0.00			
	May	1955643	316174	0	2271817	86.08	13.92	0.00	0.00			
	Jun	1907339	315159	0	2222497	85.82	14.18	0.00	0.00			
	Jul	1970472	329226	0	2299698	85.68	14.32	0.00	0.00			
	Aug	2050670	326752	0	2377422	86.26	13.74	0.00	0.00			
	Sep	2001249	316135	0	2317384	86.36	13.64	0.00	0.00		27555	
	Oct	2047077	319626	0	2364725	86.57	13.52	0.00	0.08			
	Nov	1971950	321735	0	2291144	86.07	14.04	0.00	0.11			
	Dec	2000740	326915	0	2325374	86.04	14.06	0.00	0.10	436385		5.33
1995	Jan	2052759	335840	0	2388599	85.94	14.06	0.00	0.00			
	Feb	2132406	348313	0	2480719	85.96	14.04	0.00	0.00			
	Mar	2195526	352525	0	2548050	86.16	13.84	0.00	0.00			
	Apr	2259415	361821	0	2621236	86.20	13.80	0.00	0.00			
	May	2348662	404807	0	2753469	85.30	14.70	0.00	0.00			
	Jun	2403856	412383	0	2816239	85.36	14.64	0.00	0.00			
	Jul	2483904	405819	0	2889724	85.96	14.04	0.00	0.00			
	Aug	2490611	416781	0	2907275	85.67	14.34	0.00	0.00			
	Sep	2594967	424074	0	3019042	85.95	14.05	0.00	0.00		27143	
	Oct	2585885	439579	0	3022209	85.56	14.54	0.00	0.11			
	Nov	2699664	450524	0	3145867	85.82	14.32	0.00	0.14			
	Dec	2749608	462778	0	3207636	85.72	14.43	0.00	0.15	496068		6.47
1996	Jan	2844194	462269	0	3306464	86.02	13.98	0.00	0.00			
	Feb	2871499	440930	0	3312428	86.69	13.31	0.00	0.00			
	Mar	2899065	431822	0	3330887	87.04	12.96	0.00	0.00			
	Apr	2941681	428255	0	3369936	87.29	12.71	0.00	0.00			
	May	3017577	441522	0	3459069	87.24	12.76	0.00	0.00			
	Jun	3029949	451821	0	3481770	87.02	12.98	0.00	0.00			
	Jul	2895116	455682	0	3350798	86.40	13.60	0.00	0.00			
	Aug	2956492	451175	0	3407468	86.77	13.24	0.00	0.01			
	Sep	3122647	464259	0	3586907	87.06	12.94	0.00	0.00		29903	
	Oct	3208208	486176	0	3693189	86.87	13.16	0.00	0.03			
	Nov	3451711	503241	0	3952611	87.33	12.73	0.00	0.06			
	Dec	3384057	490358	0	3871963	87.40	12.66	0.00	0.06	566950		6.83

Table 5.1 (*Cont'd*)

Monthly Evolution of the Social Security Trust Fund if It Had Been Invested in US Treasury Bonds, Large Company US Stocks, and (Since 2002) International Stocks, 1937–2010.
(other things being equal)
(Dollar amounts rounded to nearest million)

Year	Month	Soc. Sec. receipts less int. income	Soc. Sec. outlays less int. expense	Net SS cash inflow/ outflow	Amount of short term loan	Debt at end of month	30-day interest rate	Amount of debt repaid	New US stock investm.	Comm. rate for US stocks	Value of cont. stock portf.	Beg. of month US stock portfolio
1997	Jan	39195	30376	8819	0	0	0.0055	2465	0	0.006	3384057	3384057
	Feb	31141	29951	1190	0	0	0.0049	0	0	0.006	3594207	3594207
	Mar	34751	30221	4530	0	0	0.0053	0	0	0.006	3623320	3623320
	Apr	42927	30289	12638	0	0	0.0053	0	0	0.006	3472590	3472590
	May	31905	30421	1484	0	0	0.0059	0	0	0.006	3679904	3679904
	Jun	37997	34057	3940	0	0	0.0047	0	0	0.006	3905850	3905850
	Jul	31878	30537	1341	0	0	0.0053	0	0	0.006	4080051	4080051
	Aug	33127	30572	2555	0	0	0.0051	0	0	0.006	4404007	4404007
	Sep	36472	30446	6026	0	0	0.0054	0	0	0.006	4159144	4159144
	Oct	31018	30571	447	0	0	0.0052	0	0	0.006	4387065	4387065
	Nov	30302	30532	-230	230	231	0.0049	0	0	0.006	4240537	4240537
	Dec	33170	31134	2036	0	0	0.0058	232	0	0.006	4436874	4436874
1998	Jan	41912	31279	10633	0	0	0.0053	0	0	0.006	4513188	4513188
	Feb	33543	31252	2291	0	0	0.0049	0	0	0.006	4563285	4563285
	Mar	37920	31473	6447	0	0	0.0049	0	0	0.006	4892297	4892297
	Apr	46701	31302	15399	0	0	0.0053	0	0	0.006	5142783	5142783
	May	34073	31451	2622	0	0	0.0050	0	0	0.006	5194725	5194725
	Jun	43472	35391	8081	0	0	0.0051	0	0	0.006	5105376	5105376
	Jul	34861	31655	3206	0	0	0.0050	0	0	0.006	5312654	5312654
	Aug	33200	31415	1785	0	0	0.0053	0	0	0.006	5256340	5256340
	Sep	31803	31837	-34	34	34	0.0056	0	0	0.006	4496273	4496273
	Oct	33784	31638	2146	0	0	0.0042	34	0	0.006	4784484	4784484
	Nov	32722	31568	1154	0	0	0.0041	0	0	0.006	5173463	5173463
	Dec	35890	31996	3894	0	0	0.0048	0	0	0.006	5486975	5486975
1999	Jan	45333	32187	13146	0	0	0.0045	0	0	0.006	5803025	5803025
	Feb	34937	32083	2854	0	0	0.0045	0	0	0.006	6045591	6045591
	Mar	38449	32275	6174	0	0	0.0053	0	0	0.006	5857573	5857573
	Apr	49810	32304	17506	0	0	0.0047	0	0	0.006	6091876	6091876
	May	36553	32286	4267	0	0	0.0044	0	0	0.006	6327632	6327632
	Jun	43190	36287	6903	0	0	0.0050	0	0	0.006	6178300	6178300
	Jul	36832	32432	4400	0	0	0.0048	0	0	0.006	6521195	6521195
	Aug	35418	32390	3028	0	0	0.0049	0	0	0.006	6317734	6317734
	Sep	39741	32573	7168	0	0	0.0049	0	0	0.006	6286145	6286145
	Oct	36706	32726	3980	0	0	0.0049	0	0	0.006	6113905	6113905
	Nov	35095	32533	2562	0	0	0.0046	0	0	0.006	6500915	6500915
	Dec	39052	32831	6221	0	0	0.0054	0	0	0.006	6632884	6632884
2000	Jan	48890	33410	15480	0	0	0.0051	0	0	0.004	7023560	7023560
	Feb	38219	33443	4776	0	0	0.0053	0	0	0.004	6670978	6670978
	Mar	41630	33619	8011	0	0	0.0057	0	0	0.004	6544896	6544896
	Apr	53751	33669	20082	0	0	0.0056	0	0	0.004	7184987	7184987
	May	39181	35467	3714	0	0	0.0060	0	0	0.004	6968719	6968719
	Jun	47204	38190	9014	0	0	0.0050	0	0	0.004	6825860	6825860
	Jul	40884	34258	6626	0	0	0.0058	0	0	0.004	6993776	6993776
	Aug	37378	34431	2947	0	0	0.0060	0	0	0.004	6884673	6884673
	Sep	43461	34825	8636	0	0	0.0061	0	0	0.004	7312212	7312212
	Oct	37749	34546	3203	0	0	0.0066	0	0	0.004	6926127	6926127
	Nov	37075	34192	2883	0	0	0.0061	0	0	0.004	6897037	6897037
	Dec	38540	35070	3470	0	0	0.0060	0	0	0.004	6353551	6353551
2001	Jan	52036	35873	16163	0	0	0.0064	0	0	0.004	6384683	6384683
	Feb	40599	35853	4746	0	0	0.0048	0	0	0.004	6611339	6611339
	Mar	46626	35885	10741	0	0	0.0052	0	0	0.004	6008385	6008385
	Apr	57083	36130	20953	0	0	0.0049	0	0	0.004	5627454	5627454
	May	41519	36284	5235	0	0	0.0042	0	0	0.004	6064707	6064707
	Jun	52093	39495	12598	0	0	0.0038	0	0	0.004	6105340	6105340
	Jul	41928	37119	4809	0	0	0.0040	0	0	0.004	5956980	5956980
	Aug	39262	35901	3361	0	0	0.0041	0	0	0.004	5898602	5898602
	Sep	42588	36579	6009	0	0	0.0038	0	0	0.004	5529350	5529350
	Oct	39183	36242	2941	0	0	0.0032	0	0	0.004	5082578	5082578
	Nov	38539	36590	1949	0	0	0.0027	0	0	0.004	5179655	5179655
	Dec	37653	36965	688	0	0	0.0025	0	0	0.004	5576935	5576935

Table 5.1 (Cont'd)

Monthly Evolution of the Social Security Trust Fund if It Had Been Invested in US Treasury Bonds, Large Company US Stocks, and (Since 2002) International Stocks, 1937–2010.
(other things being equal)
(Dollar amounts rounded to nearest million)

Year	Month	New gov't bond investm.	Market impact for bonds	Value of cont. bond portfolio	Beg. of month bond portfolio	New EAFE+ Canada investm.	Comm. for EAFE+ stocks	Value of cont. EAFE+ portfolio	Beg. of month EAFE+ portfolio	Return on large US stocks	Return on LT US gov't bonds	Return on EAFE+ stocks
1997	Jan	0	0.003	490358	490358	0	0.010	0	0	0.0621	-0.0079	-0.0309
	Feb	6354	0.003	486484	492819	0	0.010	0	0	0.0081	0.0005	0.0154
	Mar	1190	0.003	493065	494251	0	0.010	0	0	-0.0416	-0.0252	0.0013
	Apr	4530	0.003	481796	486313	0	0.010	0	0	0.0597	0.0255	0.0064
	May	12638	0.003	498714	511314	0	0.010	0	0	0.0614	0.0095	0.0662
	Jun	1484	0.003	516171	517651	0	0.010	0	0	0.0446	0.0197	0.0536
	Jul	3940	0.003	527848	531777	0	0.010	0	0	0.0794	0.0626	0.0186
	Aug	1341	0.003	565066	566403	0	0.010	0	0	-0.0556	-0.0317	-0.0734
	Sep	2555	0.003	548448	550995	0	0.010	0	0	0.0548	0.0316	0.0564
	Oct	6026	0.003	568407	574415	0	0.010	0	0	-0.0334	0.0341	-0.0752
	Nov	447	0.003	594002	594448	0	0.010	0	0	0.0463	0.0148	-0.0110
	Dec	0	0.003	603246	603246	0	0.010	0	0	0.0172	0.0184	0.0098
1998	Jan	1804	0.003	614345	616143	0	0.010	0	0	0.0111	0.0200	0.0429
	Feb	10633	0.003	628466	639067	0	0.010	0	0	0.0721	-0.0072	0.0654
	Mar	2291	0.003	634466	636750	0	0.010	0	0	0.0512	0.0025	0.0331
	Apr	6447	0.003	638342	644770	0	0.010	0	0	0.0101	0.0026	0.0080
	May	15399	0.003	646446	661799	0	0.010	0	0	-0.0172	0.0182	-0.0050
	Jun	2622	0.003	673844	676458	0	0.010	0	0	0.0406	0.0228	0.0055
	Jul	8081	0.003	691881	699938	0	0.010	0	0	-0.0106	-0.0040	0.0068
	Aug	3206	0.003	697138	700335	0	0.010	0	0	-0.1446	0.0465	-0.1275
	Sep	1785	0.003	732900	734680	0	0.010	0	0	0.0641	0.0395	-0.0283
	Oct	0	0.003	763700	763700	0	0.010	0	0	0.0813	-0.0218	0.1044
	Nov	2112	0.003	747051	749156	0	0.010	0	0	0.0606	0.0097	0.0509
	Dec	1154	0.003	756423	757574	0	0.010	0	0	0.0576	-0.0032	0.0386
1999	Jan	3894	0.003	755149	759032	0	0.010	0	0	0.0418	0.0121	0.0004
	Feb	13146	0.003	768216	781323	0	0.010	0	0	-0.0311	-0.0520	-0.0249
	Mar	2854	0.003	740694	743539	0	0.010	0	0	0.0400	-0.0008	0.0420
	Apr	6174	0.003	742944	749100	0	0.010	0	0	0.0387	0.0021	0.0431
	May	17506	0.003	750673	768126	0	0.010	0	0	-0.0236	-0.0185	-0.0503
	Jun	4267	0.003	753916	758170	0	0.010	0	0	0.0555	-0.0078	0.0393
	Jul	6903	0.003	752257	759139	0	0.010	0	0	-0.0312	-0.0079	0.0290
	Aug	4400	0.003	753142	757528	0	0.010	0	0	-0.0050	-0.0051	0.0031
	Sep	3028	0.003	753665	756684	0	0.010	0	0	-0.0274	0.0084	0.0110
	Oct	7168	0.003	763040	770187	0	0.010	0	0	0.0633	-0.0012	0.0389
	Nov	3980	0.003	769262	773230	0	0.010	0	0	0.0203	-0.0061	0.0352
	Dec	2562	0.003	768514	771068	0	0.010	0	0	0.0589	-0.0155	0.0922
2000	Jan	6221	0.002	759117	765325	0	0.008	0	0	-0.0502	0.0228	-0.0606
	Feb	15480	0.002	782774	798224	0	0.008	0	0	-0.0189	0.0264	0.0285
	Mar	4776	0.002	819297	824063	0	0.008	0	0	0.0978	0.0367	0.0412
	Apr	8011	0.002	854306	862301	0	0.008	0	0	-0.0301	-0.0076	-0.0517
	May	20082	0.002	855748	875790	0	0.008	0	0	-0.0205	-0.0054	-0.0240
	Jun	3714	0.002	871060	874767	0	0.008	0	0	0.0246	0.0244	0.0435
	Jul	9014	0.002	896111	905107	0	0.008	0	0	-0.0156	0.0173	-0.0380
	Aug	6626	0.002	920765	927378	0	0.008	0	0	0.0621	0.0240	0.0133
	Sep	2947	0.002	949635	952576	0	0.008	0	0	-0.0528	-0.0157	-0.0516
	Oct	8636	0.002	937621	946240	0	0.008	0	0	-0.0042	0.0187	-0.0271
	Nov	3203	0.002	963934	967131	0	0.008	0	0	-0.0788	0.0319	-0.0401
	Dec	2883	0.002	997982	1000860	0	0.008	0	0	0.0049	0.0243	0.0352
2001	Jan	3470	0.002	1025181	1028644	0	0.008	0	0	0.0355	0.0005	0.0019
	Feb	16163	0.002	1029158	1045289	0	0.008	0	0	-0.0912	0.0191	-0.0791
	Mar	4746	0.002	1065254	1069990	0	0.008	0	0	-0.0634	0.0074	-0.0674
	Apr	10741	0.002	1062072	1072792	0	0.008	0	0	0.0777	-0.0313	0.0702
	May	20953	0.002	1039213	1060124	0	0.008	0	0	0.0067	0.0037	-0.0321
	Jun	5235	0.002	1064047	1069271	0	0.008	0	0	-0.0243	0.0085	-0.0404
	Jul	12598	0.002	1078360	1090933	0	0.008	0	0	-0.0098	0.0376	-0.0175
	Aug	4809	0.002	1131952	1136751	0	0.008	0	0	-0.0626	0.0206	-0.0265
	Sep	3361	0.002	1160169	1163523	0	0.008	0	0	-0.0808	0.0081	-0.1007
	Oct	6009	0.002	1172947	1178944	0	0.008	0	0	0.0191	0.0464	0.0245
	Nov	2941	0.002	1233647	1236582	0	0.008	0	0	0.0767	-0.0471	0.0394
	Dec	1949	0.002	1178339	1180285	0	0.008	0	0	0.0088	-0.0183	0.0065

Table 5.1 (Cont'd)

Monthly Evolution of the Social Security Trust Fund if It Had Been Invested in US Treasury Bonds, Large Company US Stocks, and (Since 2002) International Stocks, 1937–2010.
(other things being equal)
(Dollar amounts rounded to nearest million)

Year	Month	Ending value of US stock portfolio	Ending value of gov't bond portfolio	Ending value of EAFE+ portfolio	End Value of SS Trust Fund	Percent in large US stocks	Percent in LT gov't bonds	Percent in EAFE+ Canada stocks	Percent of debt	Official value ot SS Trust Fund	Net SS inflows by fiscal year	Ratio of invested to actual Trust Fund
1997	Jan	3594207	486484	0	4080691	88.08	11.92	0.00	0.00			
	Feb	3623320	493065	0	4116385	88.02	11.98	0.00	0.00			
	Mar	3472590	481796	0	3954386	87.82	12.18	0.00	0.00			
	Apr	3679904	498714	0	4178617	88.07	11.93	0.00	0.00			
	May	3905850	516171	0	4422021	88.33	11.67	0.00	0.00			
	Jun	4080051	527848	0	4607899	88.54	11.46	0.00	0.00			
	Jul	4404007	565066	0	4969073	88.63	11.37	0.00	0.00			
	Aug	4159144	548448	0	4707592	88.35	11.65	0.00	0.00			
	Sep	4387065	568407	0	4955472	88.53	11.47	0.00	0.00		40103	
	Oct	4240537	594002	0	4834539	87.71	12.29	0.00	0.00			
	Nov	4436874	603246	0	5039888	88.04	11.97	0.00	0.00			
	Dec	4513188	614345	0	5127534	88.02	11.98	0.00	0.00	655510		7.82
1998	Jan	4563285	628466	0	5191751	87.89	12.11	0.00	0.00			
	Feb	4892297	634466	0	5526764	88.52	11.48	0.00	0.00			
	Mar	5142783	638342	0	5781125	88.96	11.04	0.00	0.00			
	Apr	5194725	646446	0	5841171	88.93	11.07	0.00	0.00			
	May	5105376	673844	0	5779220	88.34	11.66	0.00	0.00			
	Jun	5312654	691881	0	6004535	88.48	11.52	0.00	0.00			
	Jul	5256340	697138	0	5953478	88.29	11.71	0.00	0.00			
	Aug	4496273	732900	0	5229173	85.98	14.02	0.00	0.00			
	Sep	4784484	763700	0	5548150	86.24	13.76	0.00	0.00		52683	
	Oct	5173463	747051	0	5920514	87.38	12.62	0.00	0.00			
	Nov	5486975	756423	0	6243398	87.88	12.12	0.00	0.00			
	Dec	5803025	755149	0	6558174	88.49	11.51	0.00	0.00	762460		8.60
1999	Jan	6045591	768216	0	6813807	88.73	11.27	0.00	0.00			
	Feb	5857573	740694	0	6598267	88.77	11.23	0.00	0.00			
	Mar	6091876	742944	0	6834820	89.13	10.87	0.00	0.00			
	Apr	6327632	750673	0	7078305	89.39	10.61	0.00	0.00			
	May	6178300	753916	0	6932216	89.12	10.88	0.00	0.00			
	Jun	6521195	752257	0	7273452	89.66	10.34	0.00	0.00			
	Jul	6317734	753142	0	7070876	89.35	10.65	0.00	0.00			
	Aug	6286145	753665	0	7039810	89.29	10.71	0.00	0.00			
	Sep	6113905	763040	0	6876945	88.90	11.10	0.00	0.00		72640	
	Oct	6500915	769262	0	7270177	89.42	10.58	0.00	0.00			
	Nov	6632884	768514	0	7401397	89.62	10.38	0.00	0.00			
	Dec	7023560	759117	0	7782677	90.25	9.75	0.00	0.00	896133		8.68
2000	Jan	6670978	782774	0	7453752	89.50	10.50	0.00	0.00			
	Feb	6544896	819297	0	7364193	88.87	11.13	0.00	0.00			
	Mar	7184987	854306	0	8039293	89.37	10.63	0.00	0.00			
	Apr	6968719	855748	0	7824467	89.06	10.94	0.00	0.00			
	May	6825860	871060	0	7696920	88.68	11.32	0.00	0.00			
	Jun	6993776	896111	0	7889887	88.64	11.36	0.00	0.00			
	Jul	6884673	920765	0	7805439	88.20	11.80	0.00	0.00			
	Aug	7312212	949635	0	8261847	88.51	11.49	0.00	0.00			
	Sep	6926127	937621	0	7863748	88.07	11.92	0.00	0.00		92049	
	Oct	6897037	963934	0	7860971	87.74	12.26	0.00	0.00			
	Nov	6353551	997982	0	7351533	86.42	13.58	0.00	0.00			
	Dec	6384683	1025181	0	7409864	86.16	13.84	0.00	0.00	1049445		7.06
2001	Jan	6611339	1029158	0	7640497	86.53	13.47	0.00	0.00			
	Feb	6008385	1065254	0	7073639	84.94	15.06	0.00	0.00			
	Mar	5627454	1062072	0	6689526	84.12	15.88	0.00	0.00			
	Apr	6064707	1039213	0	7103920	85.37	14.63	0.00	0.00			
	May	6105340	1064047	0	7169387	85.16	14.84	0.00	0.00			
	Jun	5956980	1078360	0	7035341	84.67	15.33	0.00	0.00			
	Jul	5898602	1131952	0	7030554	83.90	16.10	0.00	0.00			
	Aug	5529350	1160169	0	6689518	82.66	17.34	0.00	0.00			
	Sep	5082578	1172947	0	6255525	81.25	18.75	0.00	0.00		94171	
	Oct	5179655	1233647	0	6413303	80.76	19.24	0.00	0.00			
	Nov	5576935	1178339	0	6755274	82.56	17.44	0.00	0.00			
	Dec	5626012	1158685	0	6784697	82.92	17.08	0.00	0.00	1212533		5.60

Table 5.1   (*Cont'd*)

Monthly Evolution of the Social Security Trust Fund if It Had Been Invested in US Treasury Bonds, Large Company US Stocks, and (Since 2002) International Stocks, 1937–2010. (other things being equal)
(Dollar amounts rounded to nearest million)

Year	Month	Soc. Sec. receipts less int. income	Soc. Sec. outlays less int. expense	Net SS cash inflow/ outflow	Amount of short term loan	Debt at end of month	30-day interest rate	Amount of debt repaid	New US stock investm.	Comm. rate for US stocks	Value of cont. stock portf.	Beg. of month US stock portfolio
2002	Jan	53973	37402	16571	0	0	0.0024	0	0	0.004	5626012	5626012
	Feb	42027	38195	3832	0	0	0.0023	0	0	0.004	5543872	5543872
	Mar	46335	38080	8255	0	0	0.0023	0	0	0.004	5436875	5436875
	Apr	59121	37841	21280	0	0	0.0025	0	0	0.004	5641302	5641302
	May	43050	38053	4997	0	0	0.0024	0	0	0.004	5299439	5299439
	Jun	49273	41645	7628	0	0	0.0023	0	0	0.004	5260223	5260223
	Jul	43386	38100	5286	0	0	0.0025	0	0	0.004	4885695	4885695
	Aug	40321	38414	1907	0	0	0.0024	0	0	0.004	4504611	4504611
	Sep	45284	38383	6901	0	0	0.0024	0	0	0.004	4534341	4534341
	Oct	40917	38233	2684	0	0	0.0024	0	0	0.004	4041459	4041459
	Nov	40142	38631	1511	0	0	0.0022	0	0	0.004	4397107	4397107
	Dec	42892	38677	4215	0	0	0.0021	0	0	0.004	4656097	4656097
2003	Jan	53799	39168	14631	0	0	0.0020	0	0	0.004	4382318	4382318
	Feb	42100	39057	3043	0	0	0.0019	0	0	0.004	4267501	4267501
	Mar	45099	39317	5782	0	0	0.0020	0	0	0.004	4203489	4203489
	Apr	59042	39283	19759	0	0	0.0020	0	0	0.004	4244263	4244263
	May	43657	39712	3945	0	0	0.0019	0	0	0.004	4593990	4593990
	Jun	50029	43393	6636	0	0	0.0020	0	0	0.004	4836093	4836093
	Jul	43270	39549	3721	0	0	0.0017	0	0	0.004	4897995	4897995
	Aug	41345	39819	1526	0	0	0.0017	0	0	0.004	4984200	4984200
	Sep	44412	39883	4529	0	0	0.0018	0	0	0.004	5081392	5081392
	Oct	42131	39757	2374	0	0	0.0017	0	0	0.004	5027529	5027529
	Nov	41282	39705	1577	0	0	0.0017	0	0	0.004	5312087	5312087
	Dec	40793	40444	349	0	0	0.0018	0	0	0.004	5358833	5358833
2004	Jan	56108	40564	15544	0	0	0.0017	0	0	0.004	5639636	5639636
	Feb	42427	41189	1238	0	0	0.0016	0	0	0.004	5743406	5743406
	Mar	46357	41148	5209	0	0	0.0019	0	0	0.004	5823239	5823239
	Apr	61625	41602	20023	0	0	0.0018	0	0	0.004	5735308	5735308
	May	45119	41531	3588	0	0	0.0016	0	0	0.004	5645264	5645264
	Jun	48938	45087	3851	0	0	0.0018	0	0	0.004	5722604	5722604
	Jul	45315	40990	4325	0	0	0.0020	0	0	0.004	5833622	5833622
	Aug	42754	42141	613	0	0	0.0021	0	0	0.004	5640530	5640530
	Sep	47543	41368	6175	0	0	0.0021	0	0	0.004	5663092	5663092
	Oct	45236	41744	3492	0	0	0.0021	0	0	0.004	5724253	5724253
	Nov	43218	41840	1378	0	0	0.0025	0	0	0.004	5811834	5811834
	Dec	44104	42440	1664	0	0	0.0026	0	0	0.004	6047213	6047213
2005	Jan	59278	43050	16228	0	0	0.0026	0	0	0.004	6252819	6252819
	Feb	44253	43326	927	0	0	0.0026	0	0	0.004	6100250	6100250
	Mar	50264	43581	6683	0	0	0.0031	0	0	0.004	6228355	6228355
	Apr	63890	43923	19967	0	0	0.0031	0	0	0.004	6118113	6118113
	May	46495	43776	2719	0	0	0.0034	0	0	0.004	6001869	6001869
	Jun	60017	47835	12182	0	0	0.0033	0	0	0.004	6192728	6192728
	Jul	48939	43919	5020	0	0	0.0034	0	0	0.004	6201398	6201398
	Aug	46351	44034	2317	0	0	0.0040	0	0	0.004	6432090	6432090
	Sep	52868	43809	9059	0	0	0.0039	0	0	0.004	6373558	6373558
	Oct	45466	44117	1349	0	0	0.0037	0	0	0.004	6425184	6425184
	Nov	44866	43844	1022	0	0	0.0041	0	0	0.004	6317884	6317884
	Dec	44819	44723	96	0	0	0.0042	0	0	0.004	6556700	6556700
2006	Jan	62867	46058	16809	0	0	0.0045	0	0	0.004	6558667	6558667
	Feb	48781	45731	3050	0	0	0.0044	0	0	0.004	6732471	6732471
	Mar	56526	46224	10302	0	0	0.0047	0	0	0.004	6750649	6750649
	Apr	69766	46463	23303	0	0	0.0046	0	0	0.004	6834357	6834357
	May	50206	46420	3786	0	0	0.0053	0	0	0.004	6925937	6925937
	Jun	60080	50738	9342	0	0	0.0050	0	0	0.004	6726470	6726470
	Jul	51151	46564	4587	0	0	0.0050	0	0	0.004	6735887	6735887
	Aug	47761	41059	6702	0	0	0.0052	0	0	0.004	6777650	6777650
	Sep	53718	46552	7166	0	0	0.0051	0	0	0.004	6938958	6938958
	Oct	48044	46722	1322	0	0	0.0051	0	0	0.004	7117983	7117983
	Nov	46879	46537	342	0	0	0.0052	0	0	0.004	7350029	7350029
	Dec	46673	46352	321	0	0	0.0050	0	0	0.004	7489680	7489680

Table 5.1 (*Cont'd*)

Monthly Evolution of the Social Security Trust Fund if It Had Been Invested in US Treasury Bonds, Large Company US Stocks, and (Since 2002) International Stocks, 1937–2010.
(other things being equal)
(Dollar amounts rounded to nearest million)

Year	Month	New gov't bond investm.	Market impact for bonds	Value of cont. bond portfolio	Beg. of month bond portfolio	New EAFE+ Canada investm.	Comm. for EAFE+ stocks	Value of cont. EAFE+ portfolio	Beg. of month EAFE+ portfolio	Return on large US stocks	Return on LT US gov't bonds	Return on EAFE+ stocks
2002	Jan	688	0.002	1158685	1159372	0	0.008	0	0	-0.0146	0.0138	-0.0508
	Feb	16571	0.002	1175371	1191909	0	0.008	0	0	-0.0193	0.0115	0.0062
	Mar	3832	0.002	1205616	1209440	0	0.008	0	0	0.0376	-0.0436	0.0537
	Apr	8255	0.002	1156709	1164947	0	0.008	0	0	-0.0606	0.0410	0.0065
	May	21280	0.002	1212710	1233948	0	0.008	0	0	-0.0074	0.0015	0.0140
	Jun	4997	0.002	1235799	1240786	0	0.008	0	0	-0.0712	0.0187	-0.0403
	Jul	3814	0.002	1263988	1267795	3814	0.008	0	3783	-0.0780	0.0303	-0.0993
	Aug	2643	0.002	1306209	1308847	2643	0.008	3408	6030	0.0066	0.0464	-0.0013
	Sep	954	0.002	1369577	1370529	954	0.008	6022	6968	-0.1087	0.0417	-0.1058
	Oct	3451	0.002	1427680	1431123	3451	0.008	6230	9653	0.0880	-0.0294	0.0526
	Nov	1342	0.002	1389048	1390388	1342	0.008	10161	11492	0.0589	-0.0122	0.0462
	Dec	756	0.002	1373425	1374179	756	0.008	12023	12773	-0.0588	0.0507	-0.0322
2003	Jan	2108	0.002	1443850	1445953	2108	0.008	12361	14452	-0.0262	-0.0106	-0.0380
	Feb	7316	0.002	1430626	1437927	7316	0.008	13902	21159	-0.0150	0.0329	-0.0196
	Mar	1522	0.002	1485234	1486753	1522	0.008	20745	22254	0.0097	-0.0135	-0.0185
	Apr	2891	0.002	1466682	1469567	2891	0.008	21842	24709	0.0824	0.0102	0.0971
	May	9880	0.002	1484557	1494416	9880	0.008	27108	36908	0.0527	0.0592	0.0629
	Jun	1973	0.002	1582886	1584854	1973	0.008	39231	41187	0.0128	-0.0154	0.0249
	Jul	3318	0.002	1560448	1563759	3318	0.008	42212	45503	0.0176	-0.0982	0.0231
	Aug	1861	0.002	1410198	1412055	1861	0.008	46554	48400	0.0195	0.0166	0.0260
	Sep	763	0.002	1435495	1436256	763	0.008	49657	50414	-0.0106	0.0546	0.0302
	Oct	2265	0.002	1514676	1516936	2265	0.008	51937	54184	0.0566	-0.0283	0.0627
	Nov	1187	0.002	1474006	1475191	1187	0.008	57581	58759	0.0088	0.0027	0.0228
	Dec	789	0.002	1479174	1479961	789	0.008	60100	60882	0.0524	0.0139	0.0768
2004	Jan	175	0.002	1500532	1500707	175	0.008	65555	65728	0.0184	0.0187	0.0140
	Feb	7772	0.002	1528770	1536526	7772	0.008	66649	74359	0.0139	0.0230	0.0232
	Mar	619	0.002	1571866	1572484	619	0.008	76082	76696	-0.0151	0.0141	0.0054
	Apr	2605	0.002	1594656	1597255	2605	0.008	77110	79694	-0.0157	-0.0588	-0.0254
	May	10012	0.002	1503337	1513328	10012	0.008	77673	87604	0.0137	-0.0051	0.0056
	Jun	1794	0.002	1505610	1507401	1794	0.008	88096	89876	0.0194	0.0121	0.0235
	Jul	1926	0.002	1525640	1527562	1926	0.008	91988	93898	-0.0331	0.0155	-0.0303
	Aug	2163	0.002	1551239	1553397	2163	0.008	91049	93194	0.0040	0.0395	0.0044
	Sep	307	0.002	1614757	1615062	307	0.008	93604	93908	0.0108	0.0096	0.0293
	Oct	3088	0.002	1630567	1633648	3088	0.008	96660	99723	0.0153	0.0154	0.0360
	Nov	1746	0.002	1658807	1660549	1746	0.008	103315	105047	0.0405	-0.0234	0.0668
	Dec	689	0.002	1621692	1622380	689	0.008	112063	112746	0.0340	0.0250	0.0423
2005	Jan	832	0.002	1662939	1663770	832	0.008	117519	118345	-0.0244	0.0300	-0.0196
	Feb	8114	0.002	1713683	1721781	8114	0.008	116024	124074	0.0210	-0.0128	0.0447
	Mar	464	0.002	1699742	1700204	464	0.008	129622	130082	-0.0177	-0.0072	-0.0223
	Apr	3342	0.002	1687963	1691298	3342	0.008	127180	130495	-0.0190	0.0373	-0.0244
	May	9984	0.002	1754383	1764347	9984	0.008	127308	137211	0.0318	0.0297	0.0028
	Jun	1360	0.002	1816748	1818104	1360	0.008	137600	138948	0.0014	0.0167	0.0168
	Jul	6091	0.002	1848467	1854546	6091	0.008	141277	147319	0.0372	-0.0288	0.0324
	Aug	2510	0.002	1801135	1803640	2510	0.008	152087	154577	-0.0091	0.0333	0.0279
	Sep	1159	0.002	1863701	1864857	1159	0.008	158891	160040	0.0081	-0.0338	0.0459
	Oct	4530	0.002	1801825	1806345	4530	0.008	167379	171872	-0.0167	-0.0196	-0.0322
	Nov	675	0.002	1770941	1771614	675	0.008	166331	167000	0.0378	0.0076	0.0268
	Dec	511	0.002	1785078	1785588	511	0.008	171470	171977	0.0003	0.0267	0.0465
2006	Jan	48	0.002	1833264	1833311	48	0.008	179967	180015	0.0265	-0.0118	0.0633
	Feb	8405	0.002	1811678	1820066	8405	0.008	191415	199752	0.0027	0.0238	-0.0032
	Mar	1525	0.002	1863384	1864906	1525	0.008	199116	200629	0.0124	-0.0539	0.0322
	Apr	5151	0.002	1764387	1769528	5151	0.008	207089	212199	0.0134	-0.0247	0.0485
	May	23303	0.002	1725821	1749077	0	0.008	222495	222495	-0.0288	0.0010	-0.0368
	Jun	1893	0.002	1750826	1752715	1893	0.008	214297	216175	0.0014	0.0092	-0.0008
	Jul	4671	0.002	1768840	1773502	4671	0.008	215992	220626	0.0062	0.0199	0.0095
	Aug	2294	0.002	1808795	1811083	2294	0.008	222721	224997	0.0238	0.0299	0.0287
	Sep	3351	0.002	1865235	1868579	3351	0.008	231457	234781	0.0258	0.0170	-0.0006
	Oct	3583	0.002	1900345	1903921	3583	0.008	234643	238197	0.0326	0.0077	0.0396
	Nov	661	0.002	1918581	1919241	661	0.008	247634	248290	0.0190	0.0207	0.0301
	Dec	171	0.002	1958969	1959140	171	0.008	255758	255928	0.0140	-0.0236	0.0288

Table 5.1 (*Cont'd*)

Monthly Evolution of the Social Security Trust Fund if It Had Been Invested in US Treasury
Bonds, Large Company US Stocks, and (Since 2002) International Stocks, 1937–2010.
(other things being equal)
(Dollar amounts rounded to nearest million)

Year	Month	Ending value of US stock portfolio	Ending value of gov't bond portfolio	Ending value of EAFE+ portfolio	End Value of SS Trust Fund	Percent in large US stocks	Percent in LT gov't bonds	Percent in EAFE+ Canada stocks	Percent of debt	Official value ot SS Trust Fund	Net SS inflows by fiscal year	Ratio of invested to actual Trust Fund
2002	Jan	5543872	1175371	0	6719243	82.51	17.49	0.00	0.00			
	Feb	5436875	1205616	0	6642492	81.85	18.15	0.00	0.00			
	Mar	5641302	1156709	0	6798011	82.98	17.02	0.00	0.00			
	Apr	5299439	1212710	0	6512149	81.38	18.62	0.00	0.00			
	May	5260223	1235799	0	6496022	80.98	19.02	0.00	0.00			
	Jun	4885695	1263988	0	6149684	79.45	20.55	0.00	0.00			
	Jul	4504611	1306209	3408	5814228	77.48	22.47	0.06	0.00			
	Aug	4534341	1369577	6022	5909940	76.72	23.17	0.10	0.00			
	Sep	4041459	1427680	6230	5475369	73.81	26.07	0.11	0.00		82235	
	Oct	4397107	1389048	10161	5796316	75.86	23.96	0.18	0.00			
	Nov	4656097	1373425	12023	6041545	77.07	22.73	0.20	0.00			
	Dec	4382318	1443850	12361	5838529	75.06	24.73	0.21	0.00	1377965		4.24
2003	Jan	4267501	1430626	13902	5712030	74.71	25.05	0.24	0.00			
	Feb	4203489	1485234	20745	5709468	73.62	26.01	0.36	0.00			
	Mar	4244263	1466682	21842	5732786	74.03	25.58	0.38	0.00			
	Apr	4593990	1484557	27108	6105654	75.24	24.31	0.44	0.00			
	May	4836093	1582886	39231	6458210	74.88	24.51	0.61	0.00			
	Jun	4897995	1560448	42212	6500655	75.35	24.00	0.65	0.00			
	Jul	4984200	1410198	46554	6440952	77.38	21.89	0.72	0.00			
	Aug	5081392	1435495	49657	6566544	77.38	21.86	0.76	0.00			
	Sep	5027529	1514676	51937	6594142	76.24	22.97	0.79	0.00		71982	
	Oct	5312087	1474006	57581	6843675	77.62	21.54	0.84	0.00			
	Nov	5358833	1479174	60100	6898107	77.69	21.44	0.87	0.00			
	Dec	5639636	1500532	65555	7205724	78.27	20.82	0.91	0.00	1530764		4.71
2004	Jan	5743406	1528770	66649	7338824	78.26	20.83	0.91	0.00			
	Feb	5823239	1571866	76082	7471188	77.94	21.04	1.02	0.00			
	Mar	5735308	1594656	77110	7407075	77.43	21.53	1.04	0.00			
	Apr	5645264	1503337	77673	7226273	78.12	20.80	1.07	0.00			
	May	5722604	1505610	88096	7316310	78.22	20.58	1.20	0.00			
	Jun	5833622	1525640	91988	7451251	78.29	20.47	1.23	0.00			
	Jul	5640530	1551239	91049	7282817	77.45	21.30	1.25	0.00			
	Aug	5663092	1614757	93604	7371452	76.82	21.91	1.27	0.00			
	Sep	5724253	1630567	96660	7451480	76.82	21.88	1.30	0.00		64866	
	Oct	5811834	1658807	103315	7573955	76.73	21.90	1.36	0.00			
	Nov	6047213	1621692	112063	7780968	77.72	20.84	1.44	0.00			
	Dec	6252819	1662939	117519	8033277	77.84	20.70	1.46	0.00	1686839		4.76
2005	Jan	6100250	1713683	116024	7929957	76.93	21.61	1.46	0.00			
	Feb	6228355	1699742	129622	8057719	77.30	21.09	1.61	0.00			
	Mar	6118113	1687963	127180	7933256	77.12	21.28	1.60	0.00			
	Apr	6001869	1754383	127308	7883560	76.13	22.25	1.61	0.00			
	May	6192728	1816748	137600	8147076	76.01	22.30	1.69	0.00			
	Jun	6201398	1848467	141277	8191142	75.71	22.57	1.72	0.00			
	Jul	6432090	1801135	152087	8385312	76.71	21.48	1.81	0.00			
	Aug	6373558	1863701	158891	8396150	75.91	22.20	1.89	0.00			
	Sep	6425184	1801825	167379	8394388	76.54	21.46	1.99	0.00		81636	
	Oct	6317884	1770941	166331	8255156	76.53	21.45	2.01	0.00			
	Nov	6556700	1785078	171470	8513248	77.02	20.97	2.01	0.00			
	Dec	6558667	1833264	179967	8571898	76.51	21.39	2.10	0.00	1858660		4.61
2006	Jan	6732471	1811678	191415	8735564	77.07	20.74	2.19	0.00			
	Feb	6750649	1863384	199116	8813148	76.60	21.14	2.26	0.00			
	Mar	6834357	1764387	207089	8805834	77.61	20.04	2.35	0.00			
	Apr	6925937	1725821	222495	8874253	78.05	19.45	2.51	0.00			
	May	6726470	1750826	214297	8691593	77.39	20.14	2.47	0.00			
	Jun	6735887	1768840	215992	8720720	77.24	20.28	2.48	0.00			
	Jul	6777650	1808795	222721	8809166	76.94	20.53	2.53	0.00			
	Aug	6938958	1865235	231457	9035650	76.80	20.64	2.56	0.00			
	Sep	7117983	1900345	234643	9252971	76.93	20.54	2.54	0.00		87514	
	Oct	7350029	1918581	247634	9516245	77.24	20.16	2.60	0.00			
	Nov	7489680	1958969	255758	9704407	77.18	20.19	2.64	0.00			
	Dec	7594535	1912904	263291	9770730	77.73	19.58	2.69	0.00	2048112		4.77

Table 5.1   (*Cont'd*)

Monthly Evolution of the Social Security Trust Fund if It Had Been Invested in US Treasury Bonds, Large Company US Stocks, and (Since 2002) International Stocks, 1937–2010.
(other things being equal)
(Dollar amounts rounded to nearest million)

Year	Month	Soc. Sec. receipts less int. income	Soc. Sec. outlays less int. expense	Net SS cash inflow/ outflow	Amount of short term loan	Debt at end of month	30-day interest rate	Amount of debt repaid	New US stock investm.	Comm. rate for US stocks	Value of cont. stock portf.	Beg. of month US stock portfolio
2007	Jan	66781	48363	18418	0	0	0.0054	0	0	0.004	7594535	7594535
	Feb	51672	48481	3191	0	0	0.0048	0	0	0.004	7709213	7709213
	Mar	60083	48944	11139	0	0	0.0053	0	0	0.004	7558112	7558112
	Apr	73654	48825	24829	0	0	0.0054	0	0	0.004	7642763	7642763
	May	52763	49439	3324	0	0	0.0051	0	0	0.004	7981338	7981338
	Jun	58928	53496	5432	0	0	0.0050	0	0	0.004	8259886	8259886
	Jul	54368	49024	5344	0	0	0.0050	0	0	0.004	8122772	8122772
	Aug	50456	49296	1160	0	0	0.0052	0	0	0.004	7870966	7870966
	Sep	55100	49831	5269	0	0	0.0042	0	0	0.004	7989031	7989031
	Oct	50731	49158	1573	0	0	0.0042	0	0	0.004	8287820	8287820
	Nov	49333	49363	-30	30	30	0.0044	0	0	0.004	8419597	8419597
	Dec	50848	50281	567	0	0	0.0037	30	0	0.004	8067658	8067658
2008	Jan	70179	50709	19470	0	0	0.0031	0	0	0.004	8011991	8011991
	Feb	53344	50828	2516	0	0	0.0023	0	0	0.004	7531271	7531271
	Mar	59091	51622	7469	0	0	0.0027	0	0	0.004	7286505	7286505
	Apr	75639	51327	24312	0	0	0.0028	0	0	0.004	7255173	7255173
	May	55039	51893	3146	0	0	0.0028	0	0	0.004	7608500	7608500
	Jun	62061	55735	6326	0	0	0.0027	0	0	0.004	7707410	7707410
	Jul	55695	52033	3662	0	0	0.0025	0	0	0.004	7057676	7057676
	Aug	51743	51934	-191	191	191	0.0023	0	0	0.004	6998391	6998391
	Sep	55260	52134	3126	0	0	0.0025	192	0	0.004	7099868	7099868
	Oct	51711	52086	-375	375	376	0.0018	0	0	0.004	6467270	6467270
	Nov	51438	51992	-554	554	931	0.0013	0	0	0.004	5381415	5381415
	Dec	47804	52851	-5047	5047	5984	0.0010	0	0	0.004	4995030	4995030
2009	Jan	71854	55290	16564	0	0	0.0010	5990	0	0.004	5047977	5047977
	Feb	54413	55760	-1347	1347	1348	0.0011	0	0	0.004	4622432	4622432
	Mar	58669	56135	2534	0	0	0.0012	1350	0	0.004	4130143	4130143
	Apr	77081	56596	20485	0	0	0.0011	0	0	0.004	4491944	4491944
	May	54408	56330	-1922	1922	1924	0.0010	0	0	0.004	4921823	4921823
	Jun	61156	61383	-227	227	2153	0.0011	0	0	0.004	5196953	5196953
	Jul	56345	56890	-545	545	2701	0.0011	0	0	0.004	5207347	5207347
	Aug	50657	56490	-5833	5833	8544	0.0011	0	0	0.004	5601022	5601022
	Sep	53507	57884	-4377	4377	12935	0.0011	0	0	0.004	5803219	5803219
	Oct	52677	57506	-4829	4829	17782	0.0010	0	0	0.004	6019679	6019679
	Nov	51412	57270	-5858	5858	23663	0.0010	0	0	0.004	5907713	5907713
	Dec	46961	58268	-11307	11307	35009	0.0011	0	0	0.004	6262176	6262176
2010	Jan	70920	57806	13114	0	21930	0.0010	13114	0	0.004	6383036	6383036
	Feb	50312	58002	-7690	7690	29652	0.0011	0	0	0.004	6153247	6153247
	Mar	51452	58296	-6844	6844	36536	0.0011	0	0	0.004	6343997	6343997
	Apr	76534	58948	17586	0	18991	0.0011	17586	0	0.004	6726540	6726540
	May	53783	58960	-5177	5177	24194	0.0011	0	0	0.004	6832820	6832820
	Jun	56802	63277	-6475	6475	30703	0.0011	0	0	0.004	6286877	6286877
	Jul	55855	59240	-3385	3385	34125	0.0011	0	0	0.004	5958074	5958074
	Aug	50750	59050	-8300	8300	42472	0.0011	0	0	0.004	6375735	6375735
	Sep	51995	59630	-7635	7635	50162	0.0011	0	0	0.004	8088189	8088189
	Oct	53460	59625	-6165	6165	56389	0.0011	0	0	0.004	6631255	6631255
	Nov	50927	59420	-8493	8493	64954	0.0011	0	0	0.004	6883243	6883243
	Dec	40841	60274	-19433	19433	84479	0.0011	0	0	0.004	6883931	6883931

Table 5.1 (*Cont'd*)

Monthly Evolution of the Social Security Trust Fund if It Had Been Invested in US Treasury Bonds, Large Company US Stocks, and (Since 2002) International Stocks, 1937–2010.
(other things being equal)
(Dollar amounts rounded to nearest million)

Year	Month	New gov't bond investm.	Market impact for bonds	Value of cont. bond portfolio	Beg. of month bond portfolio	New EAFE+ Canada investm.	Comm. for EAFE+ stocks	Value of cont. EAFE+ portfolio	Beg. of month EAFE+ portfolio	Return on large US stocks	Return on LT US gov't bonds	Return on EAFE+ stocks
2007	Jan	321	0.002	1912904	1913224	0	0.008	263291	263291	0.0151	-0.0102	0.0062
	Feb	18418	0.002	1893709	1912091	0	0.008	264922	264922	-0.0196	0.0335	0.0082
	Mar	1596	0.002	1976146	1977738	1596	0.008	267083	268666	0.0112	-0.0145	0.0261
	Apr	11139	0.002	1949061	1960177	0	0.008	275679	275679	0.0443	0.0085	0.0464
	May	24829	0.002	1976839	2001618	0	0.008	288461	288461	0.0349	-0.0200	0.0235
	Jun	3324	0.002	1961586	1964903	0	0.008	295235	295235	-0.0166	-0.0091	0.0013
	Jul	5432	0.002	1947023	1952444	0	0.008	295632	295632	-0.0310	0.0284	-0.0137
	Aug	5344	0.002	2007893	2013227	0	0.008	291580	291580	0.0150	0.0199	-0.0142
	Sep	1160	0.002	2053290	2054447	0	0.008	287434	287434	0.0374	0.0012	0.0570
	Oct	5269	0.002	2056913	2062171	0	0.008	303828	303828	0.0159	0.0155	0.0436
	Nov	1573	0.002	2094135	2095705	0	0.008	317074	317074	-0.0418	0.0468	-0.0388
	Dec	0	0.002	2193784	2193784	0	0.008	304760	304760	-0.0069	-0.0029	-0.0187
2008	Jan	268	0.002	2187422	2187690	268	0.008	299062	299328	-0.0600	0.0213	-0.0900
	Feb	9735	0.002	2234287	2244003	9735	0.008	272376	282033	-0.0325	0.0018	0.0184
	Mar	1258	0.002	2248042	2249298	1258	0.008	287234	288482	-0.0043	0.0106	-0.0138
	Apr	3735	0.002	2273140	2276867	3735	0.008	284506	288211	0.0487	-0.0288	0.0568
	May	12156	0.002	2211293	2223425	12156	0.008	304581	316640	0.0130	-0.0164	0.0170
	Jun	1573	0.002	2186961	2188531	1573	0.008	322009	323570	-0.0843	0.0220	-0.0775
	Jul	3163	0.002	2236678	2239835	3163	0.008	298486	301624	-0.0084	-0.0025	-0.0355
	Aug	1831	0.002	2234236	2236063	1831	0.008	290924	292740	0.0145	0.0242	-0.0384
	Sep	0	0.002	2290176	2290176	0	0.008	281501	281501	-0.0891	0.0112	-0.1440
	Oct	1467	0.002	2315826	2317290	1467	0.008	240958	242413	-0.1679	-0.0383	-0.2079
	Nov	0	0.002	2228537	2228537	0	0.008	192009	192009	-0.0718	0.1443	-0.0537
	Dec	0	0.002	2550115	2550115	0	0.008	181689	181689	0.0106	0.0967	0.0529
2009	Jan	0	0.002	2796712	2796712	0	0.008	191298	191298	-0.0843	-0.1124	-0.0931
	Feb	5287	0.002	2482361	2487638	5287	0.008	173486	178731	-0.1065	-0.0056	-0.1009
	Mar	0	0.002	2473707	2473707	0	0.008	160699	160699	0.0876	0.0641	0.0664
	Apr	592	0.002	2632272	2632862	592	0.008	171375	171962	0.0957	-0.0649	0.1305
	May	10243	0.002	2461990	2472212	10243	0.008	194398	204559	0.0559	-0.0248	0.1282
	Jun	0	0.002	2410901	2410901	0	0.008	230781	230781	0.0020	0.0083	-0.0100
	Jul	0	0.002	2430911	2430911	0	0.008	228466	228466	0.0756	0.0019	0.0941
	Aug	0	0.002	2435530	2435530	0	0.008	249957	249957	0.0361	0.0231	0.0481
	Sep	0	0.002	2491791	2491791	0	0.008	261982	261982	0.0373	0.0176	0.0415
	Oct	0	0.002	2535646	2535646	0	0.008	272851	272851	-0.0186	-0.0171	-0.0160
	Nov	0	0.002	2492287	2492287	0	0.008	268495	268495	0.0600	0.0208	0.0250
	Dec	0	0.002	2544126	2544126	0	0.008	275212	275212	0.0193	-0.0584	0.0161
2010	Jan	0	0.002	2395549	2395549	0	0.008	279649	279649	-0.0360	0.0264	-0.0468
	Feb	0	0.002	2458792	2458792	0	0.008	266561	266561	0.0310	0.0032	-0.0009
	Mar	0	0.002	2466660	2466660	0	0.008	266322	266322	0.0603	-0.0179	0.0650
	Apr	0	0.002	2422507	2422507	0	0.008	283632	283632	0.0158	0.0304	-0.0141
	May	0	0.002	2496151	2496151	0	0.008	279633	279633	-0.0799	0.0437	-0.1091
	Jun	0	0.002	2605233	2605233	0	0.008	249125	249125	-0.0523	0.0446	-0.0142
	Jul	0	0.002	2721426	2721426	0	0.008	245588	245588	0.0701	0.0024	0.0926
	Aug	0	0.002	2727957	2727957	0	0.008	268329	268329	-0.0451	0.0702	-0.0297
	Sep	0	0.002	2919460	2919460	0	0.008	260360	260360	0.0892	-0.0153	0.0962
	Oct	0	0.002	2874792	2874792	0	0.008	285406	285406	0.0380	-0.0317	0.0357
	Nov	0	0.002	2783661	2783661	0	0.008	295595	295595	0.0001	-0.0137	-0.0421
	Dec	0	0.002	2745525	2745525	0	0.008	283151	283151	0.0668	-0.0388	0.0807

Table 5.1   (*Cont'd*)

Monthly Evolution of the Social Security Trust Fund if It Had Been Invested in US Treasury Bonds, Large Company US Stocks, and (Since 2002) International Stocks, 1937–2010.
(other things being equal)
(Dollar amounts rounded to nearest million)

Year	Month	Ending value of US stock portfolio	Ending value of gov't bond portfolio	Ending value of EAFE+ portfolio	End Value of SS Trust Fund	Percent in large US stocks	Percent in LT gov't bonds	Percent in EAFE+ Canada stocks	Percent of debt	Official value ot SS Trust Fund	Net SS inflows by fiscal year	Ratio of invested to actual Trust Fund
2007	Jan	7709213	1893709	264922	9867844	78.12	19.19	2.68	0.00			
	Feb	7558112	1976146	267083	9801341	77.11	20.16	2.72	0.00			
	Mar	7642763	1949061	275679	9867503	77.45	19.75	2.79	0.00			
	Apr	7981338	1976839	288461	10246637	77.89	19.29	2.82	0.00			
	May	8259886	1961586	295235	10516707	78.54	18.65	2.81	0.00			
	Jun	8122772	1947023	295632	10365426	78.36	18.78	2.85	0.00			
	Jul	7870966	2007893	291580	10170439	77.39	19.74	2.87	0.00			
	Aug	7989031	2053290	287434	10329755	77.34	19.88	2.78	0.00			
	Sep	8287820	2056913	303828	10648561	77.83	19.32	2.85	0.00		80091	
	Oct	8419597	2094135	317074	10830806	77.74	19.33	2.93	0.00			
	Nov	8067658	2193784	304760	10566171	76.35	20.76	2.88	0.00			
	Dec	8011991	2187422	299062	10498474	76.32	20.84	2.85	0.00	2238500		4.69
2008	Jan	7531271	2234287	272376	10037935	75.03	22.26	2.71	0.00			
	Feb	7286505	2248042	287234	9821781	74.19	22.89	2.92	0.00			
	Mar	7255173	2273140	284506	9812819	73.94	23.17	2.90	0.00			
	Apr	7608500	2211293	304581	10124374	75.15	21.84	3.01	0.00			
	May	7707410	2186961	322009	10216381	75.44	21.41	3.15	0.00			
	Jun	7057676	2236678	298486	9592840	73.57	23.32	3.11	0.00			
	Jul	6998391	2234236	290924	9523551	73.49	23.46	3.05	0.00			
	Aug	7099868	2290176	281501	9671353	73.41	23.68	2.91	0.00			
	Sep	6467270	2315826	240958	9024053	71.67	25.66	2.67	0.00		71946	
	Oct	5381415	2228537	192009	7801586	68.98	28.57	2.46	0.00			
	Nov	4995030	2550115	181689	7725903	64.65	33.01	2.35	0.01			
	Dec	5047977	2796712	191298	8030002	62.86	34.83	2.38	0.07	2418658		3.32
2009	Jan	4622432	2482361	173486	7278280	63.51	34.11	2.38	0.00			
	Feb	4130143	2473707	160699	6763201	61.07	36.58	2.38	0.02			
	Mar	4491944	2632272	171375	7295590	61.57	36.08	2.35	0.00			
	Apr	4921823	2461990	194398	7578211	64.95	32.49	2.57	0.00			
	May	5196953	2410901	230781	7836711	66.32	30.76	2.94	0.02			
	Jun	5207347	2430911	228466	7864570	66.21	30.91	2.91	0.03			
	Jul	5601022	2435530	249957	8283808	67.61	29.40	3.02	0.03			
	Aug	5803219	2491791	261982	8548448	67.89	29.15	3.06	0.10			
	Sep	6019679	2535646	272851	8815242	68.29	28.76	3.10	0.15		19356	
	Oct	5907713	2492287	268495	8650713	68.29	28.81	3.10	0.21			
	Nov	6262176	2544126	275212	9057851	69.14	28.09	3.04	0.26			
	Dec	6383036	2395549	279649	9023225	70.74	26.55	3.10	0.39	2540348		3.55
2010	Jan	6153247	2458792	266561	8856670	69.48	27.76	3.01	0.25			
	Feb	6343997	2466660	266322	9047326	70.12	27.26	2.94	0.33			
	Mar	6726540	2422507	283632	9396143	71.59	25.78	3.02	0.39			
	Apr	6832820	2496151	279633	9589613	71.25	26.03	2.92	0.20			
	May	6286877	2605233	249125	9117041	68.96	28.58	2.73	0.27			
	Jun	5958074	2721426	245588	8894384	66.99	30.60	2.76	0.35			
	Jul	6375735	2727957	268329	9337896	68.28	29.21	2.87	0.37			
	Aug	6088189	2919460	260360	9225537	65.99	31.65	2.82	0.46			
	Sep	6631255	2874792	285406	9741292	68.07	29.51	2.93	0.51		-36800	
	Oct	6883243	2783661	295595	9906111	69.48	28.10	2.98	0.57			
	Nov	6883931	2745525	283151	9847654	69.90	27.88	2.88	0.66			
	Dec	7343778	2638999	306001	10204299	71.97	25.86	3.00	0.83	2608950	1144299	3.91

REFERENCES

Adkins, Mark (1996). How Federal Trust Funds Really Work. *Durell Journal of Money and Banking*, 8(1).

Auerbach, Alan (2004). How Much Equity Does the Government Hold? *The American Economic Review*, 94(2).

Authers, John (2011). Even with Luck, a Value Strategy Is Not Enough. *Financial Times*, November 20.

Autor, David and Mark G Duggan (2006). The Growth in Social Security Disability Rolls: A Fiscal Crisis Unfolding. *The Journal of Economic Perspectives*, 20(3).

Banham, Russ (2010). Protecting the American Dream — For Financial Security, Disability Insurance Tops the List. *The Wall Street Journal*, May 19.

Barber, Brad and Terrance Odean (2000) Trading is Hazardous to Your Wealth: The Common Stock Performance of Individual Investors. *The Journal of Finance*, 55(2).

Barber, Brad and Terrance Odean (2001). Boys Will Be Boys: Gender, Overconfidence, and Common Stock Investment. *Quarterly Journal of Economics*, 116(1).

Basler, Barbara (2007). Sick of Waiting. *AARP Bulletin, November.*

Becker, Gary (2005). A Political Case for Social Security Reform. *The Wall Street Journal*, February 15.

Berk, Jonathan (2005). The Cost of Reforming Social Security. *The Financial Times*, April 5.

Bertocchi, Marida, Sandra L Schwartz and William T Ziemba (2010). *Optimizing the Aging, Retirement, and Pensions Dilemma*. John Wiley & Sons.

Blinder, Alan (2010). Return of the Bond Market Vigilantes. *The Wall Street Journal*, May 20.

Brandon, Emily (2010). 12 Ways to Fix Social Security. *US News & World Report*, May 18.

Brown, Jeffrey, Julia Lynn Coronado and Don Fullerton (2009). Is Social Security Part of the Social Safety Net?. *National Bureau of Economic Research*, Working Book 15070, June.

Bucks, Brian (2009). Changes in U.S. Family Finances from 2004 to 2007: Evidence from the Survey of Consumer Finances. *Federal Reserve Bulletin*, February, A19, A5.

Busse, Jeffrey, Amit Goyal and Sunil Wahal (2010). Performance and Persistence in Institutional Investment Management. *The Journal of Finance*, 55(2).

Canada Pension Plan (2010). Available at http://cppib.ca/Investments/Total_Portfolio_view/asset_mix.html, May.

Cohen, Norma (2005). A Bloody Mess. *The American Prospect Online*, January 11.

Collins, Margaret (2010). Volcker Says Social Security a 'Bedrock' for Savings. Available at http://Bloomberg.com, February 19.

Cronquist, Henrik and Richard H Thaler (2004). Design Choices in Privatized Social Security Systems: Learning from the Swedish Experience. *The American Economic Review*, 95(2).

Davidson, Joe (2009). Social Security Workers Feeling Strapped. *The Washington Post*, February 12.

Davis, Bob and Matt Moffett (2005). From Nations That Have Tried Similar Pensions, Some Lessons. *The Wall Street Journal*, February 3.

Dewitt, Larry (2007). The Social Security Trust Funds and the Federal Budget. Research Note #20, Social Security Online History, June 18.

Diamond, Peter (2004). Social Security. *The American Economic Review*, 94(1).

Diamond, Peter and John Geanakoplos (2003). Social Security Investment in Equities. *The American Economic Review*, 93(4).

Diamond, Peter and Peter Orzag (2004). *Saving Social Security — A Balanced Approach*, Washington, D.C.: Brookings Institution Press.

Dichev, Ilia (2007). What are Stock Investors' Actual Historical Returns? Evidence from Dollar-Weighted Returns. *The American Economic Review*, 97(1).

Dickie, Mure (2012). Chinese Encouraged to Spend More and Save Less. *Financial Times*, May 26–27.

Dimson, Elroy, Paul Marsh and Mike Staunton (2002). *Triumph of the Optimists*, Princeton University Press.

Dimson, Elroy, Paul Marsh and Mike Staunton (2011). Equity Premia Around the World. Available at SSRN: http://ssrn.com/abstract=1940165, October 21.

Dvorak, Phred (2010). Canada's Pension Fund Records 15% Gain. *The Wall Street Journal*, May 21.

Eckholm, Eric (2007). Disability Cases Last Far Longer as Backlog Rises. *The New York Times*, December 10.

Eddings, Cordell and Evan Applegate (2011). Bonds Notch a Rare Win Over Stocks. *Bloomberg Businessweek*, November 7–November 13.

Employee Benefit Research Institute (2010). The 2010 Retirement Confidence Survey: Confidence Stabilizing, But Preparations Continue to Erode. EBRI Issue Brief #340, March.

Farrell, Chris (2010). The Social Security Squeeze Can be Solved. *Bloomberg BusinessWeek*, July 19.

Feldstein, Martin (2007). Social Security Compromise. *The Wall Street Journal*, October 8.

Financial Times Editorial (2005). Lessons Learnt the Hard Way: US Social Security Reformers Should Study the UK Experience. *The Financial Times*, June 15.

Fleischer, Art (2011). Calling Obama's Payroll Tax Bluff. *The Wall Street Journal*, December 16.

French, Kenneth (2008). The Cost of Active Investing. *The Journal of Finance*, 63(4).

Friedman, Milton (1962). *Capitalism and Freedom*, The University of Chicago Press.

Giles, Chris and Andrew Balls (2005). Cheques and Balances: America Takes Heed of the British Pensions Disaster. *The Financial Times*, March 1.

Gokhale, Jagadeesh and Kent Smetters (2003). America's Book-keeping Scandal. *The Financial Times*, September 9.

Gora, Marek (2003). The New Polish Pension System. The Institute of Economic Research, Hitotsubashi University, Tokyo, PIE Discussion Book Series No. 186, August.

Hayek, Friedrich (1960). *The Constitution of Liberty*, The University of Chicago Press.

Jenkins, Holman (2005). Don't Pshaw the Shaw Plan. *The Wall Street Journal*, March 30.

Jeszeck, Charles (2010). Retirement Income: Challenges for Insuring Income Throughout Retirement. *US Government Accountability Office*, April 28.

Johnston, David Cay (2004). The Social Security Promise Not Kept. *The New York Times*, February 29.

Kreuger, Alan (2004). Some Lessons from Sweden on the Pros and Cons of Privatizing Social Security. *The New York Times*, February 5.

Kreuger, Alan (2005). The Disability Insurance Side of Social Security Raises Some Questions About Plans to Create Personal Accounts. *The New York Times*, March 3.

Kritzer, Barbara (2000). Social Security Privatization in Latin America. *Social Security Bulletin*, Vol. 62, No. 2.

Kritzer, Barbara (2008). Chile's Next Generation Pension Reform. *Social Security Bulletin*, Vol. 68, No. 2.

Krugman, Paul (2004). Buying into Failure. *The New York Times*, December 17.

Lowenstein, Roger (2005). A Question of Numbers. *The New York Times Magazine*, January 16.

Malkiel, Burton (2010). Entitlement Reform and the Global Budget Crisis. *The Wall Street Journal*, June 3.

Mercer.com (2009). New Global Index Shows Singapore's Pension System Faces Challenges Despite High Contributions, October 15.

Mesa-Lago, Carmelo (2008). *Reassembling Social Security — A Survey of Pensions and Health Care Reforms in Latin America*, Oxford University Press.

Moffett, Matt (2005). Pension Reform Pied Piper Loves Private Accounts. *The Wall Street Journal*, March 3.

Morningstar, Inc. (2011). *Ibbotson SBBI 2010 Classic Yearbook — Market Results for Stocks, Bonds, Bills, and Inflation 1926–2010*, Chicago: Morningstar, Inc.

Morningstar, Inc. (2012). *Ibbotson SBBI 2011 Classic Yearbook — Market Results for Stocks, Bonds, Bills, and Inflation 1926–2011*, Chicago: Morningstar, Inc.

MSCIBarra.com/IndexPerformance

Nataraj, Sita and John B Shoven (2004). Has the Unified Budget Undermined the Federal Government Trust Funds? Working Book 10953, National Bureau of Economic Research, December.

New York Times Editorial (2008). How Immigrants Saved Social Security. *The New York Times*, April 2.

Office of Management and Budget (2010). *Budget of the United States Government, Fiscal Year 2011, Historical Tables*, Washington D.C.: U.S. Government Printing Office.

O'Neill, Paul (2005). Who Wants to Be a Millionaire? *The Wall Street Journal*, January 16.

Pagrotsky, Leif and Lotta Fogde (2007). Social Security Can Secure Europe's Economy. *Financial Times*, April 10.

Peterson, Peter (2010). Tax Aversion Syndrome and Our Deficit Future. *The Wall Street Journal*, July 24.

Piñera, José (2004). Retiring in Chile. *The New York Times*, December 1.

Porter, Eduardo (2005). Illegal Immigrants are Bolstering Social Security With Billions. *The New York Times*, April 5.

Prescott, Edward (2004a). Why Does the Government Patronize Us? *The Wall Street Journal*, November 11.

Prescott, Edward (2004b). It's Irrational to Save. *The Wall Street Journal,* December 29.

Rattner, Steven (2007). Fudging the Budget. *The New York Times,* February 6.

Reich, Robert (2011). Protecting Social Security from Politicians' Hatchets. *San Francisco Chronicle,* July 11, p. E4.

Reinhart, Carmen and Kenneth S Rogoff (2009). *This Time is Different: Eight Centuries of Financial Folly,* Princeton University Press.

Rice-Oxley, Mark and Jennifer Ross (2005). In Britain and Chile, Lessons for Revamping Social Security. *The Christian Science Monitor,* March 14.

Rohter, Larry (2005). Chile's Retirees Find Shortfall in Private Plan. *The New York Times,* January 27.

Sharpe, William F (2010). Adaptive Asset Allocation Policies. *Financial Analysts Journal,* 66(3).

Shilling, John (2008). Time to Honor America's Debt to the Retired. *Financial Times,* March 28.

Siegel, Jeremy (2010). *Stocks for the Long Run,* 4th ed., McGraw-Hill.

Sloan, Allan (2009). The Next Great Bailout. *Fortune,* August 17.

Sloan, Allan (2011). Legg Mason's Miller Shows the Risks in a Mutual Fund's Hot Hand. *The Washington Post,* December 6.

Smith, Adam (1776). *An Inquiry into the Nature and Causes of the Wealth of Nations,* The Easton Press, 1991.

Smith, Adam (1790). *The Theory of Moral Sentiments,* Sixth Edn., Penguin Books, 2009.

Social Security Administration (2010). *Income of the Population 55 or Older, 2008,* Research, Statistics, and Policy Analysis, April.

Social Security Administration (2010). *The 2010 Annual Report of the Board Trustees of the Federal Old-Age and Survivors insurance and Federal Disability Insurance Trust Funds,* U.S. Government Printing Office, May 10.

Tully, Sharon (2010). Robert Arnott's Magic Formula. *Fortune,* June 14.

Turner, John (2004). Individual Accounts: Lessons from Sweden. *International Social Security Review,* Vol. 57, 1.

Walsh, Mary Williams (2008). Insurers Faulted as Overloading Social Security. *The New York Times,* April 1.

Willoughby, Jack (2010). Lifting Beyond Their Weight Class. *Barron's,* July 12.

Yang, Jia Lynn (2011). Payroll Tax Cut Raises Worries about Social Security's Future Funding. *The Washington Post,* December 29.

Yermo, J (2008). Governance and Investment of Public Reserve Funds in Selected OECD Countries, OECD Working Books on Insurance and Private Pensions, No. 15, OECD Publishing, doi: 10.1787/244270553278.

Zweig, Jason (2011). A Star Exits After Value Falls: The Long Climb and Steep Descent of Legg Mason's Top Stock Picker. *The Wall Street Journal,* November 18.

ACKNOWLEDGMENTS

I would like to thank Minder Cheng for valuable discussions, Ben Fredrickson and Nils A. Hakansson for research assistance, and Sandhya Venkatesh for excellent editorial support.

INDEX

About the Author

Nils H. Hakansson is the Sylvan C. Coleman Professor of Finance and Accounting, Emeritus, University of California, Berkeley. He has lectured widely around the world and received an honorary doctorate from the Stockholm School of Economics. He was a trustee of the Laudus Mutual Funds and chair of its audit committee, 1990–2009.